Hyperledger Cookbook

Over 40 recipes implementing the latest Hyperledger
blockchain frameworks and tools

Xun (Brian) Wu
Chuanfeng Zhang
Andrew Zhang

BIRMINGHAM - MUMBAI

Hyperledger Cookbook

Copyright © 2019 Packt Publishing

Commissioning Editor: Sunith Shetty
Acquisition Editor: Joshua Nadar
Content Development Editor: Karan Thakkar
Technical Editor: Suwarna Patil
Copy Editor: Safis Editing
Language Support Editor: Storm Mann
Project Coordinator: Hardik Bhinde
Proofreader: Safis Editing
Indexer: Pratik Shirodkar
Graphics: Jisha Chirayil
Production Coordinator: Deepika Naik

First published: April 2019

Production reference: 1300419

Published by Packt Publishing Ltd.
Livery Place
35 Livery Street
Birmingham
B3 2PB, UK.

ISBN 978-1-78953-488-7

www.packtpub.com

mapt.io

Mapt is an online digital library that gives you full access to over 5,000 books and videos, as well as industry leading tools to help you plan your personal development and advance your career. For more information, please visit our website.

Why subscribe?

- Spend less time learning and more time coding with practical eBooks and Videos from over 4,000 industry professionals

- Improve your learning with Skill Plans built especially for you

- Get a free eBook or video every month

- Mapt is fully searchable

- Copy and paste, print, and bookmark content

Packt.com

Did you know that Packt offers eBook versions of every book published, with PDF and ePub files available? You can upgrade to the eBook version at www.packt.com and as a print book customer, you are entitled to a discount on the eBook copy. Get in touch with us at customercare@packtpub.com for more details.

At www.packt.com, you can also read a collection of free technical articles, sign up for a range of free newsletters, and receive exclusive discounts and offers on Packt books and eBooks.

Contributors

About the authors

Xun (Brian) Wu is an author, software architect, and advisor with over 17 years' extensive hands-on experience in blockchain design and development, big data, AI, the cloud, UIs, and system infrastructures. He has worked for top investment banks including J.P. Morgan, Citigroup, and Bank of America. He is a coauthor of *Blockchain Quick Start Guide, Blockchain By Example*, and *Seven NoSQL Databases in a Week,* and has worked as a technical reviewer on over 50 technical computer books for Packt. He owns several blockchain patents, and currently serves as a board advisor for several blockchain start-up companies. Brian holds an NJIT computer science master's degree. He lives in New Jersey with his two beautiful daughters, Bridget and Charlotte.

> *I would like to thank my parents, wife and kids for their patience and support throughout this endeavor.*

Chuanfeng Zhang is enthusiastic and passionate about technologies and trading and data analysis, with 20 years' experience in both the technology and finance sectors. He has worked at top investment banks and technology firms including Goldman Sachs, Credit Suisse, and IBM. He has led, designed, and successfully developed many enterprise-scale systems with diverse architectures for algorithmic trading, order management, risk management, business intelligence, and more.

> *I would like to especially thank my lovely wife and kids (Kathleen and Kevin) for their support for this project.*

Andrew Zhang is an IBM Watson Cloud Advocate. He has many years of experience in cloud platforms, big data analytics, and machine learning. He works with start-ups and enterprise clients in the government, education, healthcare, and life science industries. His current interests are in embedding AI and blockchain open source technologies for consumer and enterprise applications. In his spare time, Andrew enjoys reading, traveling, and spending time with his family and friends.

Contributing author

Belinda Li is a seasoned software engineer. Her recent endeavors include MLaaS, AI enabled applications, and permissioned blockchain technologies. She is entrepreneurial and has over 15 years of hands-on enterprise software design and development experience in wealth management brokerage and trading platforms, investment portfolio optimization and analytics, call center training and operations, single sign-on security, and more. Belinda has held various positions in top-tier financial firms including Morgan Stanley and Citigroup. She started her career as a C/C++ programmer in the math department in Intergraph Corporation, a pioneer in GIS and the global leader in CAD software. She enjoys Zumba, folk dancing, and traveling in her free time.

About the reviewer

Rameshwar Nigam is the director and founder of Pytriot Solutions LLP. He oversees the design and deployment of blockchain services. With strategic thinking, sharp analytical skills, and business acumen, Rameshwar can identify business opportunities and develop solutions for managing business challenges. His in-depth knowledge of blockchain and associated domains aids organizations in the seamless and risk-free adoption of these technologies. He continues to build awareness and recognition of blockchain as a technology in various corporates by providing training, proofs-of-concept, and so on.

Packt is searching for authors like you

If you're interested in becoming an author for Packt, please visit `authors.packtpub.com` and apply today. We have worked with thousands of developers and tech professionals, just like you, to help them share their insight with the global tech community. You can make a general application, apply for a specific hot topic that we are recruiting an author for, or submit your own idea.

Table of Contents

Preface

Hyperledger is an umbrella project of modular open source frameworks and tools for building and experimenting with blockchains. The *Hyperledger Cookbook* provides hands-on experiences and in-depth illustrations covering the full spectrum of Hyperledger offerings. You will not only learn a range of permissioned business blockchain technologies, including Fabric, Sawtooth, Burrow, Iroha, and Indy, but also a set of tools to work with these blockchain frameworks, including Composer, Explorer, and Caliper.

Each chapter contains a set of recipes that helps the reader to become more familiar with Hyperledger blockchain and its tools. The examples in this book will help readers to apply Hyperledger technologies to their own problems.

Who this book is for

This book is for blockchain developers who want to learn about the permissioned blockchain technologies for business offered by Hyperledger. With an abundance of recipes covering distributed ledger networks, smart contract engines, client libraries, and various tools in Hyperledger technologies, blockchain developers can apply them to rapidly develop decentralized DLT systems for their enterprises. For more experienced blockchain developers, the recipes covered in this book might expose them to new ways of thinking in terms of how to select and build enterprise blockchain for their business use cases.

What this book covers

Chapter 1, *Working with Hyperledger Fabric*, concentrates on the fundamental Fabric architecture and components. The recipes cover installation, building a Fabric network, adding an org to a channel, integrating with CouchDB, and writing your first Fabric application.

Chapter 2, *Implementing Hyperledger Fabric*, is dedicated to building a simple device asset management DApp. The example covers recipes designed to show how to design and write a chaincode smart contract, compile and deploy Fabric chaincode, run and test the smart contract, develop a DApp, and interact with Hyperledger Fabric chaincode through the client SDK API.

Chapter 3, *Modeling a Business Network Using Hyperledger Composer*, contains recipes designed to show how to use the Composer tool to rapidly develop use cases, build blockchain business networks using the Composer model language, deploy, test and export BNA using the Composer CLI tool, and interact with Composer through the SDK.

Chapter 4, *Integrating Hyperledger Fabric with Explorer*, this includes installing, setting up, and configuring Hyperledger Explorer, integrating with the Hyperledger framework, and running the Hyperledger Explorer application.

Chapter 5, *Working with Hyperledger Sawtooth*, includes recipes for installing, deploying, and running DApps with Hyperledger Sawtooth. With the help of Hyperledger Sawtooth's modular architecture, distributed ledger, distributed data storage, and decentralized consensus, several examples demonstrate how to build a transaction processor, design a namespace and address, grant permission on the Sawtooth network, and develop client applications with the Sawtooth RestAPI and SDK.

Chapter 6, *Operating an Ethereum Smart Contract with Hyperledger Burrow*, contains recipes about how to write smart contracts with Solidity, deploy and interact with Ethereum smart contracts on Burrow, invoke smart contracts with Seth CLI and RPC, and create externally owned accounts on Seth. This chapter also covers the permissioning of Ethereum EOA and contract accounts on Seth.

Chapter 7, *Working with Hyperledger Iroha*, covers several recipes associated with working with Hyperledger Iroha, including installing and configuring Hyperledger Iroha, and interacting with Hyperledger Iroha using the client library. This chapter also provides an example demonstrating how to use Iroha CLI to create a cryptocurrency.

Chapter 8, *Exploring the CLI with Hyperledger Indy*, covers the installation of Hyperledger Indy and the exploration of Indy CLI with Hyperledger Indy.

Chapter 9, *Hyperledger Blockchain Scalability and Security*, contains recipes about how to measure Hyperledger blockchain performance using the Hyperledger Caliper tool, how to design and implement highly scalable Hyperledger blockchain, and how to build a secure Hyperledger consortium network with Fabric CA.

Appendix, *Hyperledger Blockchain Ecosystem*, mainly targets those individuals who are relatively new to distributed ledger technology and permissioned blockchains. It covers Hyperledger blockchain concepts, the important technical design methodology of the Hyperledger ecosystem, and explores when to apply these technologies through real-world use cases.

To get the most out of this book

To better understand and follow the recipes in this book, it will help if you have some basic knowledge of blockchain technology and cryptograph concepts, have a basic understanding of programming languages for JavaScript, Go, and Python, some basic Unix skills, in particular, shell command, and are familiar with basic flows for launching and running applications in the cloud, such as Amazon AWS.

Download the example code files

You can download the example code files for this book from your account at `www.packt.com`. If you purchased this book elsewhere, you can visit `www.packt.com/support` and register to have the files emailed directly to you.

You can download the code files by following these steps:

1. Log in or register at `www.packt.com`.
2. Select the **SUPPORT** tab.
3. Click on **Code Downloads & Errata**.
4. Enter the name of the book in the **Search** box and follow the onscreen instructions.

Once the file is downloaded, please make sure that you unzip or extract the folder using the latest version of:

- WinRAR/7-Zip for Windows
- Zipeg/iZip/UnRarX for Mac
- 7-Zip/PeaZip for Linux

The code bundle for the book is also hosted on GitHub at `https://github.com/PacktPublishing/Hyperledger-Cookbook`. In case there's an update to the code, it will be updated on the existing GitHub repository.

We also have other code bundles from our rich catalog of books and videos available at `https://github.com/PacktPublishing/`. Check them out!

Conventions used

There are a number of text conventions used throughout this book.

`CodeInText`: Indicates code words in text, database table names, folder names, filenames, file extensions, pathnames, dummy URLs, user input, and Twitter handles. Here is an example: "Install Node.js, `npm`, and Python."

A block of code is set as follows:

```
type Chaincode interface {
    Init (stub ChaincodeStubInterface) pb.Response
    Invoke (stub ChaincodeStubInterface) pb.Response
}
```

Any command-line input or output is written as follows:

```
$ sudo apt-get update
```

Bold: Indicates a new term, an important word, or words that you see on screen. For example, words in menus or dialog boxes appear in the text like this. Here is an example: "Click on the **Query Chaincode** button."

 Warnings or important notes appear like this.

 Tips and tricks appear like this.

Sections

In this book, you will find several headings that appear frequently (*Getting ready*, *How to do it...*, *How it works...*, *There's more...*, and *See also*).

To give clear instructions on how to complete a recipe, use these sections as follows:

Getting ready

This section tells you what to expect in the recipe and describes how to set up any software or any preliminary settings required for the recipe.

How to do it...

This section contains the steps required to follow the recipe.

How it works...

This section usually consists of a detailed explanation of what happened in the previous section.

There's more...

This section consists of additional information about the recipe in order to increase your knowledge of it.

See also

This section provides helpful links to other useful information for the recipe.

Get in touch

Feedback from our readers is always welcome.

General feedback: If you have questions about any aspect of this book, mention the book title in the subject of your message and email us at `customercare@packtpub.com`.

Errata: Although we have taken every care to ensure the accuracy of our content, mistakes do happen. If you have found a mistake in this book, we would be grateful if you would report this to us. Please visit www.packt.com/submit-errata, selecting your book, clicking on the Errata Submission Form link, and entering the details.

Piracy: If you come across any illegal copies of our works in any form on the internet, we would be grateful if you would provide us with the location address or website name. Please contact us at copyright@packt.com with a link to the material.

If you are interested in becoming an author: If there is a topic that you have expertise in, and you are interested in either writing or contributing to a book, please visit authors.packtpub.com.

Reviews

Please leave a review. Once you have read and used this book, why not leave a review on the site that you purchased it from? Potential readers can then see and use your unbiased opinion to make purchase decisions, we at Packt can understand what you think about our products, and our authors can see your feedback on their book. Thank you!

For more information about Packt, please visit packt.com.

Working with Hyperledger Fabric

1

Hyperledger Fabric is the most widely-used permissioned blockchain in the Hyperledger family. It is an open source enterprise-grade platform that leverages a highly-modular and configurable architecture. Hyperledger Fabric is optimized for a broad range of industry use cases, including the finance, banking, healthcare, insurance, and public sectors, as well as supply chains and digital asset management.

Hyperledger Fabric supports smart contact development in general-purpose programming languages, such as Java, Go, and Node.js. Hyperledger Fabric is also operating under a governance model to build trust between participants on a shared network.

In this chapter, we will cover the following recipes:

- Reviewing the Hyperledger Fabric architecture and components
- Installing Hyperledger Fabric on AWS
- Building the Fabric network
- Adding an organization to a channel
- Using CouchDB
- Writing your first application

Reviewing the Hyperledger Fabric architecture and components

We will review and examine various Hyperledger Fabric components and architectures throughout this recipe. Hyperledger Fabric has three core components, which are peers, ordering service, and Fabric CA:

- **Peer**: A node on the network that maintains the state of the ledger and manages chaincode. Any number of peers may participate in a network. A peer can be an endorser, which executes transactions, or a committer, which verifies the endorsements and validates transactions results. An endorser is always a committer. Peers form a peer-to-peer gossip network. A peer manages the events hub and delivers events to the subscribers.

- **Ordering service**: Packages transactions into blocks to be delivered to peers, since it communicates only with peers. The ordering service is the genesis of a network. Clients of the ordering service are peers and applications. A group of orderers run a communication service, called an ordering service, to provide an atomic broadcast. The ordering service accepts transactions and delivers blocks. The ordering service processes all configuration transactions to set up network policies (including readers, writers, and admins). The orderer manages a pluggable trust engine (such as CFT or BFT) that performs the ordering of the transactions.

- **Fabric CA**: Fabric CA is the certificate authority that issues PKI-based certificates to network member organizations and users. Fabric CA supports LDAP for user authentication and HSM for security. Fabric CA issues one root certificate to member organizations and one enrollment certificate to each authorized user.

Hyperledger Fabric also have several important key features and concepts:

- **Fabric ledger**: Maintained by each peer and consists of two parts: the blockchain and the world state. Transaction read/write and channel configurations sets are written to the blockchain. A separate ledger is maintained for each channel for each peer that joins. The world state has options of either LevelDB or CouchDB, where LevelDB is a simple key-value store and CouchDB is a document store that allows complex queries. The smart contract decides what is written into the world state.

- **Channel**: Provides privacy between different ledgers and exists in the scope of a channel. Channels can be shared across an entire network of peers, and peers can participate in multiple channels. Channels can be permissioned for a specific set of participants. Chaincode is installed on peers to access the world state. Chaincode is instantiated on specific channels. Channels also support concurrent execution for performance and scalability.
- **Organization**: Define boundaries within a Fabric blockchain network. Each organization defines an MSP for the identities of administrators, users, peers, and orderers. A network can include many organizations, representing a consortium. Each organization has an individual ID.
- **Endorsement policy**: The conditions by which a transaction can be endorsed. A transaction can only be considered valid if it has been endorsed according to its policy. Each chaincode is deployed with an endorsement policy. **Endorsement system chaincode** (**ESCC**) signs the proposal response on the endorsing peer and **validation system chaincode** (**VSCC**) validates the endorsement.
- **Membership services provider** (**MSP**): Manages a set of identities within a distributed Fabric network. It provides identities for peers, orderers, client applications, and administrators. Where the identities can be Fabric CA or external CA, MSP provides authentication, validation, signing and issuance. MSP support different crypto standards with a pluggable interface. A network can include multiple MSPs (typically one per organization), which can include TLS crypto material for encrypted communications.

Getting ready

We will look into a sample transaction flow on Hyperledger Fabric. Fabric uses the execute-order-validate blockchain transaction flow architecture shown in the following diagram:

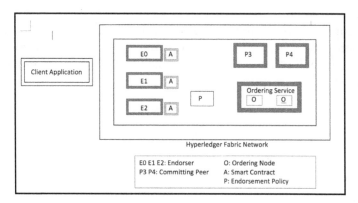

How to do it...

In this section, we will review how a transaction is created on the Hyperledger Fabric network:

1. The **Client Application** submits a transaction proposal for smart contact **A** to the network. The endorsement policy requires three endorsers—**E0**, **E1**, and **E2**—to sign together.

2. The endorsers execute proposed transactions. At this time, three endorsers—**E0**, **E1**, **E2**—will each execute the proposed transaction independently. None of these executions will update the ledger. Each execution will capture the set of **read and written** (**RW**) data, which will now flow in the fabric network. All transactions should be signed and encrypted.

3. RW sets are asynchronously returned to the client application with a transaction proposal. The RW sets are signed by each endorser and will be processed later.

4. All transactions that returned from the Fabric network are submitted for ordering. The application can submit responses as a transaction to be ordered, and ordering happens across the Fabric in parallel with transactions submitted by other applications.

5. **Ordering Service** collects transactions into proposed blocks for distribution to committing peers. This proposed blocks can then be deliver to other peers in a hierarchy. There are two ordering algorithms available: SOLO (single node for development) and Kafka (crash-fault-tolerance for production). In the production system, it is suggested to use Kafka.

6. Committing peers validate the transactions. All committing peers validate against the endorsement policy and check whether RW sets are still valid for the current world state. World state is not update if there is invalid transctions but are retained on the ledger while validated transactions are applied to the world state.

7. Client applications can register to be notified on the status of transactions, to find out whether they succeed or fail, and when blocks are added to the ledger. Client applications will be notified by each peer to which they are independently connected.

How it works...

We reviewed how transaction flow works in Fabric. Fabric uses the execute-order-validate model with the following seven steps:

1. Client application submits a transaction proposal
2. Endorsers execute the proposed transactions
3. Client applications receive transaction proposal response
4. Transactions are submitted for ordering
5. Transactions are delivered to committing peer
6. Validated transaction are applied to world state
7. Client applications get notified with the status of the transaction

In the next recipe, we will walk through how to install Hyperledger Fabric on **Amazon Web Services** (**AWS**).

Installing Hyperledger Fabric on AWS

To install and run the recipe in this chapter, you need AWS EC2 Ubuntu Server 16.04 with 4 GB of memory. We will use the Fabric 1.3 release as it is the most stable release as of writing this recipe.

Getting ready

From the Hyperledger Fabric website (`https://hyperledger-fabric.readthedocs.io/en/release-1.3/prereqs.html`), the prerequisites for this recipe are as follows:

- **Operating systems**: Ubuntu Linux 14.04 / 16.04 LTS (both 64-bit), or macOS 10.12
- **cURL tool**: The latest version
- **Docker engine**: Version 17.06.2-ce or greater
- **Docker-compose**: Version 1.14 or greater
- **Go**: Version 1.10.x
- **Node**: Version 8.9 or higher (note: version 9 is not supported)
- **npm**: Version 5.x
- **Python**: 2.7.x

We chose Amazon Ubuntu Server 16.04. If you don't have experience with installing Ubuntu in EC2, please refer to the AWS document: https://aws.amazon.com/getting-started/tutorials/launch-a-virtual-machine/.

You can also chose to install Ubuntu in your local machine virtual box. A tutorial for this can be found at http://www.psychocats.net/ubuntu/virtualbox or https://askubuntu.com/questions/142549/how-to-install-ubuntu-on-virtualbox.

How to do it...

To install Hyperledger on AWS, follow these steps:

1. Execute the following commands to update the software on your system:

   ```
   $ sudo apt-get update
   ```

2. Install curl and the golang software package:

   ```
   $ sudo apt-get install curl
   $ sudo apt-get install golang
   $ export GOPATH=$HOME/go
   $ export PATH=$PATH:$GOPATH/bin
   ```

3. Install Node.js, npm, and Python:

   ```
   $ sudo apt-get install nodejs
   $ sudo apt-get install npm
   $ sudo apt-get install python
   ```

4. Install and upgrade docker and docker-compose:

   ```
   $ sudo apt-get install docker
   $ curl -fsSL https://download.docker.com/linux/ubuntu/gpg |
     sudo apt-key add -
   $ sudo add-apt-repository "deb [arch=amd64]
     https://download.docker.com/linux/ubuntu
   $(lsb_release -cs) stable"
   $ sudo apt-get update
   $ apt-cache policy docker-ce
   $ sudo apt-get install -y docker-ce
   $ sudo apt-get install docker-compose
   $ sudo apt-get upgrade
   ```

5. Let's customize and update Node.js and `golang` to the proper versions:

```
$ wget https://dl.google.com/go/go1.11.2.linux-amd64.tar.gz
$ tar -xzvf go1.11.2.linux-amd64.tar.gz
$ sudo mv go/ /usr/local
$ export GOPATH=/usr/local/go
$ export PATH=$PATH:$GOPATH/bin
$ curl -sL https://deb.nodesource.com/setup_8.x | sudo bash -
$ sudo apt-get install -y nodejs
```

6. Verify the installed software package versions:

```
$ curl --version
$ /usr/local/go/bin/go version
$ python -V
$ node -v
$ npm --version
$ docker --version
$ docker-compose --version
```

The result should look like this:

```
curl 7.47.0 (x86_64-pc-linux-gnu) libcurl/7.47.0 GnuTLS/3.4.10 zlib/1.2.8 libidn/1.32 librtmp/2.3
Protocols: dict file ftp ftps gopher http https imap imaps ldap ldaps pop3 pop3s rtmp rtsp smb smbs smtp smtps telnet tftp
Features: AsynchDNS IDN IPv6 Largefile GSS-API Kerberos SPNEGO NTLM NTLM_WB SSL libz TLS-SRP UnixSockets
go version go1.11.2 linux/amd64
Python 2.7.12
v8.15.0
6.4.1
Docker version 18.09.0, build 4d60db4
docker-compose version 1.8.0, build unknown
```

7. Install Hyperledger Fabric 1.3:

```
$ curl -sSL http://bit.ly/2ysbOFE | sudo bash -s 1.3.0
```

It will take a few minutes to download the Docker images. When it is done, the results should look like this:

```
===> List out hyperledger docker images
hyperledger/fabric-ca          1.4.0-rc2    921e03d2731e    2 weeks ago     244MB
hyperledger/fabric-ca          latest       921e03d2731e    2 weeks ago     244MB
hyperledger/fabric-zookeeper   0.4.14       d36da0db87a4    2 months ago    1.43GB
hyperledger/fabric-zookeeper   latest       d36da0db87a4    2 months ago    1.43GB
hyperledger/fabric-kafka       0.4.14       a3b095201c66    2 months ago    1.44GB
hyperledger/fabric-kafka       latest       a3b095201c66    2 months ago    1.44GB
hyperledger/fabric-couchdb     0.4.14       f14f97292b4c    2 months ago    1.5GB
hyperledger/fabric-couchdb     latest       f14f97292b4c    2 months ago    1.5GB
hyperledger/fabric-javaenv     1.3.0        2476cefaf833    2 months ago    1.7GB
hyperledger/fabric-javaenv     latest       2476cefaf833    2 months ago    1.7GB
hyperledger/fabric-tools       1.3.0        c056cd9890e7    2 months ago    1.5GB
hyperledger/fabric-tools       latest       c056cd9890e7    2 months ago    1.5GB
hyperledger/fabric-ccenv       1.3.0        953124d80237    2 months ago    1.38GB
hyperledger/fabric-ccenv       latest       953124d80237    2 months ago    1.38GB
hyperledger/fabric-orderer     1.3.0        f430f581b46b    2 months ago    145MB
hyperledger/fabric-orderer     latest       f430f581b46b    2 months ago    145MB
hyperledger/fabric-peer        1.3.0        f3ea63abddaa    2 months ago    151MB
hyperledger/fabric-peer        latest       f3ea63abddaa    2 months ago    151MB
```

This completes the installation of the Hyperledger Fabric on the AWS EC2 machine. We will build up the network in the next recipe.

How it works...

We installed several prerequisites, so let's explain what each software package is and how they work together to build the Hyperledger Fabric platform:

- **cURL**: A tool used to transfer data from or to a server, using one of the supported protocols (HTTP, HTTPS, FTP, FTPS, SCP, SFTP, TFTP, DICT, TELNET, LDAP, or FILE). The command is designed to work without user interaction.
- **Docker**: A tool to create, deploy, and run applications using containers. Containers allow developers to package applications with all of the parts it needs, such as libraries and other dependencies, and ship it out as one package.
- **Docker Compose**: It is a tool which is used for defining and running Multi-container application. You can create and start all the services with help of a single command from your configuration YAML file.
- **Go:** An open source programming language that makes it easy to build simple, reliable, and efficient software. Hyperledger Fabric is primarily developed using the Go language.

- **Node.js**: A platform built on Chrome's JavaScript runtime to easily build fast and scalable network applications. Node.js is considered to be more lightweight and efficient since it uses event-driven, non-blocking I/O models, which make it more feasible for data-intensive real-time applications.
- **npm package manager**: A tool that will allow you to install third-party libraries (other people's code) using the command line.
- **Python**: A general-purpose programming language for developing both desktop and web applications. Python is also used to develop complex scientific and numeric applications. It is designed with features to facilitate data analysis and visualization.

With this Hyperledger Fabric installation, it will download and install samples and binaries to your system. The sample applications installed are useful for learning the capabilities and operations of Hyperledger Fabric:

- `balance-transfer`: A sample Node.js app to demonstrate `fabric-client` and `fabric-ca-client` Node.js SDK APIs.
- `basic-network`: A basic network with certificates and key materials, predefined transactions, and one channel, `mychannel`.
- `bin`: Binary and scripts for `fabric-ca`, `orderer`, and `peer`.
- `chaincode`: Chaincode developed for `fabcar`, marbles, and a few other examples.
- `chaincode-docker-devmode`: Develops chaincode in `dev mode` for rapid `code/build/run/debug`.
- `config`: YAML files to define transaction, orderer, organization, and chaincode.
- `fabcar`: A sample Node.js app to demonstrate the capabilities with chaincode deployment, query, and updating the ledger.
- `fabric-ca`: Uses the Fabric CA client and server to generate all crypto material and learn how to use attribute-based access control.
- `first-network`: Builds the first hyperledger fabric network with `byfn.sh` and `eyfn.sh`.
- `Jenkinsfile`: Jenkins is a suite of plugins that supports implementing and integrating continuous-delivery pipelines. The definition of a Jenkins pipeline is typically written into a text file, `Jenkinsfile`, which in turn is checked into a project's source-control repository.
- `scripts`: There are two scripts in this directory: `bootstrap.sh` and `Jenkins_Scripts`.

Now that we have successfully installed Hyperledger Fabric on an AWS EC2 virtual machine, in the next recipe, we will set up the first Hyperledger Fabric network.

Building the Fabric network

To run this recipe, you need to complete the *Reviewing the Hyperledger Fabric architecture and components* recipe in this chapter to install Hyperledger Fabric with samples and binaries on the AWS EC2 instance.

How to do it...

There is a **Build your first network** (**BYFN**) sample installed with Hyperledger Fabric. We will use that to provision a sample Hyperledger Fabric network that consists of two organizations, each maintaining two peer nodes, and a `solo` ordering service. To do this, follow these steps:

1. Log in as a default user and execute the `byfn.sh` script to generate certificates and keys for the network:

   ```
   $ cd ~
   $ sudo chmod 777 -R fabric-samples
   $ cd fabric-samples/first-network
   $ sudo ./byfn.sh generate
   ```

2. Bring up the Fabric network by executing the `byfn.sh` script using the `up` option:

   ```
   $ cd ~
   $ cd fabric-samples/first-network
   $ sudo ./byfn.sh up
   ```

   You should see the following output, which states that the network has started successfully:

```
ubuntu@ip-172-31-78-117:~/fabric-samples/first-network$ sudo ./byfn.sh up
Starting for channel 'mychannel' with CLI timeout of '10' seconds and CLI delay of '3' seconds
Continue? [Y/n] Y
proceeding ...
LOCAL_VERSION=1.3.0
DOCKER_IMAGE_VERSION=1.3.0
Creating network "net_byfn" with the default driver
Creating volume "net_peer0.org2.example.com" with default driver
Creating volume "net_peer1.org2.example.com" with default driver
Creating volume "net_peer1.org1.example.com" with default driver
Creating volume "net_peer0.org1.example.com" with default driver
Creating volume "net_orderer.example.com" with default driver
Creating peer0.org2.example.com
Creating peer1.org1.example.com
Creating peer0.org1.example.com
Creating peer1.org2.example.com
Creating orderer.example.com
Creating cli
```

```
Build your first network (BYFN) end-to-end test
```

3. Bring down the Fabric network by executing the `byfn.sh` script using the `down` option to shut down and clean up the network. This kills the containers, removes the crypto material and artifacts, and deletes the chaincode images. The following code shows how to do this:

```
$ cd ~
$ cd fabric-samples/first-network
$ sudo ./byfn.sh down
```

Let's review the `byfn.sh` script, shown as follows. This script is well documented, and you should read about it in detail to understand each execution step during the network startup process:

```
# Print the usage message
function printHelp() {
  echo "Usage: "
  echo "  byfn.sh <mode> [-c <channel name>] [-t <timeout>] [-d <delay>] [-f <docker-compose-file>] [-s <dbtype>] [-l <language>] [-i <imagetag>] [-v]"
  echo "    <mode> - one of 'up', 'down', 'restart', 'generate' or 'upgrade'"
  echo "      - 'up' - bring up the network with docker-compose up"
  echo "      - 'down' - clear the network with docker-compose down"
  echo "      - 'restart' - restart the network"
  echo "      - 'generate' - generate required certificates and genesis block"
  echo "      - 'upgrade'  - upgrade the network from version 1.2.x to 1.3.x"
  echo "    -c <channel name> - channel name to use (defaults to \"mychannel\")"
  echo "    -t <timeout> - CLI timeout duration in seconds (defaults to 10)"
  echo "    -d <delay> - delay duration in seconds (defaults to 3)"
  echo "    -f <docker-compose-file> - specify which docker-compose file use (defaults to docker-compose-cli.yaml)"
  echo "    -s <dbtype> - the database backend to use: goleveldb (default) or couchdb"
  echo "    -l <language> - the chaincode language: golang (default) or node"
  echo "    -i <imagetag> - the tag to be used to launch the network (defaults to \"latest\")"
  echo "    -v - verbose mode"
  echo "  byfn.sh -h (print this message)"
  echo
  echo "Typically, one would first generate the required certificates and "
  echo "genesis block, then bring up the network. e.g.:"
  echo
  echo "        byfn.sh generate -c mychannel"
  echo "        byfn.sh up -c mychannel -s couchdb"
  echo "        byfn.sh up -c mychannel -s couchdb -i 1.2.x"
  echo "        byfn.sh up -l node"
  echo "        byfn.sh down -c mychannel"
  echo "        byfn.sh upgrade -c mychannel"
  echo
  echo "Taking all defaults:"
  echo "        byfn.sh generate"
  echo "        byfn.sh up"
  echo "        byfn.sh down"
```

We will review and exam the Hyperledger Fabric `byfn.sh` script using the command-line interface.

4. Use the tool for crypto and certificate generation, called cryptogen, which uses a YAML configuration file as the base to generate the certificates:

```
OrdererOrgs:
  - Name: Orderer
    Domain: example.com
    Specs:
      - Hostname: orderer
PeerOrgs:
  - Name: Org1
    Domain: org1.example.com
    EnableNodeOUs: true
    Template:
      Count: 2
    Users:
      Count: 1
  - Name: Org2
    Domain: org2.example.com
```

```
EnableNodeOUs: true
  Template:
    Count: 2
  Users:
    Count: 1
```

The following command will generate the YAML file:

```
$ cd ~
$ cd fabric-samples/first-network
$ sudo ../bin/cryptogen generate --config=./crypto-config.yaml
```

On execution of the previous command, you will find a new directory crypto-config is created, and inside there are directories that correspond to ordererOrganizations and peerOrganizations. We have two organizations, (Org1.example.com and Org2.example.com) network artifacts.

5. Let's generate the configuration transaction. The tool to generate the configuration transaction is called configtxgen. The artifacts generated in this step are the orderer genesis block, the channel configuration transaction, and one anchor peer transaction for each peer organization. There will also be a configtx.yaml file that is broken into several sections: profiles (describe the organizational structure of the network), organizations (the details regarding individual organizations), orderer (the details regarding the orderer parameters), and application (application defaults—not needed for this recipe).

The profiles that are needed for this recipe are shown as follows:

```
Profiles:

TwoOrgsOrdererGenesis:
    <<: *ChannelDefaults
    Orderer:
        <<: *OrdererDefaults
        Organizations:
            - *OrdererOrg
        Capabilities:
            <<: *OrdererCapabilities
    Consortiums:
        SampleConsortium:
            Organizations:
                - *Org1
                - *Org2
TwoOrgsChannel:
    Consortium: SampleConsortium
    Application:
```

```
<<: *ApplicationDefaults
Organizations:
    - *Org1
    - *Org2
Capabilities:
    <<: *ApplicationCapabilities
```

Let's go with the detailed command-line steps to understand what is happening:

```
$ export FABRIC_CFG_PATH=$PWD
$ sudo ../bin/configtxgen -profile TwoOrgsOrdererGenesis -
outputBlock ./channel-artifacts/genesis.block
$ export CHANNEL_NAME=mychannel
$ sudo ../bin/configtxgen -profile TwoOrgsChannel
    -outputCreateChannelTx ./channel-artifacts/channel.tx
    -channelID $CHANNEL_NAME
$ sudo ../bin/configtxgen -profile TwoOrgsChannel
    -outputAnchorPeersUpdate ./channel-artifacts/Org1MSPanchors.tx
    -channelID $CHANNEL_NAME -asOrg Org1MSP
$ sudo ../bin/configtxgen -profile TwoOrgsChannel
    -outputAnchorPeersUpdate ./channel-artifacts/Org2MSPanchors.tx
    -channelID $CHANNEL_NAME -asOrg Org2MSP
```

Here, we write the blockchain genesis block, create the first channel transaction, and write anchor peer updates. You may not care how exactly it is done, but this is how Fabric is built from the bottom up. You can see that four new files are generated and stored in the channel-artifacts directory:

- genesis.block
- channel.tx
- Org1MSPanchors.tx
- Org2MSPanchors.tx

6. The Docker Compose tool is used to bring up Docker containers. We use docker-compose-cli.yaml to keep track of all Docker containers that we bring up:

```
$ cd ~
$ cd fabric-samples/first-network
$ sudo docker-compose -f docker-compose-cli.yaml up -d
```

7. We have brought up six nodes: `cli`, `orderer.example.com`, `peer0.org1.example.com`, `peer0.org2.example.com`, `peer1.org1.example.com`, and `peer1.org2.example.com`:

```
ubuntu@ip-172-31-78-117:~/fabric-samples/first-network$ sudo docker-compose -f docker-compose-cli.yaml up -d
Creating network "net_byfn" with the default driver
Creating volume "net_peer0.org2.example.com" with default driver
Creating volume "net_peer1.org2.example.com" with default driver
Creating volume "net_peer1.org1.example.com" with default driver
Creating volume "net_peer0.org1.example.com" with default driver
Creating volume "net_orderer.example.com" with default driver
Creating peer1.org1.example.com
Creating peer1.org2.example.com
Creating peer0.org2.example.com
Creating peer0.org1.example.com
Creating orderer.example.com
Creating cli
```

8. Use the peer CLI to set up the network. Using the peer command line within the Docker CLI container for this step, we will create the channel using `channel.tx` so that peers can join the channel. Please note that some commands are extremely long as we need to set up peer environment variables (note that the default is `peer0.org1`), as follows:

```
$ cd ~
$ cd fabric-samples/first-network
$ sudo docker exec -it cli bash
$ export CHANNEL_NAME=mychannel

$ peer channel create -o orderer.example.com:7050 -c
$CHANNEL_NAME -f ./channel-artifacts/channel.tx --tls --
  cafile/opt/gopath/src/github.com/hyperledger/fabric/peer/
crypto/ordererOrganizations/example.com/orderers/
orderer.example.com/msp/tlscacerts/tlsca.example.com-cert.pem
$ peer channel join -b mychannel.block

// for peer0.org2
$
CORE_PEER_MSPCONFIGPATH=/opt/gopath/src/github.com/hyperledger/
      fabric/peer/crypto/peerOrganizations/org2.example.com/
        users/Admin@org2.example.com/msp
      CORE_PEER_ADDRESS=peer0.org2.example.com:7051
      CORE_PEER_LOCALMSPID="Org2MSP"
      CORE_PEER_TLS_ROOTCERT_FILE=/opt/gopath/src/github.com/
hyperledger/fabric/peer/crypto/peerOrganizations/org2.example.com/
      peers/peer0.org2.example.com/tls/ca.crt
      $ peer channel join -b mychannel.block
```

```
// for peer1.org1
CORE_PEER_MSPCONFIGPATH=/opt/gopath/src/github.com/
hyperledger/fabric/peer/crypto/peerOrganizations/
org1.example.com/users/Admin@org1.example.com/msp
CORE_PEER_ADDRESS=peer1.org1.example.com:7051
CORE_PEER_LOCALMSPID="Org1MSP"
CORE_PEER_TLS_ROOTCERT_FILE=/opt/gopath/src/github.com/
hyperledger/fabric/peer/crypto/peerOrganizations/
org1.example.com/peers/peer1.org1.example.com/tls/ca.crt
peer channel join -b mychannel.block
```

```
// for peer1.org2
CORE_PEER_MSPCONFIGPATH=/opt/gopath/src/github.com/hyperledger/fabric/p
eer/crypto/peerOrganizations/org2.example.com/users/Admin@org2.example.
com/msp CORE_PEER_ADDRESS=peer1.org2.example.com:7051
CORE_PEER_LOCALMSPID="Org2MSP"
CORE_PEER_TLS_ROOTCERT_FILE=/opt/gopath/src/github.com/hyperledger/fabr
ic/peer/crypto/peerOrganizations/org2.example.com/peers/peer1.org2.exam
ple.com/tls/ca.crt peer channel join -b mychannel.block
```

This will create a connection between all four peers:

9. Update the anchor peer on each organization. We use the files we created in the *Installing Hyperledger Fabric on AWS* section (Org1MSPanchors.tx and Org2MSPanchors.tx) and apply them to Peer0 of both Org1 and Org2:

```
$ peer channel update -o orderer.example.com:7050 -c $CHANNEL_NAME
-f ./channel-artifacts/Org1MSPanchors.tx --tls --cafile
/opt/gopath/src/github.com/hyperledger/fabric/peer/crypto/
ordererOrganizations/example.com/orderers/orderer.example.com/
msp/tlscacerts/tlsca.example.com-cert.pem
```

```
$ CORE_PEER_MSPCONFIGPATH=/opt/gopath/src/github.com/hyperledger/
fabric/peer/crypto/peerOrganizations/org2.example.com/
```

```
users/Admin@org2.example.com/msp
CORE_PEER_ADDRESS=peer0.org2.example.com:7051
CORE_PEER_LOCALMSPID="Org2MSP"
CORE_PEER_TLS_ROOTCERT_FILE=/opt/gopath/src/github.com/
hyperledger/fabric/peer/crypto/peerOrganizations/
org2.example.com/peers/peer0.org2.example.com/tls/ca.crt
peer channel update -o orderer.example.com:7050 -c
$CHANNEL_NAME -f ./channel-artifacts/Org2MSPanchors.tx
--tls --cafile /opt/gopath/src/github.com/hyperledger/fabric/peer/
crypto/ordererOrganizations/example.com/orderers/
orderer.example.com/msp/tlscacerts/tlsca.example.com-cert.pem
```

10. Using the CLI, we need to install the chaincode to `peer0 Org1` and `peer0 Org2`. The chaincode is specified in the `-p` option in the command and the chaincode name is `mycc`. This is shown in the following code:

```
$ peer chaincode install -n mycc -v 1.0 -p
github.com/chaincode/chaincode_example02/go/

$
CORE_PEER_MSPCONFIGPATH=/opt/gopath/src/github.com/hyperledger/
fabric/peer/crypto/peerOrganizations/org2.example.com/users/Adm
in@org2.example.com/msp
CORE_PEER_ADDRESS=peer0.org2.example.com:7051
CORE_PEER_LOCALMSPID="Org2MSP"
CORE_PEER_TLS_ROOTCERT_FILE=/opt/gopath/src/github.com/hyperled
ger/fabric/peer/crypto/peerOrganizations/org2.example.com/peers
/peer0.org2.example.com/tls/ca.crt peer chaincode install -n
mycc -v 1.0 -p
github.com/chaincode/chaincode_example02/go//orderers/orderer.e
xample.com/msp/tlscacerts/tlsca.example.com-cert.pem
```

11. Instantiate the chaincode from `peer0.org2`. We will use `-c` to initialize this with a value of `100`, and `b` with `200`. We use `-p` to define the endorsement policy. This is shown in the following code:

```
$
CORE_PEER_MSPCONFIGPATH=/opt/gopath/src/github.com/hyperledger/
fabric/peer/crypto/peerOrganizations/org2.example.com/users/Adm
in@org2.example.com/msp
CORE_PEER_ADDRESS=peer0.org2.example.com:7051
CORE_PEER_LOCALMSPID="Org2MSP"
CORE_PEER_TLS_ROOTCERT_FILE=/opt/gopath/src/github.com/hyperled
ger/fabric/peer/crypto/peerOrganizations/org2.example.com/peers
/peer0.org2.example.com/tls/ca.crt peer chaincode instantiate -
o orderer.example.com:7050 --tls --cafile
/opt/gopath/src/github.com/hyperledger/fabric/peer/crypto/order
```

```
erOrganizations/example.com/orderers/orderer.example.com/msp/tl
scacerts/tlsca.example.com-cert.pem -C $CHANNEL_NAME -n mycc -v
1.0 -c '{"Args":["init","a", "100", "b","200"]}' -P "AND
('Org1MSP.peer','Org2MSP.peer')"
```

12. Execute a query on `peer0 Org1` on the `a` value. We should get the correct value of `100` back:

```
$ peer chaincode query -C $CHANNEL_NAME -n mycc -c
'{"Args":["query","a"]}'
```

```
2019-01-25 16:52:06.751 UTC [chaincodeCmd] checkChaincodeCmdParams -> INFO 002 Using default vscc
Error: could not assemble transaction, err proposal response was not successful, error code 500, msg chaincode with name 'mycc' already exists
root@c4dedc504f0a:/opt/gopath/src/github.com/hyperledger/fabric/peer# peer chaincode query -C $CHANNEL_NAME -n mycc -c '{"Args":["query","a"]}'
100
```

13. Using the CLI, create a transaction by invoking chaincode. In this example, we will move `10` from `a` to `b`. Install chaincode on `peer1 org2`, and then query from `peer1 org2` for the latest value of `a`:

```
$
CORE_PEER_MSPCONFIGPATH=/opt/gopath/src/github.com/hyperledger/
fabric/peer/crypto/peerOrganizations/org2.example.com/users/Adm
in@org2.example.com/msp
CORE_PEER_ADDRESS=peer1.org2.example.com:7051
CORE_PEER_LOCALMSPID="Org2MSP"
CORE_PEER_TLS_ROOTCERT_FILE=/opt/gopath/src/github.com/hyperled
ger/fabric/peer/crypto/peerOrganizations/org2.example.com/peers
/peer1.org2.example.com/tls/ca.crt peer chaincode install -n
mycc -v 1.0 -p github.com/chaincode/chaincode_example02/go/

$CORE_PEER_MSPCONFIGPATH=/opt/gopath/src/github.com/hyperledger
/fabric/peer/crypto/peerOrganizations/org2.example.com/users/Ad
min@org2.example.com/msp
CORE_PEER_ADDRESS=peer1.org2.example.com:7051
CORE_PEER_LOCALMSPID="Org2MSP"
CORE_PEER_TLS_ROOTCERT_FILE=/opt/gopath/src/github.com/hyperled
ger/fabric/peer/crypto/peerOrganizations/org2.example.com/peers
/peer1.org2.example.com/tls/ca.crt peer chaincode query -C
$CHANNEL_NAME -n mycc -c '{"Args":["query","a"]}'
```

This takes some time, but we will eventually receive the result of 90, which is correct after 10 is removed from 100:

```
root@93079f1bf920:/opt/gopath/src/github.com/hyperledger/fabric/peer# peer chaincode invoke -o orderer.example.com:7050 --tls true --cafile /opt/gopath/src/github.com/hyperledger
/fabric/peer/crypto/ordererOrganizations/example.com/orderers/orderer.example.com/msp/tlscacerts/tlsca.example.com-cert.pem -C $CHANNEL_NAME -n mycc --peerAddresses peer0.org1.ex
ample.com:7051 --tlsRootCertFiles /opt/gopath/src/github.com/hyperledger/fabric/peer/crypto/peerOrganizations/org1.example.com/peers/peer0.org1.example.com/tls/ca.crt --peerAddre
sses peer0.org2.example.com:7051 --tlsRootCertFiles /opt/gopath/src/github.com/hyperledger/fabric/peer/crypto/peerOrganizations/org2.example.com/peers/peer0.org2.example.com/tls/
ca.crt -c '{"Args":["invoke","a","b","10"]}'
2019-01-25 17:46:10.093 UTC [chaincodeCmd] chaincodeInvokeOrQuery -> INFO 001 Chaincode invoke successful. result: status:200
root@93079f1bf920:/opt/gopath/src/github.com/hyperledger/fabric/peer# CORE_PEER_MSPCONFIGPATH=/opt/gopath/src/github.com/hyperledger/fabric/peer/crypto/peerOrganizations/org2.exa
mple.com/users/Admin@org2.example.com/msp CORE_PEER_ADDRESS=peer1.org2.example.com:7051 CORE_PEER_LOCALMSPID="Org2MSP" CORE_PEER_TLS_ROOTCERT_FILE=/opt/gopath/src/github.com/hype
rledger/fabric/peer/crypto/peerOrganizations/org2.example.com/peers/peer1.org2.example.com/tls/ca.crt peer chaincode install -n mycc -v 1.0 -p github.com/chaincode/chaincode_exam
ple02/go/
2019-01-25 17:46:24.021 UTC [chaincodeCmd] checkChaincodeCmdParams -> INFO 001 Using default escc
2019-01-25 17:46:24.021 UTC [chaincodeCmd] checkChaincodeCmdParams -> INFO 002 Using default vscc
2019-01-25 17:46:24.668 UTC [chaincodeCmd] install -> INFO 003 Installed remotely response:<status:200 payload:"OK" >
root@93079f1bf920:/opt/gopath/src/github.com/hyperledger/fabric/peer# CORE_PEER_MSPCONFIGPATH=/opt/gopath/src/github.com/hyperledger/fabric/peer/crypto/peerOrganizations/org2.exa
mple.com/users/Admin@org2.example.com/msp CORE_PEER_ADDRESS=peer1.org2.example.com:7051 CORE_PEER_LOCALMSPID="Org2MSP" CORE_PEER_TLS_ROOTCERT_FILE=/opt/gopath/src/github.com/hype
rledger/fabric/peer/crypto/peerOrganizations/org2.example.com/peers/peer1.org2.example.com/tls/ca.crt peer chaincode query -C $CHANNEL_NAME -n mycc -c '{"Args":["query","a"]}'
90
```

This concludes building our first Fabric network. We will look at how to make changes to the existing network and add an organization to a channel in the next recipe.

How it works...

We covered the following steps to build our Fabric network:

- Generating the crypto/certificate using cryptogen
- Generating the configuration transaction using configtxgen
- Bring up the nodes based on what is defined in the docker-compose file
- Using the CLI to set up the first network
- Using the CLI to install and instantiate the chaincode
- Using the CLI to invoke and query the chaincode

This recipe helps you to understand the Hyperledge Fabric components and shows how we can quickly set up a Hyperledger Fabric network using sample chaincode (mycc). You should be able to modify the scripts and run other samples, such as fabcar and marble02, which are provided under the fabric-sample/chaincode directory.

Fabric provides the following commands used in the byfn.sh script. In the following chapters and recipes, these commands will be used to operate and manage the Fabric network environment:

- **peer**: Operates and configures a peer
- **peer chaincode**: Manages chaincode on the peer
- **peer channel**: Manages channels on the peer
- **peer node**: Manages the peer

- **peer version**: Returns the peer version
- **cryptogen**: Utility for generating crypto material
- **configtxgen**: Creates configuration data, such as the genesis block
- **configtxlator**: Utility for generating channel configurations
- **fabric-ca-client**: Manage identities
- **fabric-ca-server**: Manages the fabric-ca server

Now that we have set up our first network, let's add an organization to the channel.

Adding an organization to a channel

This recipe serves as an extension to the BYFN recipe. We will demonstrate how to add a new organization – Org3 – to the application's channel (`mychannel`).

Getting ready...

To run this recipe, you need complete the *Reviewing the Hyperledger Fabric architecture and components* recipe in this chapter to install Hyperledger Fabric with samples and binaries on the AWS EC2 instance.

How to do it...

Since we need add the new organization, Org3, to BYFN, we will first bring up the BYFN network. Follow these steps:

1. Bring up the first network using the following command:

```
$ cd ~
$ cd fabric-samples/first-network
$ sudo ./byfn.sh generate
$ sudo ./byfn.sh up
```

2. Execute the script to add `Org3` into the `mychannel` channel:

```
$ cd ~
$ cd fabric-samples/first-network
$ sudo ./eyfn.sh up
```

The following screenshot confirms `org3` is added to `mychannel` successfully:

```
========= Finished adding Org3 to your first network! =========


 /‾‾|  |‾ ‾| /\  |‾ ‾| |‾ ‾|
 \__\ | |  /_\  | |_) | | |
  _) | | | /   \ |  _ <  | |
 |___/ |_| /_/ \_\|_| \_\ |_|

Extend your first network (EYFN) test

Channel name : mychannel
Querying chaincode on peer0.org3...
=================== Querying on peer0.org3 on channel 'mychannel'... ===================
Attempting to Query peer0.org3 ...3 secs
+ peer chaincode query -C mychannel -n mycc -c '{"Args":["query","a"]}'
+ res=0
+ set +x

90
=================== Query successful on peer0.org3 on channel 'mychannel' ===================
```

We can test this by running a query against `Org3 peer0`.

3. To shut down and clean up the network, execute the following:

```
$ cd fabric-samples/first-network
$ sudo ./eyfn.sh down
$ sudo ./byfn.sh down
```

How it works...

Like what we did in the *Building the Fabric network* recipe, the `eyfn.sh` script is a good resource to understand how things work.

We will also look into the command-line steps to see the internal building blocks to add an organization to a channel:

```
# Print the usage message
function printHelp () {
  echo "Usage: "
  echo "  eyfn.sh up|down|restart|generate [-c <channel name>] [-t <timeout>] [-d <delay>] [-f <docker-compose-file>] [-s <dbtype>]"
  echo "  eyfn.sh -h|--help (print this message)"
  echo "    <mode> - one of 'up', 'down', 'restart' or 'generate'"
  echo "      - 'up' - bring up the network with docker-compose up"
  echo "      - 'down' - clear the network with docker-compose down"
  echo "      - 'restart' - restart the network"
  echo "      - 'generate' - generate required certificates and genesis block"
  echo "    -c <channel name> - channel name to use (defaults to \"mychannel\")"
  echo "    -t <timeout> - CLI timeout duration in seconds (defaults to 10)"
  echo "    -d <delay> - delay duration in seconds (defaults to 3)"
  echo "    -f <docker-compose-file> - specify which docker-compose file use (defaults to docker-compose-cli.yaml)"
  echo "    -s <dbtype> - the database backend to use: goleveldb (default) or couchdb"
  echo "    -l <language> - the chaincode language: golang (default) or node"
  echo "    -i <imagetag> - the tag to be used to launch the network (defaults to \"latest\")"
  echo "    -v - verbose mode"
  echo
  echo "Typically, one would first generate the required certificates and "
  echo "genesis block, then bring up the network. e.g.:"
  echo
  echo "        eyfn.sh generate -c mychannel"
  echo "        eyfn.sh up -c mychannel -s couchdb"
  echo "        eyfn.sh up -l node"
  echo "        eyfn.sh down -c mychannel"
  echo
  echo "Taking all defaults:"
  echo "        eyfn.sh generate"
  echo "        eyfn.sh up"
  echo "        eyfn.sh down"
}
```

4. Generate the `org3` certificates:

   ```
   $ cryptogen generate --config=./org3-crypto.yaml
   ```

5. Generate the `org3` configuration materials:

   ```
   $ configtxgen -printOrg Org3MSP
   ```

6. Generate and submit the transaction configuration for organization 3:

   ```
   $ peer channel fetch config config_block.pb -o
   orderer.example.com:7050 -c mychannel --tls --cafile
   /opt/gopath/src/github.com/hyperledger/fabric/peer/
   crypto/ordererOrganizations/example.com/orderers/
   orderer.example.com/msp/tlscacerts/tlsca.example.com-cert.pem
   $ configtxlator proto_encode --input config.json
     --type common.Config
   $ configtxlator proto_encode --input modified_config.json
     --type common.Config
   $ configtxlator compute_update --channel_id mychannel
   --original original_config.pb --updated modified_config.pb
   $ configtxlator proto_decode --input config_update.pb
   --type common.ConfigUpdate
   ```

7. Configure the transaction to add `org3`, which has been created:

```
$ peer channel signconfigtx -f org3_update_in_envelope.pb
```

8. Submit the transaction from a different peer (`peer0.org2`), who also signs it:

```
$ peer channel update -f org3_update_in_envelope.pb -c mychannel -o
orderer.example.com:7050 --tls --cafile
/opt/gopath/src/github.com/hyperledger/fabric/peer/
crypto/ordererOrganizations/example.com/orderers/
orderer.example.com/msp/tlscacerts/tlsca.example.com-cert.pem
```

9. Get the `org3` peer to join the network:

```
$ peer channel fetch 0 mychannel.block -o orderer.example.com:7050
-c mychannel --tls --cafile /opt/gopath/src/github.com/
  hyperledger/fabric/peer/crypto/ordererOrganizations/
  example.com/orderers/orderer.example.com/
  msp/tlscacerts/tlsca.example.com-cert.pem
$ peer channel join
 -b mychannel.blockcd fabric-samples/first-network
```

10. Install and update the chaincode:

```
$ peer chaincode install -n mycc -v 2.0 -l golang -p
 github.com/chaincode/chaincode_example02/go/
$ peer chaincode upgrade -o orderer.example.com:7050
--tls true --cafile /opt/gopath/src/github.com/hyperledger/
fabric/peer/crypto/ordererOrganizations/example.com/orderers/
orderer.example.com/msp/tlscacerts/tlsca.example.com-cert.pem
-C mychannel -n mycc -v 2.0 -c
'{"Args":["init","a","90","b","210"]}'
-P 'AND ('\''Org1MSP.peer'\'','\''Org2MSP.peer'\'',
 '\''Org3MSP.peer'\'')'
```

11. Query `peer0 org3`:

```
$ peer chaincode query -C mychannel -n mycc
-c '{"Args":["query","a"]}'
```

12. Invoke the transaction to move 10 from a to b again on a different peer:

```
$ peer chaincode invoke -o orderer.example.com:7050 --tls true
--cafile /opt/gopath/src/github.com/hyperledger/fabric/peer/
crypto/ordererOrganizations/example.com/orderers/
orderer.example.com/msp/tlscacerts/tlsca.example.com-cert.pem
-C mychannel -n mycc --peerAddresses peer0.org1.example.com:7051
--tlsRootCertFiles /opt/gopath/src/github.com/hyperledger/
```

```
fabric/peer/crypto/peerOrganizations/org1.example.com/peers/
peer0.org1.example.com/tls/ca.crt
--peerAddresses peer0.org2.example.com:7051
--tlsRootCertFiles /opt/gopath/src/github.com/hyperledger/
fabric/peer/crypto/peerOrganizations/org2.example.com/peers/
 peer0.org2.example.com/tls/ca.crt
--peerAddresses peer0.org3.example.com:7051
--tlsRootCertFiles/opt/gopath/src/github.com/hyperledger/
fabric/peer/crypto/peerOrganizations/org3.example.com/peers/
peer0.org3.example.com/tls/ca.crt
-c '{"Args":["invoke","a","b","10"]}'
```

This concludes how to add an organization to an existing network in a channel. We will look at how to use CouchDB to review transactions in the next recipe.

Following all the previous steps will create our first network, which consists of two organizations, two peers per organization, and single Solo ordering service. In this recipe, we showed you how to add a third organization to an application channel with its own peers to an already running first network, and then join it to the new channel.

When you view the log file, you will be able to see details in the following order:

- Generating Org3 config material
- Generating and submitting config tx to add Org3
- Creating config transaction to add Org3 to the network
- Installing jq
- Config transaction to add Org3 to the network
- Signing the config transaction
- Submitting the transaction from a different peer (peer0.org2), which also signs it
- Configure transaction to add Org3 to network submitted
- Having Org3 peers join the network
- Getting Org3 on to your first network
- Fetching the channel config block from orderer
- peer0.org3 joined the mychannel channel
- peer1.org3 joined the mychannel channel
- Installing chaincode 2.0 on peer0.org3
- Upgrading chaincode to have Org3 peers on the network
- Finishing adding Org3 to your first network
- Chaincode is installed on peer0.org1
- Chaincode is installed on peer0.org2

- Chaincode is upgraded on `peer0.org1` on the `mychannel` channel
- Finished adding Org3 to your first network!

Updating modification policies or altering batch sizes or any other channel configuration can be updated using the same approach but for now we will focus solely on the integration of a new organization.

There's more...

The following block shows the `org3-crypto.yaml` section for `Org3`:

```
# ---------------------------------------------------------------------
-
# "PeerOrgs" - Definition of organizations managing peer nodes
# ---------------------------------------------------------------------
--
PeerOrgs:
# ---------------------------------------------------------------------
--
# Org3
# ---------------------------------------------------------------------
--
- Name: Org3
Domain: org3.example.com
EnableNodeOUs: true
Template:
Count: 2
Users:
Count: 1
```

The following block shows the `configtx.yaml` section for `Org3`:

```
#####################################################################
######
# Section: Organizations
#
# - This section defines the different organizational identities which will
# be referenced later in the configuration.
#
#####################################################################
#####
Organizations:
- &Org3
# DefaultOrg defines the organization which is used in the sampleconfig
# of the fabric.git development environment
Name: Org3MSP
```

```
# ID to load the MSP definition as
ID: Org3MSP
MSPDir: crypto-config/peerOrganizations/org3.example.com/msp
AnchorPeers:
# AnchorPeers defines the location of peers which can be used for cross org
gossip #communication. Note, this value is only
# encoded in the genesis block in the Application section context
- Host: peer0.org3.example.com
Port: 7051
```

In the next recipe, we will look at how smart contracts work with CouchDB.

Using CouchDB

In this recipe, we will explore how to start up a network using CouchDB and then look at transactions applied into CouchDB from a web UI. To successfully execute this recipe, you need install the Hyperledger Fabric with samples and binaries on the AWS EC2 instance.

How to do it...

To use CouchDB, follow these steps:

1. Make sure network is not up. If it is up, shut down the network, as shown here:

```
$ cd fabric-samples/first-network
$ sudo ./byfn.sh down
```

2. Start up the BYFN network using CouchDB:

Here we will start up the network by using the CouchDB database.

```
$ cd fabric-samples/first-network
$ sudo ./byfn.sh up -c mychannel -s couchdb
```

Following screenshot shows our network starting up:

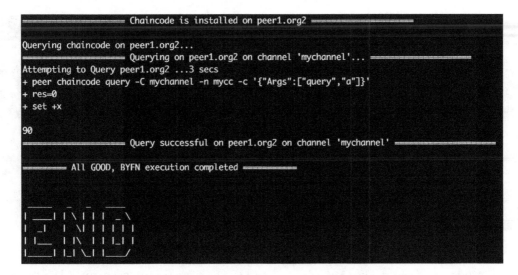

3. Install chaincode by navigating into the CLI container using the command-line interface:

```
$ sudo docker exec -it cli bash
$ peer chaincode install -n marbles -v 1.0
  -p github.com/chaincode/marbles02/go
```

4. Instantiate the chaincode:

```
$ export CHANNEL_NAME=mychannel
$ peer chaincode instantiate -o orderer.example.com:7050
--tls --cafile /opt/gopath/src/github.com/hyperledger/fabric/peer/
  crypto/ordererOrganizations/example.com/orderers/
  orderer.example.com/msp/tlscacerts/tlsca.example.com-cert.pem
  -C $CHANNEL_NAME -n marbles -v 1.0 -c '{"Args":["init"]}' -P "OR
  ('Org0MSP.peer','Org1MSP.peer')"
```

5. Invoke the chaincode. The following commands invoke chaincode to create marble.

```
$ peer chaincode invoke -o orderer.example.com:7050 --tls
--cafile /opt/gopath/src/github.com/hyperledger/fabric/peer/
  crypto/ordererOrganizations/example.com/orderers/
  orderer.example.com/msp/tlscacerts/tlsca.example.com-cert.pem
  -C $CHANNEL_NAME -n marbles -c
  '{"Args":["initMarble","marble5","blue","35","tom"]}'
```

Following screenshot shows successful creation of chanincode:

```
ubuntu@ip-172-31-37-157:~/fabric-samples/first-network$ docker exec -it cli bash
Got permission denied while trying to connect to the Docker daemon socket at unix:///var/run/docker.sock: Get http://%2Fvar%2Frun%2Fdocker.sock/
v1.39/containers/cli/json: dial unix /var/run/docker.sock: connect: permission denied
ubuntu@ip-172-31-37-157:~/fabric-samples/first-network$ sudo docker exec -it cli bash
root@f317f76b6c31:/opt/gopath/src/github.com/hyperledger/fabric/peer# peer chaincode install -n marbles -v 1.0 -p github.com/chaincode/marbles02
/go
2019-01-22 16:54:34.470 UTC [chaincodeCmd] checkChaincodeCmdParams -> INFO 001 Using default escc
2019-01-22 16:54:34.470 UTC [chaincodeCmd] checkChaincodeCmdParams -> INFO 002 Using default vscc
2019-01-22 16:54:34.713 UTC [chaincodeCmd] install -> INFO 003 Installed remotely response:<status:200 payload:"OK" >
root@f317f76b6c31:/opt/gopath/src/github.com/hyperledger/fabric/peer#
root@f317f76b6c31:/opt/gopath/src/github.com/hyperledger/fabric/peer# export CHANNEL_NAME=mychannel
root@f317f76b6c31:/opt/gopath/src/github.com/hyperledger/fabric/peer# peer chaincode instantiate -o orderer.example.com:7050 --tls --cafile /opt
/gopath/src/github.com/hyperledger/fabric/peer/crypto/ordererOrganizations/example.com/orderers/orderer.example.com/msp/tlscacerts/tlsca.example
.com-cert.pem -C $CHANNEL_NAME -n marbles -v 1.0 -c '{"Args":["init"]}' -P "OR ('Org0MSP.peer','Org1MSP.peer')"
2019-01-22 16:56:08.495 UTC [chaincodeCmd] checkChaincodeCmdParams -> INFO 001 Using default escc
2019-01-22 16:56:08.495 UTC [chaincodeCmd] checkChaincodeCmdParams -> INFO 002 Using default vscc

root@f317f76b6c31:/opt/gopath/src/github.com/hyperledger/fabric/peer#
root@f317f76b6c31:/opt/gopath/src/github.com/hyperledger/fabric/peer# peer chaincode invoke -o orderer.example.com:7050 --tls --cafile /opt/gopa
th/src/github.com/hyperledger/fabric/peer/crypto/ordererOrganizations/example.com/orderers/orderer.example.com/msp/tlscacerts/tlsca.example.com-
cert.pem -C $CHANNEL_NAME -n marbles -c '{"Args":["initMarble","marble5","blue","35","tom"]}'
2019-01-22 16:56:57.478 UTC [chaincodeCmd] chaincodeInvokeOrQuery -> INFO 001 Chaincode invoke successful. result: status:200
root@f317f76b6c31:/opt/gopath/src/github.com/hyperledger/fabric/peer#
```

6. Open the CouchDB UI by navigating
   to `http://host-ip:5984/_utils/#/_all_dbs` (in my case, my AWS public
   IP address is `3.91.245.92`, so the URL is
   `http://3.91.245.92:5984/_utils/#/_all_dbs`):

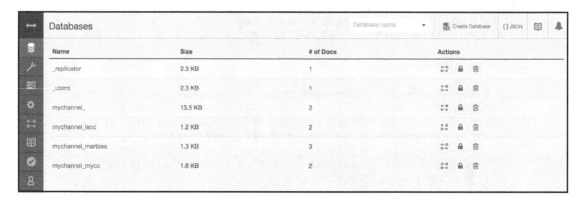

In order to allow public access to CouchDB, we need open port `5984`. Navigate to
the AWS security group under the instance, launch the wizard, and choose
Action | Edit Inbound Rules | Add Inbound Rule. This is shown as follows.
After this, click **Save**. You can follow the below example to allow all IP address to
access CouchDB:

7. From **mychannel_marbles**, we can query and see the transaction ID with **marble5**:

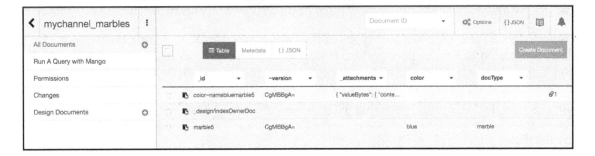

8. Click **marble5**, and you will see the default **marble5** files:

```
mychannel_marbles > marble5

  Save Changes    Cancel

1  {
2      "_id": "marble5",
3      "_rev": "1-42ccde40ce1f9b56aa5737cce1738d1c",
4      "color": "blue",
5      "docType": "marble",
6      "name": "marble5",
7      "owner": "tom",
8      "size": 35,
9      "~version": "\u0000CgMBBgA="
10 }
```

Here, we saw how to use CouchDB to view how transactions get created, and updated them on the Fabric network. We will write a smart contract and deploy it as an application in the next recipe.

How it works...

In this recipe, we learned how to use CouchDB as the state database with Hyperledger Fabric. We also looked at how to use CouchDB to deploy Marbles to the network.

Hyperledger Fabric supports two types of peer databases: LevelDB is the default state database embedded in the peer node and stores chaincode data as simple key-value pairs; and CouchDB is an optional alternate state database that supports rich queries when chaincode data values are modeled as JSON. This recipe describes the steps required to use CouchDB as the state database with Fabric. CouchDB is a JSON document datastore rather than a pure key-value store, therefore enabling indexing of the contents of the documents in the database.

In the last recipe, we will show you how to write your first smart contract application and deploy it into the blockchain.

Writing your first application

In this recipe, we will explore how to create a smart contract and then deploy it into the blockchain.

To run this recipe, you need to have completed the *Installing Hyperledger Fabric on AWS* recipe in this chapter to install Hyperledger Fabric with samples and binaries on the AWS EC2 instance.

How to do it...

To write your first application, follow these steps:

1. Set up the development environment:

```
$ cd ~
cd fabric-samples/first-network
sudo docker ps
sudo ./byfn.sh down
sudo docker rm -f $(sudo docker ps -aq)
sudo docker network prune
cd ../fabcar && ls
```

You will notice that there are a few **Node.js** file present in `fabcar` folder such as `enrollAdmin.js`, `invoke.js`, `query.js`, `registerUser.js`, and `package.json` and all others packaged into one `startFabric.sh` file.

2. Install the Fabric client:

```
$ sudo npm install -g npm@5.3.0
$ sudo npm update
```

You will notice from the following screenshot that the Fabric client 1.3.0 and Fabric CA client 1.30 packages are installed:

```
CXX(target) Release/obj.target/pkcs11/src/pkcs11/param_ecdh.o
CXX(target) Release/obj.target/pkcs11/src/pkcs11/pkcs11.o
CXX(target) Release/obj.target/pkcs11/src/async.o
CXX(target) Release/obj.target/pkcs11/src/node.o
SOLINK_MODULE(target) Release/obj.target/pkcs11.node
COPY Release/pkcs11.node
make: Leaving directory '/home/ubuntu/fabric-samples/fabcar/node_modules/pkcs11js/build'
npm notice created a lockfile as package-lock.json. You should commit this file.
npm WARN ajv-keywords@2.1.1 requires a peer of ajv@^5.0.0 but none was installed.
npm WARN fabcar@1.0.0 No repository field.

+ grpc@1.18.0
+ fabric-ca-client@1.3.0
+ fabric-client@1.3.0
added 743 packages in 44.441s
```

3. Execute the following command to launch the network:

```
$ sudo ./startFabric.sh node
```

4. Open a new Terminal to stream the Docker logs:

```
$ sudo docker logs -f ca.example.com
```

This will open the Docker file, which will look similar to the following screenshot:

```
# don't rewrite paths for Windows Git Bash users
export MSYS_NO_PATHCONV=1

docker-compose -f docker-compose.yml down
Removing network net_basic
WARNING: Network net_basic not found.

docker-compose -f docker-compose.yml up -d ca.example.com orderer.example.com peer0.org1.example.com couchdb
Creating network "net_basic" with the default driver
Creating orderer.example.com
Creating couchdb
Creating ca.example.com
Creating peer0.org1.example.com

# wait for Hyperledger Fabric to start
# incase of errors when running later commands, issue export FABRIC_START_TIMEOUT=<larger number>
export FABRIC_START_TIMEOUT=10
#echo ${FABRIC_START_TIMEOUT}
sleep ${FABRIC_START_TIMEOUT}

# Create the channel
docker exec -e "CORE_PEER_LOCALMSPID=Org1MSP" -e "CORE_PEER_MSPCONFIGPATH=/etc/hyperledger/msp/users/Admin@org1.example.com/msp" peer0.org1.
example.com peer channel create -o orderer.example.com:7050 -c mychannel -f /etc/hyperledger/configtx/channel.tx
2019-01-05 19:27:29.498 UTC [channelCmd] InitCmdFactory -> INFO 001 Endorser and orderer connections initialized
2019-01-05 19:27:29.544 UTC [cli/common] readBlock -> INFO 002 Received block: 0
# Join peer0.org1.example.com to the channel.
docker exec -e "CORE_PEER_LOCALMSPID=Org1MSP" -e "CORE_PEER_MSPCONFIGPATH=/etc/hyperledger/msp/users/Admin@org1.example.com/msp" peer0.org1.
example.com peer channel join -b mychannel.block
2019-01-05 19:27:29.963 UTC [channelCmd] InitCmdFactory -> INFO 001 Endorser and orderer connections initialized
2019-01-05 19:27:30.073 UTC [channelCmd] executeJoin -> INFO 002 Successfully submitted proposal to join channel
Creating cli
2019-01-05 19:27:31.654 UTC [chaincodeCmd] checkChaincodeCmdParams -> INFO 001 Using default escc
2019-01-05 19:27:31.654 UTC [chaincodeCmd] checkChaincodeCmdParams -> INFO 002 Using default vscc
2019-01-05 19:27:31.680 UTC [chaincodeCmd] install -> INFO 003 Installed remotely response:<status:200 payload:"OK" >
2019-01-05 19:27:32.002 UTC [chaincodeCmd] checkChaincodeCmdParams -> INFO 001 Using default escc
2019-01-05 19:27:32.002 UTC [chaincodeCmd] checkChaincodeCmdParams -> INFO 002 Using default vscc
2019-01-05 19:28:12.288 UTC [chaincodeCmd] chaincodeInvokeOrQuery -> INFO 001 Chaincode invoke successful. result: status:200

Total setup execution time : 58 secs ...

Start by installing required packages run 'npm install'
Then run 'node enrollAdmin.js', then 'node registerUser'

The 'node invoke.js' will fail until it has been updated with valid arguments
The 'node query.js' may be run at anytime once the user has been registered
```

Next, we will use the Node.js script to run, query, and update the records on Fabric network.

Accessing the API with SDK

In this recipe, the application uses an SDK to access the APIs that permit queries and updates to the ledger. Now we will perform the following steps:

1. Enroll an admin user with the enrollAdmin.js script:

```
$ sudo node enrollAdmin.js
```

When we launch the network, an admin user needs to be registered with certificate authority. We send an enrollment call to the CA server and retrieve the **enrollment certificate (eCert)** for this user. We then use this admin user to subsequently register and enroll other users:

```
ubuntu@ip-172-31-45-218:~/fabric-samples/fabcar$ sudo node enrollAdmin.js
 Store path:/home/ubuntu/fabric-samples/fabcar/hfc-key-store
(node:4356) DeprecationWarning: grpc.load: Use the @grpc/proto-loader module with grpc.loadPackageDefinition instead
Successfully enrolled admin user "admin"
Assigned the admin user to the fabric client ::{"name":"admin","mspid":"Org1MSP","roles":null,"affiliation":"","enrollmentSecret":"","enroll
ment":{"signingIdentity":"8312cd0dbdeeddf02397eaab8e36ff1f4b44507777313e55667d68e9dcce5853","identity":{"certificate":"-----BEGIN CERTIFICAT
E-----\nMIICATCCAaigAwIBAgIUE2CeOFH7I6tsjOxaTXWmd1uFeMkwCgYIKoZIzj0EAwIw\nczELMAkGA1UEBhMCVVMxEzARBgNVBAgTCkNhbGlmb3JuaWExFjAUBgNVBAcTDVNh\n
biBGcmFuY2lzY28xGTAXBgNVBAoTEG9yZzEuZXhhbXBsZS5jb20xHDAaBgNVBAMT\nE2NhLm9yZzEuZXhhbXBsZS5jb20wHhcNMTkwMTA1MTkzNjAwWhcNMjAwMTA1MTk0\nMTAwWjAh
MQ8wDQYDVQQLEwZjbGllbnQxDjAMBgNVBAMTBWFkbWluMFkwEwYHKoZI\nzj0CAQYIKoZIzj0DAQcDQgAEjEewCJzMAxWIAvnELX1tTRxAZfY3aOUZG1wU1A7w\nnxR9q1XOfUG15+doD
N7YCYSLW41EGa+QaW8b4CqNNt/irIaNsMGowDgYDVR0PAQH/\nBAQDAgeAMAwGA1UdEwEB/wQCMAAwHQYDVR0OBBYEFCxsDPYQBdFkAA+lcnGmqOpz\nnq7tcMCsGA1UdIwQkMCKAIEI5
qg3NdtruuLoMZnAYUdFFBNMarRst3dusalc2Xk18\nMAoGCCqGSM49BAMCA0cAMEQCID9+iCfAq4xkrsUNphUCGJMqb0dbSENezFXIZgFy\nKdRUAiBOuIC8SWrNMHA3gPTg6tJA1xS6
+tut0mK6rpzZB5hm4Q==\n-----END CERTIFICATE-----\n"}}}
```

2. Register and enroll a user called user1 using the registerUser.js script:

```
$ sudo node registerUser.js
```

3. With the newly-generated eCert for the admin user, let's communicate with the CA server once more to register and enroll user1. We can use the ID of user1 to query and update the ledger:

```
 Store path:/home/ubuntu/fabric-samples/fabcar/hfc-key-store
(node:4370) DeprecationWarning: grpc.load: Use the @grpc/proto-loader module with grpc.loadPackageDefinition instead
Successfully loaded admin from persistence
Successfully registered user1 - secret:ZLBOPPJGbJOY
Successfully enrolled member user "user1"
User1 was successfully registered and enrolled and is ready to interact with the fabric network
```

4. Let's run a query against the ledger:

```
$ sudo node query.js
```

5. It returns the following screenshot. You will find that there are 10 cars on the network, from CAR0 to CAR9. Each has a color, doctype, make, model, and owner:

```
 Store path:/home/ubuntu/fabric-samples/fabcar/hfc-key-store
(node:4384) DeprecationWarning: grpc.load: Use the @grpc/proto-loader module with grpc.loadPackageDefinition instead
Successfully loaded user1 from persistence
Query has completed, checking results
Response is  [{"Key":"CAR0","Record":{"color":"blue","docType":"car","make":"Toyota","model":"Prius","owner":"Tomoko"}},{"Key":"CAR1","Recor
d":{"color":"red","docType":"car","make":"Ford","model":"Mustang","owner":"Brad"}},{"Key":"CAR2","Record":{"color":"green","docType":"car","
make":"Hyundai","model":"Tucson","owner":"Jin Soo"}},{"Key":"CAR3","Record":{"color":"yellow","docType":"car","make":"Volkswagen","model":"P
assat","owner":"Max"}},{"Key":"CAR4","Record":{"color":"black","docType":"car","make":"Tesla","model":"S","owner":"Adriana"}},{"Key":"CAR5",
"Record":{"color":"purple","docType":"car","make":"Peugeot","model":"205","owner":"Michel"}},{"Key":"CAR6","Record":{"color":"white","docTyp
e":"car","make":"Chery","model":"S22L","owner":"Aarav"}},{"Key":"CAR7","Record":{"color":"violet","docType":"car","make":"Fiat","model":"Pun
to","owner":"Pari"}},{"Key":"CAR8","Record":{"color":"indigo","docType":"car","make":"Tata","model":"Nano","owner":"Valeria"}},{"Key":"CAR9"
,"Record":{"color":"brown","docType":"car","make":"Holden","model":"Barina","owner":"Shotaro"}}]
```

6. The following chaincode constructs the query using the `queryAllCars` function to query all cars:

```
// queryCar chaincode function - requires 1 argument,
   ex: args: ['CAR4'],
// queryAllCars chaincode function - requires no arguments,
   ex: args: [''],
 const request = {
    //targets : --- letting this default to the
      peers assigned to the channel
    chaincodeId: 'fabcar',
    fcn: 'queryAllCars',
    args: ['']
 }
```

7. Update the ledger. To do this, we will update the `invoke.js` script. This time, the `fabcar` chaincode uses the `createCar` function to insert a new car, CAR10, into the ledger:

```
var request = {
    //targets: let default to the peer assigned to the client
    chaincodeId: 'fabcar',
     fcn: 'createCar',
    args: ['CAR10', 'Chevy', 'Volt', 'Red', 'Nick'],
    chainId: 'mychannel',
    txId: tx_id
};

sudo node invoke.js
```

Here we will complete the transaction when CAR10 is created.

8. Execute a query to verify the changes made. Change `query.js` using the `queryCar` function to query CAR10:

```
var request = {
   //targets: let default to the peer assigned to the client
   chaincodeId: 'fabcar',
   fcn: 'queryCar',
   args: ['CAR10'],
   chainId: 'mychannel',
   txId: tx_id
};
```

9. Run `query.js` again. We can now extract `CAR10` from the ledger with the response as
`{"color":"Red","docType":"car","make":"Chevy","model":"Volt","owner":"Nick"}`:

```
sudo node query.js
```

This will result in the following query:

```
Store path:/home/ubuntu/fabric-samples/fabcar/hfc-key-store
(node:9047) DeprecationWarning: grpc.load: Use the @grpc/proto-loader module with grpc.loadPackageDefinition instead
Successfully loaded user1 from persistence
Query has completed, checking results
Response is  {"color":"Red","docType":"car","make":"Chevy","model":"Volt","owner":"Nick"}
```

10. Shut down the Fabric network:

```
sudo docker stop $(sudo docker ps -a -q)
sudo docker rm $(sudo docker ps -a -q)
sudo docker ps
```

We have gone through the steps to query and update the transaction using smart contract chaincode. Now, let's see how it works under the hood.

How it works...

This concludes the recipe to create and deploy your first smart contract chaincode.

In the previous steps, we used `query.js` to query the key-value pair store. We can also query for the values of one or more keys, or perform complex searches on JSON data-storage formats. The following diagram shows how the query works:

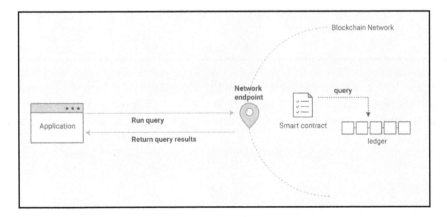

The following is a representation of different functions in chaincode, which explains that we should first define the code functions to all the available APIs in the chaincode interface:

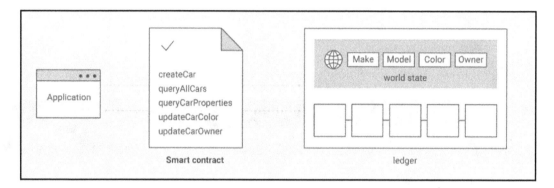

The following diagram shows the process of updating the ledger. Once an update to the ledger is proposed and endorsed, it will be returned to the application, and will in turn send the updated ledger to be ordered and written to every peer's ledger:

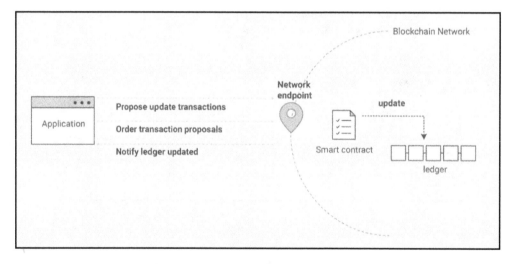

We learned how to write a small smart contract chaincode on the Fabric network to perform a transaction data query and update. In the next chapter, you will learn how to write an end-to-end Hyperledger Fabric application using all that we have learned in this chapter.

See also

- *Fabric Explored: A Technical Deep-Dive* on Hyperledger Fabric, IBM blockchain, IBM September 17, 2018 (`https://www.slideshare.net/MattLucas3/ blockchain-hyperledger-fabric-explored-v45`)
- The *hyperledger-fabricdocs Documentation*, release master, January 27, 2019: `https://media.readthedocs.org/pdf/hyperledger-fabric/latest/ hyperledger-fabric.pdf`

2
Implementing Hyperledger Fabric

In the previous chapter, we learned about how to set up and configure Hyperledger Fabric. We explored its key components, including channels, **Membership Service Providers** (**MSPs**), the ordering service, and Fabric **Certificate Authority** (**CA**).

In this chapter, we are going to build a simple device asset management DApp. We will exploit this example by writing chaincode implemented by various programming languages and we'll also build, test, and deploy our DApp.

First, we will look at inventory asset management, and then the rest of the chapter will be divided into the following recipes:

- Writing chaincode as a smart contract
- Compiling and deploying Fabric chaincode
- Running and testing the smart contract
- Developing an application with Hyperledger Fabric through the SDK

Inventory asset management

Blockchain technology is considered to be a game-changer for building an immutable, decentralized, trustless, and peer-to-peer ledger for business logic. Records in the blockchain are linked using cryptography. Each block contains a block timestamp, transaction data, and the previous block's cryptographic hash information.

IT asset management is an important part of an organization's strategy. It usually involves incorporating detailed IT assets and inventory information for business practices, such as hardware purchases and redistribution. Typical business practices include the request and approval process, procurement management, life cycle management, and so on.

Today, there are many participants in an asset's life cycle—from the manufacturer, the transporter, the IT service department, all the way to the end user—with each having their own management system. As a result, it's quite difficult to integrate all of these different bits of data to maintain a single version of the truth for the asset's entire life cycle.

By design, blockchain is a shared ledger technology. It is really good at registering, controlling, and transferring assets. Applying blockchain in an asset-tracking management system allows us to track digital transactions more securely and transparently. It provides new opportunities for organizations to correct problems within the asset management industry as it revolves around a *single source of truth*.

In this chapter, we will look at the processes involved in an IT asset management system. One of the main processes is tracking the complete life cycle of the assets. This includes ordering the asset, shipping the asset, receiving the asset, requesting a new asset, approving the asset, and then recycling and retiring the asset. Other record-tracking activities involve geographically locating the asset across the organization's various locations. This allows organizations to maintain the inventory better, to identify where the asset is currently located, and which asset is available at any time.

For the sake of our demonstration, we are going to simplify the entire process, as it can be very complex in a real-world scenario. In the following school IT-asset management system, we have defined three participants: the **School Administrative Office** (**SAO**), the **original equipment manufacturer** (**OEM**), and the end user, who is a student. In this scenario, the following occurs:

1. The SAO places an **Order** to the **OEM**
2. The **OEM** receives the **Order**, makes the products, and ships the orders
3. The school receives the **Order** and distributes the products to the students

The overall process is shown in the following diagram:

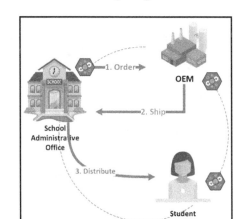

In the following recipe, we will implement this flow using Fabric chaincode.

Writing chaincode as a smart contract

Chaincode in Hyperledger Fabric is similar to smart contracts. It is a program that implements the business logic and is run on top of blockchain. The application can interact with the blockchain by invoking chaincode to manage the ledger state and keep the transaction record in the ledger. This chaincode needs to be installed on each endorsing peer node that runs in a secured Docker container. The Hyperledger Fabric chaincode can be programmed in Go, Node.js, and Java.

Every chaincode program must implement the `Chaincode` interface. In this section, we will explore chaincode implementation using Go.

Getting ready

In `Chapter 1`, *Working with Hyperledger Fabric*, we set up our Hyperledger Fabric and the runtime environments. If you haven't done this, please revisit the previous chapter. After that, you can start following this recipe.

Writing chaincode using Go

Every chaincode needs to implement a `Chaincode` interface. There are two methods defined in the interface:

```
type Chaincode interface {
  Init (stub ChaincodeStubInterface) pb.Response
  Invoke (stub ChaincodeStubInterface) pb.Response
}
```

Here, the `Init` method is called to allow the chaincode to create an initial state and the data initialization after the `chaincode` container has been established for the first time. The `Invoke` method is called to interact with the ledger (to query or update the asset) in the proposed transaction.

`ChaincodeStubInterface` provides the API for apps to access and modify their ledgers. Here are some important APIs:

```
type ChaincodeStubInterface interface {
    InvokeChaincode(chaincodeName string, args [][]byte, channel string)
pb.Response
    GetState(key string) ([]byte, error)
    PutState(key string, value []byte) error
    DelState(key string) error
    GetQueryResult(query string) (StateQueryIteratorInterface, error)
    GetTxTimestamp() (*timestamp.Timestamp, error)
    GetTxID() string
    GetChannelID() string
}
```

Examples of important APIs include the following:

- `InvokeChaincode`: Calls the chaincode function
- `GetState`: Returns the value of the specified `key` from the ledger
- `PutState`: Adds the key and the value to the ledger

Now that we understand some basic chaincode APIs, let's start to write our chaincode for IT asset management.

How to do it...

We will implement our school IT-asset management system using chaincode, and define the `Asset` object, and the `Init`, `Invoke`, and `query` functions. To do this, follow these steps:

1. Since we will use Go to write chaincode, install it in Unix (Ubuntu). Make sure Go version 1.10.x is installed. If you haven't yet installed Go, run the following command:

   ```
   wget https://dl.google.com/go/go1.11.4.linux-amd64.tar.gz
   sudo tar -zxvf go1.11.4.linux-amd64.tar.gz -C /usr/local/
   ```

2. Create a local folder called `itasset` and navigate to that folder:

   ```
   mkdir ~/itasset && cd ~/itasset
   ```

3. To set up the `PATH` variable for Go, enter the following command:

   ```
   ubuntu@ip-172-31-0-111:~$ export GOPATH=/home/ubuntu/itasset/
   ubuntu@ip-172-31-0-111:~$ export
   PATH=/usr/local/go/bin:$GOPATH/bin/:$PATH
   ubuntu@ip-172-31-0-111:~$ cd /home/ubuntu/itasset/
   ubuntu@ip-172-31-0-111:~/itasset$ mkdir -p $GOPATH/src/assetmgr
   ubuntu@ip-172-31-0-111:~/itasset$ cd $GOPATH/src/assetmgr
   ```

4. Create the chaincode source file, `assetmgr.go`, for writing IT asset management:

   ```
   touch assetmgr.go
   ```

5. Our `assetmgr` chaincode needs to implement the `Chaincode` interface and the business functions for IT asset management. As we discussed in the previous section, we will implement three chaincode functions in blockchain, shown as follows:

   ```
   Order: function called by school administer to order a device from
   OEM
   Ship: function called by OEM to transport the device to school
   Distribute: function called by School to distribute the device to
   students.
   ```

Once the student receives the device, the asset management process is completed. We will keep track of the device's asset information, so we also need to define the device with related tracking information in the chaincode.

6. Based on our chaincode implementation analysis, let's define the skeleton of the `AssetMgr` chaincode. Define the `import` section:

```
package main
import (
               "encoding/json"
               "fmt"
               "github.com/hyperledger/fabric/core/chaincode/shim"
               pb "github.com/hyperledger/fabric/protos/peer"
)
type AssetMgr struct {
}
```

7. Define the asset:

```
//define organization asset information, the record can be trace in
bloackchain
type OrgAsset struct {
}
```

8. Define the `Init` and `Invoke` methods:

```
func (c *AssetMgr) Init(stub shim.ChaincodeStubInterface)
pb.Response {
               return shim.Success(nil)
}
func (c *AssetMgr) Invoke(stub shim.ChaincodeStubInterface)
pb.Response {
               return shim.Error("Invalid function name")
}
func (c *AssetMgr) Order(stub shim.ChaincodeStubInterface, args
[]string) pb.Response {
}
func (c *AssetMgr) Ship(stub shim.ChaincodeStubInterface, args
[]string) pb.Response {
}
func (c *AssetMgr) Distribute(stub shim.ChaincodeStubInterface,
args []string) pb.Response {
}
```

9. Define the chaincode's `main` function:

```
func main() {
        err := shim.Start(new(AssetMgr))
        if err != nil {
                fmt.Printf("Error creating new
AssetMgr Contract: %s", err)
        }
}
```

We have now defined our `AssetMgr` skeleton. Next, we need to implement all of these unimplemented functions in our chaincode. We will start by defining the `OrgAsset` entity.

The OrgAsset entity

All assets should have an `Id` field to identify them. Each device also has a physical device ID (`DeviceId`) that indicates the type of device, such as iPhone, iPad, or macOS. During the IT asset management flow process, the device is transferred from one entity to another, and the `Location` of the device keeps changing. Each processor may want to enter `Comment` to provide additional information at each step. Based on this, we can define the `OrgAsset` entity as follows:

```
type OrgAsset struct {
        Id        string `json:"id"`        //the assetId
        AssetType string `json:"assetType"` //type of device
        Status    string `json:"status"`    //status of asset
        Location  string `json:"location"`  //device location
        DeviceId  string `json:"deviceId"`  //DeviceId
        Comment   string `json:"comment"`   //comment
        From      string `json:"from"`      //from
        To        string `json:"to"`        //to
}
```

After we have defined the `OrgAsset` entity, we will take a look at the implementation of the `Init` function.

The Init function

The implementation of our `Init` function is as follows:

```
func (c *AssetMgr) Init(stub shim.ChaincodeStubInterface) pb.Response {
  args := stub.GetStringArgs()
  if len(args) != 3 {
    return shim.Error("Incorrect arguments. Expecting a key and a value")
```

```go
    }
    assetId := args[0]
    assetType := args[1]
    deviceId := args[2]

    //create asset
    assetData := OrgAsset{
      Id: assetId,
      AssetType: assetType,
      Status: "START",
      Location: "N/A",
      DeviceId: deviceId,
      Comment: "Initialized asset",
      From: "N/A",
      To: "N/A"}
    assetBytes, _ := json.Marshal(assetData)
    assetErr := stub.PutState(assetId, assetBytes)
    if assetErr != nil {
      return shim.Error(fmt.Sprintf("Failed to create asset: %s", args[0]))
    }
    return shim.Success(nil)
}

func (c *AssetMgr) Init(stub shim.ChaincodeStubInterface) pb.Response {
      args := stub.GetStringArgs()
              assetId := args[0]    assetType := args[1]
deviceId := args[2]
              //create asset
              assetData := OrgAsset{Id:        assetId,AssetType:
assetType,                      Status:    "START",Location:
"N/A",DeviceId:
deviceId,Comment:    "Initialized asset",From:        "N/A",                      To:
"N/A"}
              assetBytes, _ := json.Marshal(assetData)
              assetErr := stub.PutState(assetId, assetBytes)
    ...
              return shim.Success(nil)
    }
```

The Invoke function

The implementation of the `Invoke` function is as follows:

```go
func (c *AssetMgr) Invoke(stub shim.ChaincodeStubInterface) pb.Response {
              function, args := stub.GetFunctionAndParameters()
              if function == "Order" {
                      return c.Order(stub, args)
```

```
            } else if function == "Ship" {
                        return c.Ship(stub, args)
            } else if function == "Distribute" {
                        return c.Distribute(stub, args)
            } else if function == "query" {
                        return c.query(stub, args)
            } else if function == "getHistory" {
                        return c.getHistory(stub, args)
            }
            return shim.Error("Invalid function name")
}
```

The Order, Ship, and Distribute functions will be quite similar. These will update the ledger state. We will use order() as an example to show how we implement the chaincode function:

```
func (c *AssetMgr) Order(stub shim.ChaincodeStubInterface, args []string)
pb.Response {
            return c.UpdateAsset(stub, args, "ORDER", "SCHOOL", "OEM")
}
```

Here is the UpdateAsset function:

```
func (c *AssetMgr) UpdateAsset(stub shim.ChaincodeStubInterface, args
[]string, currentStatus string, from string, to string) pb.Response {
            assetId := args[0]    comment := args[1]
location := args[2]
            assetBytes, err := stub.GetState(assetId)
            orgAsset := OrgAsset{}
            ...
            if currentStatus == "ORDER" && orgAsset.Status != "START" {
            return shim.Error(err.Error())
            } else if currentStatus == "SHIP" && orgAsset.Status !=
"ORDER" {.}
else if currentStatus == "DISTRIBUTE" && orgAsset.Status != "SHIP" {.}
            orgAsset.Comment = comment
            orgAsset.Status = currentStatus
....
            orgAsset0, _ := json.Marshal(orgAsset)
            err = stub.PutState(assetId, orgAsset0)
            ...
            return shim.Success(orgAsset0)
}
```

The query and getHistory functions

`ChaincodeStubInterface` provides `GetState`, `query` functions. We can call this functions by passing `assetId`. This will trigger chaincode to get the corresponding result.

The `getHistory` function is used to view the records returned from the transaction history; all records are associated with `assetId`. Each record contains a related transaction ID and timestamp. With the timestamp, we know when the asset status was updated in the past.

Once the data is saved to blockchain, the application needs to query the chaincode data to check the `OrgAsset` information, shown as follows:

```
func (c *AssetMgr) getHistory(stub shim.ChaincodeStubInterface, args
[]string) pb.Response {
        type AuditHistory struct {
                        TxId   string   `json:"txId"`
                        Value OrgAsset `json:"value"`
        }
        var history []AuditHistory
        var orgAsset OrgAsset
        assetId := args[0]
        // Get History
        resultsIterator, err := stub.GetHistoryForKey(assetId)
        defer resultsIterator.Close()
        for resultsIterator.HasNext() {
                        historyData, err := resultsIterator.Next()
                        var tx AuditHistory
                        tx.TxId = historyData.TxId
                        json.Unmarshal(historyData.Value, &orgAsset)
                        tx.Value = orgAsset          //copy
orgAsset over
                        history = append(history, tx) //add this tx
to the list
        }
        ..
}
```

How it works...

Let's now take a closer look at what happens in each function in detail.

The Init function

The Init function is called when the chaincode is instantiated by the blockchain network and the function initializes the asset management data. In this function, we need to set up the OrgAsset initialization information. The three parameters we pass to call the Init function are assetId, assetType, and deviceId. This will set our device asset information, then we call the PutState(key, value) method to store the key and the value on the ledger.

The Invoke function

The Invoke function is called when the client invokes a specific function to process the transaction proposal. The ChaincodeStubInterface interface has the GetFunctionAndParameters method. This method extracts the function name and arguments and dispatches code to different functions based on the first argument. In our assetmgr, we need to call the Order, Ship, and Distribute functions, and then update the status for each step and the orgAsset information in the ledger. We can also define the query and query history functions, to get orgAsset information from the ledger.

You will notice that the Order method passes parameters from the command-line input. We use stub.GetState(assetId) to query the asset data from the blockchain, then we verify to make sure the current asset status is correct. We update the orgAsset info and then convert the asset data to byte data by calling json.Marshal(orgAsset). Finally, we save the data into the blockchain via stub.PutState. If there are no errors, the function will return a successful response to the client.

The query function

`ChaincodeStubInterface` defines the `GetState` method. The `query` function simply calls this function by passing `assetId`. This will trigger the chaincode to get the corresponding result.

All records returned from the transaction history are associated with `assetId`. Each record contains a related transaction ID and a timestamp. The timestamp tells us when the asset status was updated.

Compiling and deploying Fabric chaincode

We have now successfully written our asset management chaincode using the Go language. It is now time to build and deploy our `assetmgr` chaincode to Hyperledger Fabric.

Getting ready

Let's first get the `fabric` library in our environment. Navigate to the `assetmgr` directory, run the `get` chaincode library command, and then start `build`:

```
cd $GOPATH/src/assetmgr
go get -u github.com/hyperledger/fabric/core/chaincode/shim
go build
```

This will load the chaincode library and compile the Go code. Next, we will deploy the chaincode using the `dev` mode. Normally, we need to define our own channel, peer, and configuration Docker container to run our chaincode. Hyperledger, however, provides a sample `dev` network with a pre-generated `orderer` and channel artifact. This allows the user to start using chaincode for quick development and testing. You should have already set up the Fabric runtime environment with the `fabric-samples` project. If you haven't already done so, check out the previous chapter, or refer to `fabric-samples` in the GitHub link and follow the instructions: `https://github.com/hyperledger/fabric-samples`.

At the time of writing this book, 1.4 is the latest version of `fabric-samples`.

In our example project, we use the build in the `fabric-samples` project and set this same project as the default user home directory, as follows:

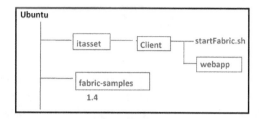

Let's now open three Terminals and navigate to the `chaincode-docker-devmode` directory of `fabric-samples`:

```
$ cd chaincode-docker-devmode
```

How to do it...

We will start a sample Fabric network to provide the Fabric runtime environment, and then package and build our Composer. Finally, we will deploy it to the network.

Starting the sample Fabric network

Open Terminal one. This Terminal will start the sample Fabric network. Issue the following command:

```
docker-compose -f docker-compose-simple.yaml up
```

This will bring up a network with the `SingleSampleMSPSolo` orderer profile. It also launches `peer` nodes, `cli`, and `chaincode` containers.

Building and deploying the chaincode

1. Open Terminal two. This Terminal will build and deploy the chaincode. Since we write and build the chaincode from our local Unix system, the chaincode is not yet in the Docker containers. Run the following command in the `chaincode-docker-devmode` folder:

```
docker exec -it chaincode bash
```

2. The output will be a list of folders:

   abac chaincode_example02 fabcar marbles02 marbles02_private sacc

3. Let's create an `assetmgr` folder:

   mkdir assetmgr

   This will create an `assetmgr` folder in the Fabric container. First, type `exit`. This will exit the container and return to the `chaincode-docker-devmode` folder. Check the Fabric `chaincode` container ID by typing `docker ps`. You will get a similar result to the following:

   In our example, the `chaincode` container ID is `dbf9a0a1da76`. The `peer` port is `7051`.

4. With the container ID, we can copy the local chaincode to the `chaincode` container. Run the following command:

   docker cp ~/itasset/src/assetmgr/assetmgr.go
   dbf9a0a1da76:/opt/gopath/src/chaincode/assetmgr

5. Launch the `chaincode` container again:

   docker exec –it chaincode bash

6. Navigate to the `assetmgr` folder and execute the `go build` command. This will compile our `assermgr.go` in the `chaincode` container, as shown in the following screenshot:

```
ubuntu@ip-172-31-0-111:~/fabric-samples/chaincode-docker-devmode$ docker exec -it chaincode bash
root@c30c857ed423:/opt/gopath/src/chaincode# ls
abac  assetmgr  chaincode_example02  fabcar  marbles02  marbles02_private  sacc
root@c30c857ed423:/opt/gopath/src/chaincode# cd assetmgr
root@c30c857ed423:/opt/gopath/src/chaincode/assetmgr# go build
root@c30c857ed423:/opt/gopath/src/chaincode/assetmgr# ls
assetmgr  assetmgr.go
```

The `assetmgr` chaincode can be found at the following
path: `/opt/gopath/src/chaincode/assetmgr`.

7. Run the chaincode by providing the `peer` address and chaincode ID name. The
   command is as follows:

   ```
   CORE_PEER_ADDRESS=peer:7052 CORE_CHAINCODE_ID_NAME=mycc:0
   ./assetmgr
   ```

8. This command will deploy the chaincode to the `peer` node at `7052`. If you don't
   see any errors, the chaincode will start with `peer`. The log indicates that
   `assetmgr.go` successfully registered with `peer`:

```
root@2cf2cdf0e844:/opt/gopath/src/chaincode# cd assetmgr
root@2cf2cdf0e844:/opt/gopath/src/chaincode/assetmgr# ls
assetmgr  assetmgr.go
root@2cf2cdf0e844:/opt/gopath/src/chaincode/assetmgr# CORE_PEER_ADDRESS=peer:7052 CORE_CHAINCODE_ID_NAME=mycc:0 ./assetmgr
2019-01-18 05:38:02.950 UTC [shim] setupChaincodeLogging -> INFO 001 Chaincode log level not provided; defaulting to: INFO
2019-01-18 05:38:02.950 UTC [shim] setupChaincodeLogging -> INFO 002 Chaincode (build level: ) starting up ...
2019-01-18 05:38:02.950 UTC [bccsp] initBCCSP -> DEBU 001 Initialize BCCSP [SW]
2019-01-18 05:38:02.950 UTC [grpc] DialContext -> DEBU 002 parsed scheme: ""
2019-01-18 05:38:02.950 UTC [grpc] DialContext -> DEBU 003 scheme "" not registered, fallback to default scheme
2019-01-18 05:38:02.950 UTC [grpc] watcher -> DEBU 004 ccResolverWrapper: sending new addresses to cc: [{peer:7052 0  <nil>}]
2019-01-18 05:38:02.950 UTC [grpc] switchBalancer -> DEBU 005 ClientConn switching balancer to "pick_first"
2019-01-18 05:38:02.950 UTC [grpc] HandleSubConnStateChange -> DEBU 006 pickfirstBalancer: HandleSubConnStateChange: 0xc000331ed0, CONNECTING
2019-01-18 05:38:02.952 UTC [grpc] HandleSubConnStateChange -> DEBU 007 pickfirstBalancer: HandleSubConnStateChange: 0xc000331ed0, READY
```

How it works...

Here, we deployed the chaincode to the `peer` node. Let's now take a look at
how `chaincode-docker-devmode` defines the blockchain configuration. `chaincode-docker-devmode` has some predefined configuration files and scripts. Here are the files
in `chaincode-docker-devmode`:

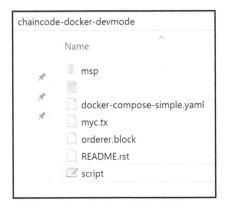

Let's take a closer look at the `docker-compose-simple.yaml` file:

- This file defines services, `peer`, `cli`, and `chaincode` container configuration.
- Services define the `orderer` service with the container name as port 7050. It points to the Docker image at `hyperledger/fabric-orderer`.
- Peer defines a `peer` node. The `peer` container port is 7051. It points to a Docker image at `hyperledger/fabric-peer`.
- The `cli` section defines the `cli` container name as `cli`. The `cli` container can issue a command to interact with the chaincode deployed in the `peer` node. It points to a Docker image at `hyperledger/fabric-tools`.
- The `chaincode` container defines the container name as `chaincode`. It points to a Docker image at `hyperledger/fabric-ccenv`.

Here is the screenshot we see after we bring up the Docker containers. We can see the previously mentioned four containers running:

The script file in `chaincode-docker-devmode` only contains the following two commands:

```
peer channel create -c myc -f myc.tx -o orderer:7050
peer channel join -b myc.block
```

The first command creates the `myc` channel using the specified configuration file in the `myc.tx` file. The `myc.tx` file is generated by the `configtxgen` tool. This tool also generates `orderer.block`.

The second command joins the created channel with `myc.block` to the `cli` container. With these four containers, we can deploy our chaincode to the Fabric in the development environment.

Let's now carry out some tests from the `cli` container.

Running and testing the smart contract

We have opened two Terminals so far and deployed the chaincode to the `peer` node. It is time to install and test our chaincode function.

How to do it...

Open the third container to issue the `cli` command and test our smart contract. In this Terminal, we will start the `cli` container and issue the `cli` command to interact with the `chaincode` container. Launch an example `cli` container as follows:

```
docker exec -it cli bash
```

Installing the assermgr chaincode

Install the `assermgr` chaincode through the `cli` container by running the following command:

```
peer chaincode install -p chaincodedev/chaincode/assetmgr -n mycc -v 0
```

Here is the result after the chaincode is installed:

Instantiating the assermgr chaincode

Next, we will instantiate the `assermgr` chaincode. As we discussed earlier, in order to create an asset record, we need to pass `assetId`, `assetType`, and `deviceId`. Let's assume that the school needs to trace an `ipad` with the `0e83ff` device ID and the `100` asset ID. We can instantiate our `ipad` asset by running the following command:

```
peer chaincode instantiate -n mycc -v 0 -c '{"Args":["100","ipad",
"0e83ff"]}' -C myc
```

The result is as follows:

We have now successfully installed and instantiated our `assetmgr` chaincode.

Invoking the assermgr chaincode

Next, we can start to invoke the remaining chaincode methods: `Order`, `Ship`, and `Distribute`.

1. To order the device from OEM, we need to pass three parameters to the chaincode—`assetId`, `Comment`, and `Location`. Here, `assetId` is `100`, and we will assume that `Location` is `New York`.

2. Now, issue `invoke` to call the `Order` method in the `assetmgr` chaincode. The command is as follows:

```
peer chaincode invoke -n mycc -c '{"Args":["Order", "100",
"initial order from
school", "New York"]}' -C myc
```

3. If all goes well, you should see the following result. The log shows that the chaincode has been invoked successfully. We can see that the result is successfully saved to blockchain:

4. In our `assetmgr`, we have defined a `query` method. We can invoke this method to verify whether the records have been saved in the Fabric blockchain. Issue the following `query` command with `assetId` as `100`:

```
peer chaincode query -C myc -n mycc -c '{"Args":["query","100"]}'
```

We can find the asset with an `assetId` of `100` from the Fabric ledger:

5. Once the OEM receives the order, it starts to work and produce the iPad device. Then, the OEM ships the device to the school. To do this, issue the following `Ship` command with `assetId`, `Comment`, and `Location`:

```
peer chaincode invoke -n mycc -c '{"Args":["Ship", "100", "OEM
deliver ipad to school", "New Jersey"]}' -C myc
```

The following screenshot will be the output of the previous code:

```
2019-01-18 05:43:16.522 UTC [grpc] DialContext -> DEBU 09c parsed scheme: ""
2019-01-18 05:43:16.522 UTC [grpc] DialContext -> DEBU 09d scheme "" not registered, fallback to default scheme
2019-01-18 05:43:16.522 UTC [grpc] watcher -> DEBU 09e ccResolverWrapper: sending new addresses to cc: [{orderer:7050 0  <nil>}]
2019-01-18 05:43:16.522 UTC [grpc] switchBalancer -> DEBU 09f ClientConn switching balancer to "pick_first"
2019-01-18 05:43:16.522 UTC [grpc] HandleSubConnStateChange -> DEBU 0a0 pickfirstBalancer: HandleSubConnStateChange: 0xc00029d470, CONNECTING
2019-01-18 05:43:16.524 UTC [grpc] HandleSubConnStateChange -> DEBU 0a1 pickfirstBalancer: HandleSubConnStateChange: 0xc00029d470, READY
2019-01-18 05:43:16.524 UTC [msp.identity] Sign -> DEBU 0a2 Sign: plaintext: 0AC9070A610B031A0C0894CF85E20510...74756446568740A08A4E65712059697726B
2019-01-18 05:43:16.524 UTC [msp.identity] Sign -> DEBU 0a3 Sign: digest: AA6E492914C398219070C001200F5310C65DCD958E9DB0897942B02ED06B36339
2019-01-18 05:43:16.534 UTC [msp.identity] Sign -> DEBU 0a4 Sign: plaintext: 0AC9070A610B031A0C08F4CE95E20510...361A44639E4FBEC37C799A3F978E2348
2019-01-18 05:43:16.534 UTC [msp.identity] Sign -> DEBU 0a5 Sign: digest: 9AF67C9DEA41C1ECFFEKC68B13B141DDC8F02B6F92C00202B8DD89SC1724F17D
2019-01-18 05:43:16.536 UTC [chaincodeCmd] chaincodeInvokeOrQuery -> DEBU 0a6 ESCC invoke result: version:1 response:<status:200 payload:"{\"id\",\"100\",\"assetType\":\"ipad\",\"status\":\
"DISTRIBUTE\",\"location\":\"New York\",\"deviceId\":\"0e83ff\",\"comment\":\"Distribute device to student\",\"from\":\"SCHOOL\",\"to\":\"STUDENT\"}" > payload:"\n \346\200\336\214\310\310y\360
\2754h\006p\031\\ 7t3\332\234\"m1> \347\327\237*7AG\022\235\003\n\337\001\022\024\n\004scc\022\014\n\n\n\004mycc\022\002\010\001\022\306\001\n\004mycc\022\275\001\n\003100\022\002\010\0
03\032\257\001\n\003100\032\247\001\"\1d\"\"100\",\"assetType\":\"ipad\",\"status\":\"DISTRIBUTE\",\"location\":\"New York\",\"deviceId\":\"0e83ff\",\"comment\":\"Distribute device to stud
ent\",\"from\":\"SCHOOL\",\"to\":\"STUDENT\"}\032\255\061\010\310\001\032\247\001{\"id\":\"100\",\"assetType\":\"ipad\",\"status\":\"DISTRIBUTE\",\"location\":\"New York\",\"deviceId\":\"0e
83ff\",\"comment\":\"Distribute device to student\"}\"from\":\"SCHOOL\",\"to\":\"STUDENT\"}\"\t\022\004mycc\032\0010" endorsement:<endorser:"\n\007DEFAULT\022\273\006-----BEGIN CERTIFICATE-
----\nMIICN1CCAd2gAwIBAgIRAMnf9/dmV5RvCCVw9pZQUIDwCqYIKoZIzj0EAwIwgYEx\nCzAJBgNVBAYTA1VTMRMwEQYDVQQIEwpDYWxp2m9ybm1hMRYwFAYDVQQGEw1TYW4g\nFRnJhbmNpc2NvMRkwFwYDVQQKExBvcmcxLmV4YW1wbGUuY29tMQw
wCgYDVQQLEwMDyY\nT:AsHDAaBgNVHAMYE2NhZasYZzRuZXhhbXRe2S5jb2OwHhcNMTcxMTExMTMxMTExEx1pNhoMMjcxMTAsMTGsMTEx8jBpMQ\nwCgYDVQQGEwJVUzETMBEGA1UEC8MKQ2FsaKZv\ncm5pYTEWMBQGA1UERxMNU2FuIFEzYW5jaXNjbzE9MA
oGA1UECxMDQ09QMR4wHQYD\nVQQDExZwZWVyMWCvcmcxLmV4YW1wbGUuY29tMFkwEwYHKoZIzj0CAQYIKoZIzj0D\nAQcDQgAEX3S4V710BJpyMIV2dwYdXXAck1trpvSrCf0HQq4O8MP9ZEcOOO7G1+Umf\nnKkmT11JXP7/AyRR8HU38oI8Ivtu4H68NMA
EswOgYDVR0PAQH/BAQDAgaAMMAwGA1Ud\nEwEB/wQCMAAwKwYDVR0jBCQwIoAg1n0RThoFEFZUhXm6eWRkm7K7Zc884/x/1A4H\nnosmDiCewCqYIKoZIzj0EAwIDRwAwRAIgV1kIIZzqfnPeGLQHMJIRVJCU7pPmEPkxr\nnPsFqeClLzGhCICpsTYlW7nwT
xF7b6tbeuJtfmrhMXQs956mD4+BoKuNI\n-----END CERTIFICATE-----\n" signature:"0E\002I\000\344X216\232\256}p\335\251\361s\004\300\314CM<\216\357\024\011JAc\267\275b\302\252\021\350\337\002 {\27
3h\347\200NF/tu\220s\366K\231\3156\032Dc\2360\276\303}y\2323\227\216BR" >
2019-01-18 05:43:16.516 UTC [chaincodeCmd] chaincodeInvokeOrQuery -> INFO 0a7 Chaincode invoke successful. result: status:200 payload:"{\"id\":\"100\",\"assetType\":\"ipad\",\"status\":\"DI
STRIBUTE\",\"location\":\"New York\",\"deviceId\":\"0e83ff\",\"comment\":\"Distribute device to student\",\"from\":\"SCHOOL\",\"to\":\"STUDENT\"}"
```

6. Once the device is received, the school will distribute the device to the student. Issue the following `Distribute` command with `assetId`, `Comment`, and `Location`:

```
peer chaincode invoke -n mycc -c '{"Args":["Distribute", "100",
"Distribute device to student", "New York"]}' -C myc
```

We should see the following result:

```
2019-01-18 05:43:48.387 UTC [msp] setupSigningIdentity -> DEBU 034 Signing identity expires at 2027-11-10 13:41:11 +0000 UTC
2019-01-18 05:43:48.387 UTC [msp] Validate -> DEBU 035 MSP DEFAULT validating identity
2019-01-18 05:43:48.388 UTC [grpc] DialContext -> DEBU 036 parsed scheme: ""
2019-01-18 05:43:48.388 UTC [grpc] DialContext -> DEBU 037 scheme "" not registered, fallback to default scheme
2019-01-18 05:43:48.389 UTC [grpc] watcher -> DEBU 038 ccResolverWrapper: sending new addresses to cc: [{peer:7051 0  <nil>}]
2019-01-18 05:43:48.389 UTC [grpc] switchBalancer -> DEBU 039 ClientConn switching balancer to "pick_first"
2019-01-18 05:43:48.389 UTC [grpc] HandleSubConnStateChange -> DEBU 03a pickfirstBalancer: HandleSubConnStateChange: 0xc00027f490, CONNECTING
2019-01-18 05:43:48.390 UTC [grpc] HandleSubConnStateChange -> DEBU 03b pickfirstBalancer: HandleSubConnStateChange: 0xc00027f490, READY
2019-01-18 05:43:48.391 UTC [grpc] DialContext -> DEBU 03c parsed scheme: ""
2019-01-18 05:43:48.391 UTC [grpc] DialContext -> DEBU 03d scheme "" not registered, fallback to default scheme
2019-01-18 05:43:48.392 UTC [grpc] watcher -> DEBU 03e ccResolverWrapper: sending new addresses to cc: [{peer:7051 0  <nil>}]
2019-01-18 05:43:48.392 UTC [grpc] switchBalancer -> DEBU 03f ClientConn switching balancer to "pick_first"
2019-01-18 05:43:48.392 UTC [grpc] HandleSubConnStateChange -> DEBU 040 pickfirstBalancer: HandleSubConnStateChange: 0xc0002ea190, CONNECTING
2019-01-18 05:43:48.393 UTC [grpc] HandleSubConnStateChange -> DEBU 041 pickfirstBalancer: HandleSubConnStateChange: 0xc0002ea190, READY
2019-01-18 05:43:48.394 UTC [msp] GetDefaultSigningIdentity -> DEBU 042 Obtaining default signing identity
2019-01-18 05:43:48.394 UTC [msp.identity] Sign -> DEBU 044 Sign: plaintext: 0AC9070A610B031A0C0894CF85E20510...9A67657446969737746F72790A03313030
[{"txId":"ee237c8254e4ad525802653ce31e6a1d9d5a078aef1afc1bd0b2d2407e54213d","value":{"id":"100","assetType":"ipad","status":"START","location":"N/A","deviceId":"0e83ff","comment":"Initializ
ed asset","from":"N/A","to":"N/A"}},{"txId":"1223d1f330ce1708a4e15edb2b9f6385a2e73417b34f0ba59df72c63cca1157","value":{"id":"100","assetType":"ipad","status":"ORDER","location":"New York",
"deviceId":"0e83ff","comment":"initial order from school","from":"SCHOOL","to":"OEM"}},{"txId":"c8597357e76ac40a0793028be5ae27549ccb3aaa49071e1d2d2337c44f5f4e1c","value":{"id":"100","assetT
ype":"ipad","status":"SHIP","location":"New Jersey","deviceId":"0e83ff","comment":"OEM deliver ipad to school","from":"OEM","to":"SCHOOL"}},{"txId":"4fc606af1c98f057031a1ad4d50bac44d02f70ff
598e31f0b9ba2d6efa7df2e3","value":{"id":"100","assetType":"ipad","status":"DISTRIBUTE","location":"New York","deviceId":"0e83ff","comment":"Distribute device to student","from":"SCHOOL","to
":"STUDENT"}}]
```

7. We have now completed the entire process for our demo use case. As we discussed earlier, blockchain is a ledger system; it will keep track of all transactions. Once records are saved to the blockchain, they cannot be altered. We should be able to see this historical transaction data. In our asset manager example, we issued the `Order`, `Ship`, and `Distribute` commands and the related chaincode was invoked. All related asset transaction records should be kept in the blockchain. Let's verify this by issuing the `getHistory` command:

```
peer chaincode query -C myc -n mycc -c
'{"Args":["getHistory","100"]}'
```

This command will provide the following results:

```
2019-01-18 05:43:48.387 UTC [msp] setupSigningIdentity -> DEBU 034 Signing identity expires at 2027-11-10 13:41:11 +0000 UTC
2019-01-18 05:43:48.387 UTC [msp] Validate -> DEBU 035 MSP DEFAULT validating identity
2019-01-18 05:43:48.388 UTC [grpc] DialContext -> DEBU 036 parsed scheme: ""
2019-01-18 05:43:48.388 UTC [grpc] DialContext -> DEBU 037 scheme "" not registered, fallback to default scheme
2019-01-18 05:43:48.389 UTC [grpc] watcher -> DEBU 038 ccResolverWrapper: sending new addresses to cc: [{peer:7051 0 <nil>}]
2019-01-18 05:43:48.389 UTC [grpc] switchBalancer -> DEBU 039 ClientConn switching balancer to "pick_first"
2019-01-18 05:43:48.389 UTC [grpc] HandleSubConnStateChange -> DEBU 03a pickfirstBalancer: HandleSubConnStateChange: 0xc00027f490, CONNECTING
2019-01-18 05:43:48.390 UTC [grpc] HandleSubConnStateChange -> DEBU 03b pickfirstBalancer: HandleSubConnStateChange: 0xc00027f490, READY
2019-01-18 05:43:48.391 UTC [grpc] DialContext -> DEBU 03c parsed scheme: ""
2019-01-18 05:43:48.391 UTC [grpc] DialContext -> DEBU 03d scheme "" not registered, fallback to default scheme
2019-01-18 05:43:48.392 UTC [grpc] watcher -> DEBU 03e ccResolverWrapper: sending new addresses to cc: [{peer:7051 0 <nil>}]
2019-01-18 05:43:48.392 UTC [grpc] switchBalancer -> DEBU 03f ClientConn switching balancer to "pick_first"
2019-01-18 05:43:48.392 UTC [grpc] HandleSubConnStateChange -> DEBU 040 pickfirstBalancer: HandleSubConnStateChange: 0xc0002ea190, CONNECTING
2019-01-18 05:43:48.393 UTC [grpc] HandleSubConnStateChange -> DEBU 041 pickfirstBalancer: HandleSubConnStateChange: 0xc0002ea190, READY
2019-01-18 05:43:48.393 UTC [msp] GetDefaultSigningIdentity -> DEBU 042 Obtaining default signing identity
2019-01-18 05:43:48.394 UTC [msp.identity] Sign -> DEBU 043 Sign: plaintext: 0AC907OA610803IA0C0894CF85S20510...0A6765744865973746F72790A0331303O
2019-01-18 05:43:48.394 UTC [msp.identity] Sign -> DEBU 044 Sign: digest: 268C36CF980D6D7023480613C85556604984D31400EA4D57E7033ACA2D60HD9F
[{"txId":"ee237c5254e4ad525802653ce316ea1d9d5a07Baef1afc1bd0b2d24007a5413d","value":{"id":"100","assetType":"ipad","status":"START","location":"N/A","deviceId":"0e83ff","comment":"Initiali
ed asset","from":"N/A","to":"N/A"}},{"txId":"1223dff330ce17083a4e15edb2b9f6385a2e7347b34f0ba59df72c63cca1157","value":{"id":"100","assetType":"ipad","status":"ORDER","location":"New York",
"deviceId":"0e83ff","comment":"initial order from school","from":"SCHOOL","to":"OEM"}},{"txId":"c8597357e76ac40a0793028be5ae27549ccb3aaa4907le1d2d2337c44f5f4e1c","value":{"id":"100","assetT
ype":"ipad","status":"SHIP","location":"New Jersey","deviceId":"0e83ff","comment":"OEM deliver ipad to school","from":"OEM","to":"SCHOOL"}},{"txId":"4fc606ef1c98f057031a1ad4d50bac44d02f70ff
596e31f0b9ba2d6efe7df2e3","value":{"id":"100","assetType":"ipad","status":"DISTRIBUTE","location":"New York","deviceId":"0e83ff","comment":"Distribute device to student","from":"SCHOOL","to
":"STUDENT"}}]
```

As we can see, the `getHistory` command returns all of the transaction records we invoked from Fabric blockchain.

How it works...

The Fabric command-line interface is built using Fabric SDK Go. The CLI provides various commands to run a `peer` node, interact with the channel and the chaincode, and to query blockchain data. Here are some functionalities provided by the CLI:

Component	Functionality	Example command
Channel	Creates a channel	`peer channel join -b myc.block`
	Joins a peer to a channel	`peer channel join -b myc.block`
Chaincode	Installs chaincode	`peer chaincode install -p chaincodedev/chaincode/assetmgr -n mycc -v 0`
	Instantiates chaincode	`peer chaincode instantiate -n mycc -v 0 -c '{"Args":["100","ipad", "0e83ff"]}' -C myc`
	Invokes the chaincode function	`peer chaincode invoke -n mycc -c '{"Args":["Order", "100", "initial order from school", "New York"]}' -C myc`
	Queries chaincode data	`peer chaincode query -C myc -n mycc -c '{"Args":["getHistory","100"]}'`

With these supported CLI commands, we can test our chaincode in the development environment.

Next, we will write client-side code and interact with the `assetmgr` chaincode in the Fabric.

Developing an application with Hyperledger Fabric through the SDK

In the previous recipes, we used the `fabric-samples` prebuilt `devmode` environment to deploy and test our asset manager chaincode using `chaincode-docker-devmode`. In this recipe, we will write UI code to interact with chaincode from blockchain. We will also build a Fabric CA container to improve the security of our application. Fortunately, `fabric-sample` provides the `basic-network` template, which can help us set up a basic Fabric network.

How to do it...

We first need to write a Fabric script to start the Fabric network and deploy the chaincode in this network. Using the `cli` container, we then install and instantiate the chaincode. The authorized client with the identity of the wallet will be able to interact with the Fabric chaincode in the network.

Creating and executing startFabric.sh

Follow these steps:

1. Navigate to the `itasset` folder
2. Create a `Client` folder
3. Under the `Client` folder, create a script file called `startFabric.sh`
4. Create a folder called `webapp`

Here is the folder structure we have created so far:

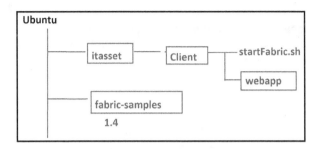

The `startFabric.sh` file contains the following commands:

```
export MSYS_NO_PATHCONV=1
starttime=$(date +%s)
CC_RUNTIME_LANGUAGE=golang
CC_SRC_PATH=github.com/assetmgr
# clean the keystore
rm -rf ./hfc-key-store
# launch network; create a channel and join peer to the channel
cd /home/ubuntu/fabric-samples/basic-network
./start.sh
```

The script calls the `start.sh` file in the `fabric-samples` section of the `basic-network` project to bring up the Fabric network. This will start the `orderer`, `couchdb`, `cli`, `peer`, and `ca` container. Then, we issue the `cli` command to install and instantiate our `assetmgr` chaincode:

```
# bring up cli cntainer to install, instantiate, invoke chaincode
docker-compose -f ./docker-compose.yml up -d cli
docker exec -e "CORE_PEER_LOCALMSPID=Org1MSP" -e
"CORE_PEER_MSPCONFIGPATH=/opt/gopath/src/github.com/hyperledger/fabric/peer
/crypto/peerOrganizations/org1.example.com/users/Admin@org1.example.com/msp
" cli peer chaincode install -n assetmgr -v 1.0 -p "$CC_SRC_PATH" -l
"$CC_RUNTIME_LANGUAGE"

docker exec -e "CORE_PEER_LOCALMSPID=Org1MSP" -e
"CORE_PEER_MSPCONFIGPATH=/opt/gopath/src/github.com/hyperledger/fabric/peer
/crypto/peerOrganizations/org1.example.com/users/Admin@org1.example.com/msp
" cli peer chaincode instantiate -o orderer.example.com:7050 -C mychannel -
n assetmgr -l "$CC_RUNTIME_LANGUAGE" -v 1.0 -c '{"Args":["100","ipad",
"0e83ff"]}' -P "OR ('Org1MSP.member','Org2MSP.member')"
```

After that, we set up our chaincode in a basic network environment. In the next step, we invoke our chaincode from `cli`:

```
docker exec -e "CORE_PEER_LOCALMSPID=Org1MSP" -e
"CORE_PEER_MSPCONFIGPATH=/opt/gopath/src/github.com/hyperledger/fabric/peer
/crypto/peerOrganizations/org1.example.com/users/Admin@org1.example.com/msp
" cli peer chaincode invoke -o orderer.example.com:7050 -C mychannel -n
assetmgr -c '{"Args":["Order", "100", "initial order from school", "New
York"]}'
```

Once the script file is created, it is ready to execute the script. First, we should make sure there aren't any other Docker containers still running. Here are the commands to clean up the Docker environment:

```
~/fabric-samples/first-network$ ./byfn.sh down
~/fabric-samples/first-network$ docker rm -f $(docker ps -aq)
~/fabric-samples/first-network$ docker network prune
```

Now, we can run the `script.sh` file:

```
~/itasset/client$ ./startFabric.sh
```

Here is the result after executing the `script.sh` file:

As we can see from the result, the Fabric CA, `client`, `peer`, `orderer`, and `counchdb` containers are running. The `assetmgr` chaincode is installed and instantiated in the blockchain. After executing the invoke order chaincode command, the `orgAsset` status is changed to `ORDER`.

Setting up a client project

Next, it is time for us to write client-side code to trigger our chaincode. As we discussed, when the client sends a request to the Fabric network to query or invoke the chaincode, these requests need to be authorized. In Fabric release 1.4, we can create a wallet by enrolling the user and importing the identity into the wallet. The client application can interact with a smart contract in blockchain by utilizing the `fabric-ca-client` and `fabric-network` APIs with the authorized wallet.

Let's create a Node.js app:

1. Navigate to the `~/itasset/client/webapp` folder, issue the `npm init` command, and fill up the related project information. This will create a basic node application:

   ```
   ubuntu@ip-172-31-9-54:~/itasset/client/webapp$ npm init
   package name: (webapp) assetmgr
   version: (1.0.0)
   description: hyperledger cookbook fabric
   entry point: (index.js)
   ```

2. Install the default `npm` libraries. This includes the `express.js`, `ejs`, `fabric-ca-client`, and `fabric-network` libraries, shown as follows:

   ```
   npm install
   npm install express -save
   ~/itasset/client/webapp$ npm i fabric-ca-client@1.4.0
   ~/itasset/client/webapp$ npm i fabric-network@1.4.0
   ~/itasset/client/webapp$ npm install ejs
   ```

3. We need to copy three files (`connection.json`, `enrollAdmin.js`, and `registerUser.js`) from the `fabric-samples/fabcar` project to our project:

   ```
   cp ~/fabric-samples/basic-network/connection.json .
   cp /home/ubuntu/fabric-samples/fabcar/javascript/enrollAdmin.js .
   cp /home/ubuntu/fabric-samples/fabcar/javascript/registerUser.js .
   Create empty wallet folder by issue below command:
   mkdir wallet
   ```

At this step, our files and folders should look as follows:

```
ubuntu@ip-172-31-9-54:~/itasset/client/webapp$ ls
app.js  connection.json  enrollAdmin.js  node_modules  package.json  package-lock.json  registerUser.js  views  wallet
ubuntu@ip-172-31-9-54:~/itasset/client/webapp$ ls -lrt
total 96
drwxrwxr-x    4 ubuntu ubuntu   4096 Jan 18 08:17 wallet
-rw-rw-r--    1 ubuntu ubuntu   1706 Jan 18 08:17 enrollAdmin.js
-rw-rw-r--    1 ubuntu ubuntu   1157 Jan 18 08:17 connection.json
-rw-rw-r--    1 ubuntu ubuntu   2395 Jan 18 08:17 registerUser.js
drwxrwxr-x  191 ubuntu ubuntu   4096 Jan 18 09:17 node_modules
-rw-rw-r--    1 ubuntu ubuntu    339 Jan 18 09:17 package.json
-rw-rw-r--    1 ubuntu ubuntu  64226 Jan 18 09:17 package-lock.json
drwxrwxr-x    2 ubuntu ubuntu   4096 Jan 18 09:38 views
-rw-rw-r--    1 ubuntu ubuntu   3965 Jan 18 09:41 app.js
```

4. Since we copied `enrollAdmin.js` and `registerUser.js` from the `fabric-samples/fabcar` folder, we also need to update the file path defined in the `enrollAdmin.js` and `registerUser.js` files. Update `path.resolve()` in the `enrollAdmin.js` and `registerUser.js` files, as follows:

   ```
   const ccpPath = path.resolve(__dirname, 'connection.json');
   ```

   The `connection.js` file we copied from `basic-network` is in the same folder as `enrollAdmin.js` and `registerUser.js`.

5. Let's create a wallet to enroll the admin and the user onto our Fabric network. To do this, issue the following command:

   ```
   ~/itasset/client/webapp$ node enrollAdmin.js
   ~/itasset/client/webapp$ node registerUser.js
   ```

   This will create a wallet for the admin and the users. The following screenshot shows the `wallet` structure for `admin` and `user1`:

```
ubuntu@ip-172-31-9-54:~/itasset/client/webapp/assetmgrweb$ ls
connection.json  enrollAdmin.js  node_modules  package.json  package-lock.json  public  README.md  registerUser.js  src  wallet
ubuntu@ip-172-31-9-54:~/itasset/client/webapp/assetmgrweb$ node enrollAdmin.js
Wallet path: /home/ubuntu/itasset/client/webapp/assetmgrweb/wallet
Successfully enrolled admin user "admin" and imported it into the wallet
ubuntu@ip-172-31-9-54:~/itasset/client/webapp/assetmgrweb$ node registerUser.js
Wallet path: /home/ubuntu/itasset/client/webapp/assetmgrweb/wallet
Successfully registered and enrolled admin user "user1" and imported it into the wallet
ubuntu@ip-172-31-9-54:~/itasset/client/webapp/assetmgrweb$ tree wallet/
wallet/
├── admin
│   ├── 5d880df4121c0e2b0584190648446eca7ffe6e217542cf98e92d864e094bdf0c-priv
│   ├── 7b8ea5cc14719f8b6ed374a882a80acc9c567799ad6760982eb67112c1e67bda-priv
│   ├── 7b8ea5cc14719f8b6ed374a882a80acc9c567799ad6760982eb67112c1e67bda-pub
│   └── admin
└── user1
    ├── 5d880df4121c0e2b0584190648446eca7ffe6e217542cf98e92d864e094bdf0c-priv
    ├── 5d880df4121c0e2b0584190648446eca7ffe6e217542cf98e92d864e094bdf0c-pub
    └── user1

2 directories, 7 files
```

Writing Node.js sever-side code

We have now set up the client environment. We should be able to connect to the remote Fabric network and trigger the chaincode API. In our Node.js app, create the `app.js` file. This file will act as a connector to create a new gateway to connect to our peer node. It also creates a new filesystem-based wallet for managing identities. Once we have connected to the peer node, the function in `app.js` can find a contract through the channel and then submit the specified transaction. To do this, follow these steps:

1. Create the `wallet` file:

```
async function ship() {
    try {
        // Create a new file system based wallet for managing
identities.
        const walletPath = path.join(process.cwd(), 'wallet');
        const wallet = new FileSystemWallet(walletPath);
    ..
}
```

2. The `wallet` file needs to make sure the user exists by using the `wallet.exist` API:

```
const userExists = await wallet.exists('user1');
if (!userExists) {
console.log('An identity for the user "user1" does not exist in the
wallet');
console.log('Run the registerUser.js application before retrying');
return;
}
```

3. Connect to blockchain through `gateway`, bypassing the `wallet` and `identity` information. Once connected to the network successfully, get the `assetmgr` contract from the network:

```
// Create a new gateway for connecting to our peer node.
const gateway = new Gateway();
await gateway.connect(ccp, { wallet, identity: 'user1', discovery:
{ enabled: false } });
// Get the network (channel) our contract is deployed to.
const network = await gateway.getNetwork('mychannel');
// Get the contract from the network.
const contract = network.getContract('assetmgr');
```

4. Submit a transaction to invoke the chaincode function:

```
// Submit the specified transaction.
await contract.submitTransaction("Ship", "100", "OEM deliver ipad
to school", "New Jersey");
```

5. Disconnect from `gateway` and return to the client caller. To do this, follow the code:

```
// Disconnect from the gateway.
await gateway.disconnect();
With node.js, you need set up your node.js server listen, of
course.
app.listen(3000, function () {
console.log('Example app listening on port 3000!');
});
```

Writing Node.js client-side code

We still need to work on one more file before we complete the end-to-end development. The Node.js client-side code provides a user interface, lets the user see the blockchain result in the browser, and invokes a method from a web page. Our Node.js client-side code can be found in `index.ejs` under the `views` folder. We can open this file and start to add some code in it.

For the `Ship` function, we use the jQuery `post` method to call the Node.js server-side `Ship` function. This will invoke the blockchain `Ship` method in the `assetmgr` chaincode, as follows:

```
<script>
$(document).ready(function(){
$("#ship").click(function(){
$.post("http://52.15.203.98:3000/ship", function(data){
var parsedJson = $.parseJSON($.parseJSON(data));
console.log(parsedJson);
});
});
});
</script>
```

The `query` function is similar to the `Ship` code; we use the jQuery `get` method to call the Node.js server-side `query` function, which will invoke the blockchain `query` method in the `assetmgr` chaincode.

Once the results return, it populates the data to the related fields on the UI:

```
$("#chainCodeQuery").click(function(){
                    $.get("http://52.15.203.98:3000/query",
                    function(data){
                                    var parsedJson =
$.parseJSON($.parseJSON(data));
$("#assetType").val(parsedJson.assetType);
                            ...
            });
});
```

We have now completed our end-to-end code. It is time to start our node server and do some quick experiments.

Running the web application

Following the steps get the web application running:

1. Run node app.js. This will bring up the node server:

```
ubuntu@ip-172-31-9-54:~/itasset/client/webapp$ node app.js
Example app listening on port 3000!
```

2. Once the node server is up, click on the **Query Chaincode** button. This will return the current orgAsset result in the blockchain. Here is the result:

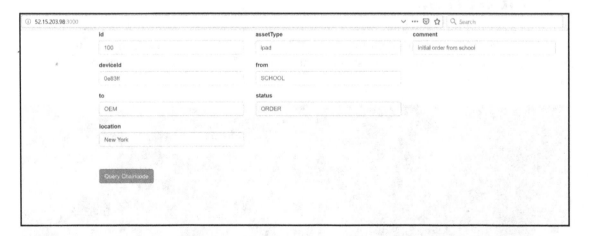

3. Click on the **Ship** button, which will call the `Ship` method in the blockchain. Once it is called successfully, click on the **Query Chaincode** button again and you will see the `updatedorgAsset` result, with the **status** updated to `SHIP`. When it has updated, the page should look like this:

Remember, since there is a delay of a few seconds, you may need to click the button a couple of times for the update to occur.

How it works...

A wallet can hold multiple identities. These identities are issued by the CA. As we have seen before, each user identity contains a certificate, X.509, which contains a private key and a public key, and some Fabric-specific metadata. The certificate file is issued from the Fabric CA service:

```
ubuntu@ip-172-31-9-54:~/itasset/client/webapp/wallet$ tree .
.
├── admin
│   ├── 5d880df4121c0e2b0584190648446eca7ffe6e217542cf98e92d864e094bdf0c-priv
│   ├── 7b8ea5cc14719f8b6ed374a882a80acc9c567799ad6760982eb67112c1e67bda-priv
│   ├── 7b8ea5cc14719f8b6ed374a882a80acc9c567799ad6760982eb67112c1e67bda-pub
│   └── admin
└── user1
    ├── 5d880df4121c0e2b0584190648446eca7ffe6e217542cf98e92d864e094bdf0c-priv
    ├── 5d880df4121c0e2b0584190648446eca7ffe6e217542cf98e92d864e094bdf0c-pub
    └── user1
```

The blockchain `admin` creates a wallet to grant user access, then calls a couple of `key` class methods, (including `X509WalletMixin.createIdentity`) to manage the wallets and identities (including `Org1MSP`). This is shown in the following code:

```
const caURL = ccp.certificateAuthorities['ca.example.com'].url;
const ca = new FabricCAServices(caURL);
// Create a new file system based wallet for managing identities.
const walletPath = path.join(process.cwd(), 'wallet');
const wallet = new FileSystemWallet(walletPath);
..
// Enroll the admin user, and import the new identity into the wallet.
const enrollment = await ca.enroll({ enrollmentID: 'admin',
enrollmentSecret: 'adminpw' });
const identity = X509WalletMixin.createIdentity('Org1MSP',
enrollment.certificate,
enrollment.key.toBytes());
wallet.import('admin', identity);
```

`X509WalletMixin.createIdentity` is used to create an `Org1MSP` identity using X.509 credentials. The function needs three input: `mspid`, the certificate, and the private key.

From the `connection.json` file, we can see that the `Org1MSP` identity is associated with `peer0.org1.example.com`:

```
"organizations": {
    "Org1": {
        "mspid": "Org1MSP",
        "peers": [
            "peer0.org1.example.com"
        ],
        "certificateAuthorities": [
            "ca.example.com"
        ]
    }
}
```

The gateway reads the connected profile, and the SDK will connect with the profile to manage the transaction submission and notification processes. In a `basic-networkdocker-compose.yml` file, the `ca.example.com` CA container starts `fabric-ca-server` to manage the Fabric CA key files:

```
ca.example.com:
image: hyperledger/fabric-ca
environment:
- FABRIC_CA_HOME=/etc/hyperledger/fabric-ca-server
- FABRIC_CA_SERVER_CA_NAME=ca.example.com
- FABRIC_CA_SERVER_CA_CERTFILE=/etc/hyperledger/fabric-ca-server-
config/ca.org1.example.com-
cert.pem
- FABRIC_CA_SERVER_CA_KEYFILE=/etc/hyperledger/fabric-ca-server-config
/4239aa0dcd76daeeb8ba0cda701851d14504d31aad1b2ddddbac6a57365e497c_sk
ports:
- "7054:7054"
command: sh -c 'fabric-ca-server start -b admin:adminpw'
volumes:
- ./crypto-
config/peerOrganizations/org1.example.com/ca/:/etc/hyperledger/fabric-ca-
server-
config
container_name: ca.example.com
networks:
- basic
```

Our `peer1.org1.com` with MSPID `Org1MSP` is associated with the `crypto-config` file to verify each transaction:

```
peer0.org1.example.com:
container_name: peer0.org1.example.com
image: hyperledger/fabric-peer
environment:
- CORE_PEER_ID=peer0.org1.example.com
- CORE_PEER_LOCALMSPID=Org1MSP
- CORE_PEER_ADDRESS=peer0.org1.example.com:7051
volumes:
- ./crypto-
config/peerOrganizations/org1.example.com/peers/peer0.org1.example.com/msp:
/etc/hyperledger/msp/peer
- ./crypto-
config/peerOrganizations/org1.example.com/users:/etc/hyperledger/msp/users
```

This will load the chaincode library and compile the Go code.

3
Modeling a Business Network Using Hyperledger Composer

Hyperledger Composer is a set of collaboration tools for business owners and developers that make it easy to write chaincode for Hyperledger Fabric and **decentralized applications** (**DApps**). With Composer, you can quickly build POC and deploy chaincode to the blockchain in a short amount of time. Hyperledger Composer consists of the following toolsets:

- **A modeling language called CTO**: A domain modeling language that defines a business model, concept, and function for a business network definition
- **Playground**: Rapid configuration, deployment, and testing of a business network
- **command-line interface (CLI) tools**: The client command-line tool is used to integrate business network with Hyperledger Fabric

In this chapter, we will explore the Composer business network and development components, including implementing models, transaction logic, access control, and query definitions. We will set up a development environment, and cover the use of the Hyperledger Playground for testing. We will also write client-side code and call chaincode using the client SDK.

In this chapter, we will cover the following recipes:

- The Hyperledger Composer business network and development components
- Setting up the Hyperledger Composer prerequisites environment
- Setting up the development environment
- Configuring a Composer business network
- Implementing models, transaction logic, access control, and query definitions

- Deploying, testing, and exporting business network archives using the Composer command-line interface
- Interacting with Composer through the RESTful API

The Hyperledger Composer business network and development components

You can use Hyperledger Composer to quickly build a business network. Here, you can define assets, participants, transactions, access-control rules, and optional events and queries in the business network. A model (.cto) file contains all of the preceding definitions in the business network. Asset is an associate with a real-world object, and participants have their own unique identity. The transactions will interact with assets. Participants can do this via transactions. The structure of a business network also includes an access control (permissions.acl), which specifies the access-control rules, a script (logic.js) file that implements transaction logic, and a package.json file that contains project metadata:

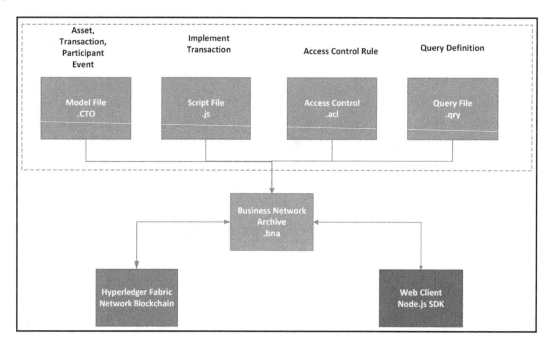

Getting ready

In this chapter, we will develop an application called **FarmaTrace Enterprise** (**FTE**), which will use the Hyperledger Composer tool. FTE will enable end-to-end tracking of medicinal products throughout the pharmaceutical supply chain. There are a variety of challenges that the pharmaceutical supply chain and its stakeholders face daily. The process is time-consuming and information about it is not efficient and transparent to all parties. Creating a flexible and holistic supply chain strategy can allow companies to have better control over processes, enhance communication, and reduce costs:

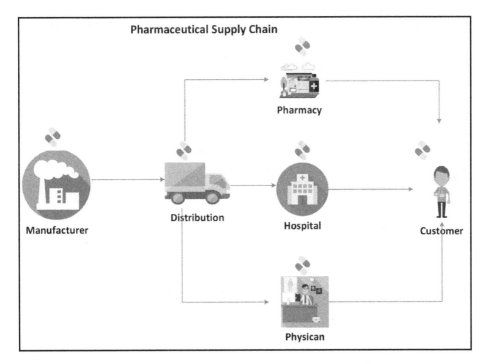

How to do it...

We aim to provide a general design and implementation approach for Composer applications. This commonly-used procedure will help you to understand how to get a kickstart. In the FarmaTrace application, we will build a business network and components. Here, we show how a typical pharmaceutical supply chain works. However, it could be much more complex in a real-world use case. The following is how the FarmaTrace process flow works.

Process flow

First, we need to understand the entire process flow:

1. The **manufacturer** produces drugs, then packages and labels them
2. The **distribution** company gathers packaged products and begins delivery
3. The **distribution** company send drugs to **pharmacies**
4. The **distribution** company send drugs to **hospitals**
5. The **distribution** company send drugs to **physicians**
6. **Customers** buy drugs from a pharmacy, hospital, or physician

Process flow can be repesented as:

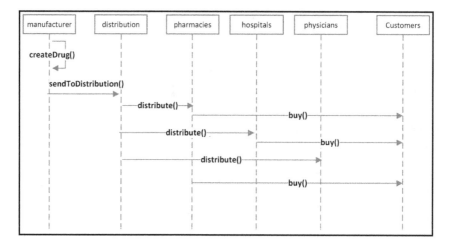

Entities

Next, we need to identify entities for a FarmaTrace application; participants are categorized into six entities:

- Manufacturer
- Distribution
- Pharmacy
- Hospital
- Physician
- Customer

Assets

We will record every transaction in the blockchain; information for these records is stored in a receipt asset object. All participants in the network can trace this receipt. The drug receipt will have all process evidence information for each transaction. This can be used to provide proof for certain steps, which need to display required documents. The asset also defines certain rules that only allow authorized parties to perform permitted transaction actions. The receipt will contain other asset information, such as the drug status, to trace the transaction proof in each step.

Query

Now we will check which parameters are needed to allow us to search for drug information:

- Drug ID
- Drug name
- FDA action date
- Marketing status (prescription, over-the-counter, or discontinued)
- Approval type (type of supplement or other regulatory action)
- Search participants by ID

We have analyzed the FarmaTrace application business use case and development components. To build a business network, we will create all of the following critical files:

- **Model file**: `org.packt.farmatrace.cto`
- **Script file**: `logic.js`
- **ACL file**: `permissions.acl`
- **Query file**: `queries.qry`

We will create these files after we set up a development environment in the *Configuring a Composer business network* recipe.

How it works...

Designing network topology is a critical step for an enterprise blockchain. For our FarmaTrace application, the deployed Composer business network will look like the following:

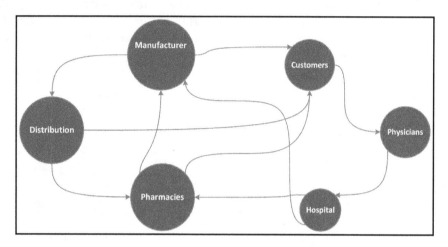

All six participants are attending the network and can communicate with each other. The methods written in `farmatrace-logic.js` will be converted into Fabric chaincode. By invoking chaincode, the Fabric order service will provide a shared communication channel and broadcast transactions to peers. Peers will verify the transactions and commit and apply the same sequence of transactions. Eventually peers will update their state in the same way.

Setting up the Hyperledger Composer prerequisites environment

A development environment consists of all Composer tools and networks that are required in order to start building Hyperledger Composer. This is not a hard task. The Hyperledger Composer can run on various operation systems including Unix (Ubuntu), macOS, or Windows. In this section, we will cover Ubuntu.

Getting ready

Before we set up a development environment, make sure you have installed the following prerequisites:

- **Operating systems**: Ubuntu Linux (64-bit) 14.04/16.04 LTS, or macOS 10.12
- **Node**: version >=8.9 and <9
- **npm**: >=v5.x
- **Git**: >=2.9.x
- **Python**: 2.7.x
- **Docker Engine**: Version 17.03 or higher
- **Docker Compose**: Version 1.8 or higher

 To run Hyperledger Composer and Hyperledger Fabric, 4 GB of memory are required. If you are running an Ubuntu system on VirtualBox, the system needs at least 12-16 GB.

Here, we are using Amazon Ubuntu Server 16.04 as our choice of OS. If you don't have experience with installing Ubuntu in EC2, please refer to the following AWS document: https://aws.amazon.com/getting-started/tutorials/launch-a-virtual-machine/.

You can also install Ubuntu in your local machine VirtualBox. A tutorial for this can be found at http://www.psychocats.net/ubuntu/virtualbox and https://askubuntu.com/questions/142549/how-to-install-ubuntu-on-virtualbox.

How to do it...

Once you have installed Ubuntu, log on to Unix and you can download and run the prerequisites from the Hyperledger GitHub site using the following commands:

```
curl -O https://hyperledger.github.io/composer/latest/prereqs-ubuntu.sh
chmod u+x prereqs-ubuntu.sh
./prereqs-ubuntu.sh
```

With the `sudo` command, you will be prompted for your password:

```
Installation completed, versions installed are:

Node:              v8.12.0
npm:               6.4.1
Docker:            Docker version 18.06.1-ce, build e68fc7a
Docker Compose:    docker-compose version 1.13.0, build 1719ceb
Python:            Python 2.7.12

Please logout then login before continuing.
```

Once installation is done, you need to log out and log on again to make all changes take effect.

How it works...

In the previous steps, you may have noticed that `prereqs-ubuntu.sh` includes a series command to install all the required libraries. Docker provides a container environment to run the tests and to run HyperLedger Fabric. Docker Compose is used to easily configure and start HyperLedger Fabric. Node.js and npm provide the main runtime environment by handling package management and dependency installation. If you're running on **Ubuntu Trusty**, it is necessary to obtain additional kernel packages to enable the use of the AUFS storage driver for Docker.

Setting up the development environment

Composer-CLI is the most important tool for Composer deployment; it contains all the essential command-line operations. Other very useful tools include **Composer REST server, generator Hyperledger Composer, Yeoman**, and **Playground**. Composer CLI provides many useful tools for developers; we will be using it in this recipe.

Composer CLI can be used to perform multiple administrative, operational, and development tasks. Here is a summary of the CLI commands:

Command	Description	Examples
composer archive <subcommand>	Composer archive command.	Composer archive list.
composer card <subcommand>	Command for managing business network cards.	Composer card list.

`composer generator` `<subcommand>`	Composer generator command to convert a business network definition into code.	Composer generator docs.
`composer identity` `<subcommand>`	Composer identity command.	Composer identity issue.
`composer network` `<subcommand>`	Composer network command.	Composer network install.
`composer participant` `<subcommand>`	Composer participant command.	Composer participant add.
`composer report`	Command for creating a report of the current .Composer environment	Composer report.
`composer transaction` `<subcommand>`	Composer transaction command.	Composer transaction submit.

The Composer REST server is used to generate a REST interface to a deployed blockchain business network.

Getting ready

In the previous recipe, we installed all the required libraries. If you haven't done this, please complete the previous setup. Now you can continue with the following installation:

```
docker kill $(docker ps -q)
docker rm $(docker ps -aq)
docker rmi $(docker images dev-* -q)
```

How to do it...

1. Install the following CLI tools:

```
npm install -g composer-cli@0.19.15
npm install -g composer-rest-server@0.19.15
npm install -g generator-hyperledger-composer@0.19.15
npm install -g yo
```

2. Install Playground:

```
npm install -g composer-playground@0.19
```

3. Set up your IDE. Download the VSCode from `https://code.visualstudio.com/download` and install it using the instructions provided onscreen.

4. Install the Composer extension. Open the VSCode extensions menu, find the **Hyperledger Composer** extension from the **EXTENSIONS: MARKETPLACE**, and then install it:

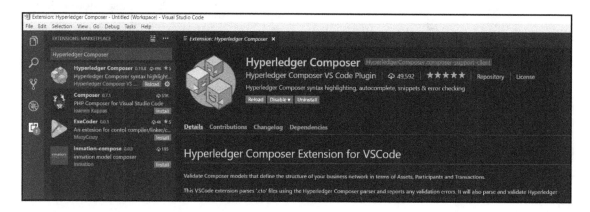

5. Install Hyperledger Fabric:

    1. Create a directory named `~/fabric-dev-servers` and download the `fabric-dev-servers.tar.gz` file:

    ```
    mkdir ~/fabric-dev-servers && cd ~/fabric-dev-servers
    curl -O
    https://raw.githubusercontent.com/hyperledger/composer-tool
    s/master/packages/fabric-dev-servers/fabric-dev-
    servers.tar.gz
    tar -xvf fabric-dev-servers.tar.gz
    ```

    2. Once the extraction is completed, use the following commands to start a local Hyperledger Fabric v1.1 runtime:

    ```
    cd ~/fabric-dev-servers
    export FABRIC_VERSION=hlfv11
    ./downloadFabric.sh
    ```

6. We have set up the typical developer environment for Hyperledger Composer. To start the development Composer application, we should be able to start and stop our Fabric runtime. When you start up a Fabric runtime for the first time, you'll need to run `startFabric.sh` by generating a **PeerAdmin** card:

```
cd ~/fabric-dev-servers
export FABRIC_VERSION=hlfv11
```

```
./startFabric.sh
./createPeerAdminCard.sh
```

7. To stop the Fabric runtime, run `stopFabric.sh` and then `~/fabric-dev-servers/teardownFabric.sh` to clean up the runtime environment.

8. To start up Playground, run the following command:

```
composer-playground
```

9. Bring up the Playground page by entering: `http://localhost:8080/login` or `http://yourserverIP:8080/login`.

Make sure your server port number, `8080`, isn't blocked (if run on the cloud server).

How it works...

The application uses the Hyperledger Composer LoopBack connector to connect to the business network, extract the models, and then model related REST APIs in the pages. Here is some code logic:

```
if (require.main === module) {
    const composerConfig = require('./composer.json');
    module.exports(composerConfig)
        .then((result) => {
            // Start the LoopBack application.
            const app = result.app, server = result.server;
            return server.listen(() => {
                app.emit('started');
                let baseUrl = app.get('url').replace(/\/$/, '');
                console.log('Web server listening at: %s', baseUrl);
                if (app.get('loopback-component-explorer')) {
                    let explorerPath = app.get('loopback-component-
explorer').mountPath;
                    console.log('Browse your REST API at %s%s', baseUrl,
explorerPath);
                }
......
                }
            });
        })
        .catch((error) => {
...
        });
}
```

`generator-hyperledger-composer` is used to create pro-forma templates for use with the Hyperledger Composer.

Yeoman provides the `generator-hyperledger-composer` utility tool to generate applications.

Hyperledger Composer Playground is a browser-based user interface that makes it possible to configure, deploy, and test a business network. You can use the Playground to model your business network, including defining assets, participants, ACL, and transactions involved in the process. Advanced Playground features permit users to manage the security of the business network, invite participants to business networks, and connect to multiple blockchain business networks.

In Hyperledger Composer, it installed a sample Hyperledger Fabric network (v1.0). PeerAdmin is the administrator for this network. It has admin rights to all peers in the network. You can access PeerAdmin by creating a PeerAdmin business network card.

Configuring a Composer business network

In the previous section, we set up a development environment. In this section, we will create the FarmaTrace business network definition including the `.cto`, `.script`, `.query`, and `.acl` files, and then package them as a `.bna` file using Composer tools.

The `yo hyperledger-composer` command has three options: Angular, business network, and CLI. These are defined as follows:

- `hyperledger-composer:businessnetwork` is used to generate a skeleton business network with an asset, participant and transaction defined, as well as a Mocha unit test.
- `hyperledger-composer:angular` is used to generate the Angular application by connecting to a running business network.
- `hyperledger-composer:cli` is used to create a standard npm module with the usual attributes of name, author, description and help to create the sample structure.

How to do it...

Follow steps to create your own bussiness network:

1. To create the FarmaTrace business network definition, we need to set up a project structure:

   ```
   mkdir farmaTrace
   cd farmaTrace
   ```

2. We will use Yeoman's `hyperledger-composer` tool to create a `businessnetwork` project template. Enter all required information for this. For example, a business network name, description, author name, author email address, license selection, and namespace:

   ```
   yo hyperledger-composer:businessnetwork
   ```

3. Select `org.packt.farmatrace` as the namespace.

4. Select `No` when asked whether to generate an empty network.

5. The Yeoman tool will generate `farmatrace-network` files, as follows:

```
.
└── farmatrace-network
    ├── features
    │   ├── sample.feature
    │   └── support
    │       └── index.js
    ├── lib
    │   └── logic.js
    ├── models
    │   └── org.packt.farmatrace.cto
    ├── package.json
    ├── permissions.acl
    ├── README.md
    └── test
        └── logic.js

6 directories, 8 files
```

How it works...

Here, we created a FramaTrace network on the local system, which contains all the required skeleton files to develop our FarmaTrace Composer application. This will help us to use Hyperledger Playground to do all our development work.

Implementing models, transaction logic, access control, and query definitions

We will use Yeoman to generate a `businessnetwork` project template. Here, we need to modify the provided template files.

Getting ready

In Playground, select an **empty-business-network** template to start our model, logic, and ACL implementation:

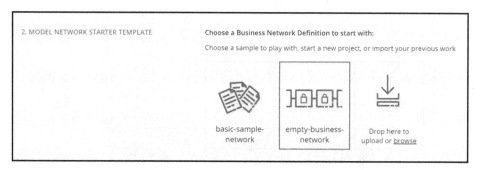

We first rename the mode file under the `models` folder to `org.packt.farmatrace.cto`. Then we add a new script file by clicking on add a file, selecting **Script File (.js)**, and adding a new **Query File (.qry)** by clicking add a file. You should then select **Query File (.qry)**:

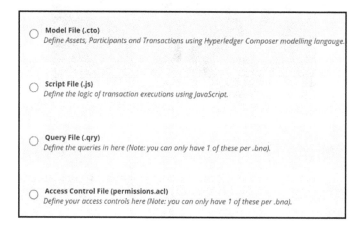

Remove the default generated content in these files. In earlier FarmaTrace use case analyses, we identified that we need to create the following businessnetwork components:

- participants: Manufacturer, distribution, pharmacy, hospital, physician, customer
- asset: drugReceipt, Evident, Drug
- transaction: Init(), makeDrug(), sendToDistribution(), three distribute() functions (to pharmacy, physician and hospital), three buy function and finally close
- query: Query participant by ID, including manufacturer, distribution, pharmacy, hospital, physician, customer, and so on
- permissions.acl: Defines participant permissions

How to do it...

Execute the following steps to generate a businessnetwork project:

1. Define participant, asset, concept, enum, transaction and event for our model file: org.packt.farmatrace.cto.
2. Define enum for ParticipantType: MANUAFACTURER, DISTRIBUTION, PHARMACY, HOSPITAL, PHYSICIAN, and CUSTOMER.
3. The model file defines the FarmaTrace flow status for the receipt, as follows:

```
enum ReceiptStatus {
o START
o CREATE_DRUG
o PICK_UP_DRUG
o DEVLIER_PHARMACY
o DEVLIER_HOSPITAL
o DEVLIER_PHYSICIAN
o CUSTOMER_RECEIVED
o CLOSED
}
```

4. The model file defines six participants in the network, as follows:

```
//address
concept Address {
  o String street
  o String city
  o String country default = "US"
```

```
}
concept Entity {
  o String name
  o String desc
  o String phone
  o Address address
}
concept Person {
  o String firstName
  o String lastName
  o String phone
 o Address address
}
participant Manufacturer identified by manufacturerId {
  o String manufacturerId
  o Entity entityInfo
}
..
```

5. Define the `Evident` asset. To do this, trace some important information, such as when a transaction happens, which participants are involved in this transaction, and what `ReceiptStatus` is, when we make this evident:

```
asset Evident identified by evidentId {
  o String evidentId
  o DateTime lastUpdate
  o ParticipantType from
  o ParticipantType to
  o String fromId
  o String toId
  o ReceiptStatus status
}
```

6. Define the `Drug` asset. The `Drug` asset defines important information, including the date of manufacture, when a drug will expire, name, and description.

7. Define the `DrugReceipt` asset. Here, the receipt will record all transactions and drug information. It maintains the current transaction status:

```
asset DrugReceipt identified by receiptId {
  o String receiptId
  o ReceiptStatus currentStatus
  --> Evident[] evidents
  --> Drug drug
  o String closeReason optional
}
```

8. Define the FarmaTrace transaction and event in the model file and implement them in the script file.

9. Create a `Drug` asset with the default set to the default manufacture date and the expiration date as `1900-01-01` (invalidated date):

```
async function initialApplication(application) {
    const factory = getFactory();
    const namespace = 'org.packt.farmatrace';
    const drugReceipt = factory.newResource(namespace,
'DrugReceipt',
application.receiptId);
    drugReceipt.currentStatus = 'START';
    drugReceipt.evidents = [];
    //initial drug
    const drug = factory.newResource(namespace, 'Drug',
application.drugId);
    drug.manu_date="1900-01-01";
    drug.expire_date="1900-01-01";
    drug.name=application.drug_name;
    drug.desc=application.drug_desc;
    drugReceipt.drug = drug;
    //save the application
...
    //save the application
..
        // emit event
...
    }
```

10. Implement the `makeDrug` function—in this step, the `makeDrug` function implements the logic for tracing `makeDrug` by manufacturer. We first verify that the receipt status is set to `START`; if not, the smart contract will throw an exception:

```
/**
 * @param {org.packt.farmatrace.makeDrug} makeDrug - Manufacturer
make a drug
 * @transaction
 */
async function makeDrug(request) {
    const factory = getFactory();
    const namespace = 'org.packt.farmatrace';
    let drugReceipt = request.drugReceipt;
    if (drugReceipt.currentStatus != 'START') {
        throw new Error ('This drug receipt should be in START');
    }
```

```
                drugReceipt.currentStatus = 'CREATE_DRUG';
  ....
  }
```

11. Query the blockchain to make sure that input from the `fromId` and `toId` parameters is valid by querying `findManufacturerById`, which is defined in `queries.qry`:

```
let fromResults = await query('findManufacturerById',{
                "manufacturerId": request.fromId
                                          });
if(fromResults.length==0) {
    throw new Error ('Can't find manufacturer');
}
```

12. Create `evident` and add it to the receipt, as follows:

```
let evidentId =  Math.random().toString(36).replace('0.', '');
let evident = factory.newResource(namespace, 'Evident',
evidentId);
evident.lastUpdate = new Date();
evident.from = 'MANUAFACTURER';
evident.to = 'MANUAFACTURER';
evident.fromId = request.fromId;
evident.toId = request.toId;
evident.status ='CREATE_DRUG'
//save the application
const evidentRegistry = await getAssetRegistry(namespace+
'.Evident');
await evidentRegistry.add(evident);
drugReceipt.evidents.push(evident);
```

13. Update the drug manufacture date and expiration date.

```
let drug = drugReceipt.drug;
var currentDate = new Date()
  drug.manu_date = currentDate.getFullYear();+ "-" +
(currentDate.getMonth() + 1) + "-"
+ currentDate.getDate();
  drug.expire_date = (currentDate.getFullYear();+ 3) + "-" +
(currentDate.getMonth() +
1)+ "-" + currentDate.getDate();
  const drugAssetRegistry = await
getAssetRegistry(drug.getFullyQualifiedType());
  await drugAssetRegistry.update(drug);
```

14. Update the receipt and emit the event in the blockchain. Other transactions in FarmaTrace will be similar.

How it works...

The Composer model's language is an object-oriented language. We first analyze and capture all critical information and then apply OOD design to define our six participants in the system. We can then define these participants using the Composer model language. There are two type of participant: one is organization-based, the other is person-based. The relationship for these participants is as follows:

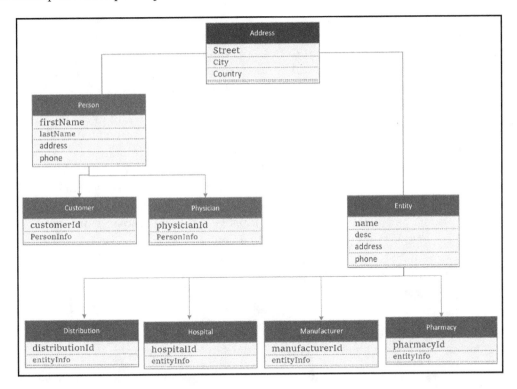

Distribution, Hospital, Manufacturer, and Pharmacy have entity information, which is an organization-based participant. Customer and Physician have person information, which is a person-based participant. Both Entity and Person contain an Address asset.

We also define transaction methods in the model file, and implement transaction logic in the logic file. The transaction function can be considered to be smart contract execution. These transactions will link to the implementation of the transaction function through annotations in the comment of the function. `@param` connects this transaction to the `makeDrug` defined in the model. `@transaction` marks this function as a transaction function:

```
/**
 * Manufacturer make a drug
 * @param {org.packt.farmatrace.makeDrug} makeDrug - Manufacturer make a
drug
 * @transaction
 */
```

The script can directly invoke a query file search function, just like a regular JavaScript post method. This can pass JSON-formatted data as a parameter. In our example, we pass the `manufacturerId` parameter and call `findManufacturerById`. If no manufacturer record is found, the transaction will throw an exception and be aborted.

There are three functions required to create or update a transaction and event record. The first one is `getFactory()`, which allows an asset or participant to be created as part of a transaction. The second is `getAssetRegistry(namespace+ '.xyzAsset)`, `getParticipantRegistry(namespace + '.xyzParticipant)`, or `factory.newEvent('org.namespace', 'xyzEvent')`. This creates `xyzAsset`, `xyzParticipant`, or `xyzEvent` defined in a specified namespace. Then the required properties on `asset`, `participant`, or `event` must be set. Finally, to emit an `event`, it should use `xyzEventRegistry.add()`. To add a new `asset` or `participant`, it should use `xyzParticipantRegistry.add()` or `xyzAssetRegistry.add()`. To update a new `asset` or `participant`, it should use `xyzParticipantRegistry.update()` or `xyzAssetRegistry.update()`:

```
        const drugReceiptAssetRegistry = await
    getAssetRegistry(request.drugReceipt.getFullyQualifiedType());
        await drugReceiptAssetRegistry.update(drugReceipt);
        // emit event
        const makeDrugEvent = factory.newEvent(namespace, 'makeDrugEvent');
        makeDrugEvent.drugReceipt = drugReceipt;
        emit(makeDrugEvent);
    emit(makeDrugEvent);
```

There's more...

We have just looked at how to use a query function to find a manufacturer by ID. There is another way to get the same result. Composer provides `getNativeAPI` to call the Hyperledger Fabric API in a Composer transaction processor function. `getNativeAPI` allows users to call the Fabric shim API, which provides APIs for the chaincode to access its state variables, transaction context, and call other chaincodes:

```
const nativeSupport = request.nativeSupport;
    const nativeFromIdKey =
getNativeAPI().createCompositeKey('Participant:org.packt.farmatrace.Manufac
turer', [request.fromId]);
    const fromIterator = await
getNativeAPI().getHistoryForKey(nativeFromIdKey);
    let fromResults = [];    let fromRes = {done : false};
    while (!fromRes.done) {
        fromRes = await fromIterator.next();
        if (fromRes && fromRes.value && fromRes.value.value) {
            let val = fromRes.value.value.toString('utf8');
            if (val.length > 0) {
                fromResults.push(JSON.parse(val));
            }
        }
        if (fromRes && fromRes.done) {
            try {
                fromIterator.close();
            }
            catch (err) {
            }
        }
    }
    if(fromResults.length==0) {
        throw new Error ('Cant find manufacturer');
    }
```

The `getState` and `putState` Hyperledger Fabric API functions will bypass the Hyperledger Composer access-control rules.

Playground uses a **Composer API** and calls the **Composer proxy Connector** to connect to a **Composer Connector Server** via **SOCKETI/O**. All Playground data in web mode is stored in the location storage. The **Composer Playground API** is an express app that directly connects to **Composer Connector Server**, which interacts with **Composer HLF Runtime**. When we load Playground, we will see some samples. These samples are taken from **NPM** libraries. The Playground UI communicates with the **Composer Playground API** via **HTTP**.

The following diagram shows how these components interact with each other:

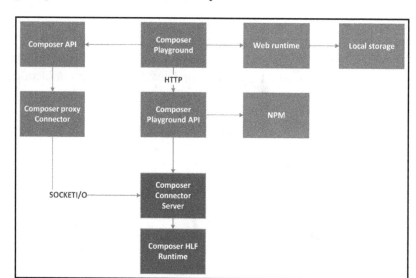

Deploying, testing, and exporting business network archives using the Composer command-line interface

We implemented all the models, transactions, and query functions in the previous recipe. It is now time for us to deploy the application to the Fabric network.

Getting ready

There are multiple ways to do this. In the Playground, there is an option to export a file as a `.bna` file. We can then upload the `.bna` file to Ubuntu server to begin deployment. We can also update all related files in the Ubuntu server's `farmatrace-network` folder, including `logic.js`, `permissions.acl`, `org.packt.farmatrace.cto`, and `queries.qry`, and then manually generate a `.bna` file.

How to do it...

Having generated a .bna file, we can start to deploy files to the blockchain using the following steps:

1. Navigate to the ~farmatrace-network directory and run the following command:

    ```
    composer archive create -t dir -n .
    ```

    This will create a .bna file called farmatrace-network@0.0.1.bna in the farmatrace-network folder. We can now deploy this .bna file to the business network

2. Install the farmatrace-network@0.0.1.bna file to our business network and run the following command:

    ```
    composer network install --card PeerAdmin@hlfv1 --archiveFile
    farmatrace-network@0.0.1.bna
    ```

3. Start the business network and run the following command:

    ```
    composer network start --networkName farmatrace-network --
    networkVersion 0.0.1 --networkAdmin admin --
    networkAdminEnrollSecret adminpw --card PeerAdmin@hlfv1 --file
    networkadmin.card
    ```

4. Import the network administrator identity as a usable business network card and run the following command:

    ```
    composer card import --file networkadmin.card
    ```

5. Ping the deployed business network to verify the successful deployment and run the following command to ping the network:

    ```
    composer network ping --card admin@farmatrace-network
    ```

    You will see the following information return from the command. Congratulations, you have successfully deployed your first business network on the blockchain:

```
ubuntu@ip-172-31-2-9:~/farmaTrace/farmatrace-network$ composer network ping --card admin@farmatrace-network
The connection to the network was successfully tested: farmatrace-network
        Business network version: 0.0.1
        Composer runtime version: 0.19.15
        participant: org.hyperledger.composer.system.NetworkAdmin#admin
        identity: org.hyperledger.composer.system.Identity#c2e3a2eec9d99a8e1b9e8ba12ff21781653d51adf3659dc96896a46b73560554

Command succeeded
```

How it works...

A business network archive contains the model definition, the JavaScript logic file, the permission file and, optionally, the query description file. Using the `composer cli archive` command, we generate a `.bna` file. This actually just ZIPs these Composer files, including `package.json`.

Once the `.bna` file has been generated, we run the Composer network install command. We then run the start command to start the Composer network to install and deploy a `.bna` file on the Hyperledger Fabric peers of the blockchain network. When deployment is completed, `networkadmin.card` is created using the PeerAdmin card we created earlier. The card stored the administrator credentials, that is, the user ID and password (or secret). Finally, we import the created `networkadmin.card` to `farmatrace-newwork`. The entire Composer deployment is shown as follows:

Interacting with Composer through the RESTful API

Once you deploy the business network archive to the blockchain network, how do you integrate it with your client application? One solution would be to use the Hyperledger Composer REST server.

The Hyperledger Composer REST server can be used to generate a Swagger REST endpoint API from a deployed Hypeledger Fabric business network. The REST server utilizes the LoopBack and converts the business network model into an open API definition. An authenticated client calls the REST server via these endpoint APIs to interact with a blockchain. Each invoked transaction must be signed by a certificate. The REST server starts this identity and signs all transactions with this. At runtime, the REST server implements **Create, Read, Update, and Delete (CRUD)** operations to manipulate the state of assets and participants and allow transactions to be submitted or retrieved with queries.

Getting ready

To launch the Composer REST server, simply type the following:

```
composer-rest-server
```

The Unix Terminal will ask you a few questions about your business network:

```
ubuntu@ip-172-31-14-42:~$ composer-rest-server
? Enter the name of the business network card to use: admin@farmatrace-network
? Specify if you want namespaces in the generated REST API: never use namespaces
? Specify if you want to use an API key to secure the REST API: No
? Specify if you want to enable authentication for the REST API using Passport: No
? Specify if you want to enable the explorer test interface: Yes
? Specify a key if you want to enable dynamic logging:
? Specify if you want to enable event publication over WebSockets: Yes
? Specify if you want to enable TLS security for the REST API: No
```

Once the server starts up, the web server will be listening at `http://localhost:3000` or `http://yourserverIP:3000`.

You can browse your REST API at `http://localhost:3000/explorer`:

Hyperledger Composer REST server			
buyFromHospital : A transaction named buyFromHospital	Show/Hide	List Operations	Expand Operations
buyFromPharmacy : A transaction named buyFromPharmacy	Show/Hide	List Operations	Expand Operations
buyFromPhysician : A transaction named buyFromPhysician	Show/Hide	List Operations	Expand Operations
Close : A transaction named Close	Show/Hide	List Operations	Expand Operations
Customer : A participant named Customer	Show/Hide	List Operations	Expand Operations
distributeToHospital : A transaction named distributeToHospital	Show/Hide	List Operations	Expand Operations
distributeToPharmacy : A transaction named distributeToPharmacy	Show/Hide	List Operations	Expand Operations

Browse around and explore the REST API. The page shows different endpoints, including all assets, participants, and transactions defined in the model and `logic.js`. The query API from `queries.qry` is also displayed on the page. You can test a simple query within the Explorer.

At this point, we can start to build a frontend application to interact with the generated REST API. We will explore a few options for this.

How to do it...

Yeoman generators support generating an Angular-based web application skeleton via the hyperledger-composer module. The Composer REST server needs to be running and connected to the Hyperledger Fabric blockchain. The Yeoman Angular command needs to run in the same directory as the .bna file. Execute the following commands:

1. Open a new Terminal and navigate to ~/farmaTrace/farmatrace-network using the following command:

   yo hyperledger-composer

2. Enter the required project information and business network card:

```
ubuntu@ip-172-31-14-42:~/farmaTrace/farmatrace-network$ yo hyperledger-composer
Welcome to the Hyperledger Composer project generator
? Please select the type of project: Angular
You can run this generator using: 'yo hyperledger-composer:angular'
Welcome to the Hyperledger Composer Angular project generator
? Do you want to connect to a running Business Network? Yes
? Project name: farmatrace-ng
? Description: farmatrace angular composer client app
? Author name: brian wu
? Author email: brian.wu@smartchart.tech
? License: Apache-2.0
? Name of the Business Network card: admin@farmatrace-network
? Do you want to generate a new REST API or connect to an existing REST API?  Connect to an existing REST API
? REST server address: http://localhost
? REST server port: 3000
? Should namespaces be used in the generated REST API? Namespaces are not used
Created application!
Completed generation process
   create app.js
   create Dockerfile
   create e2e/app.e2e-spec.ts
```

3. This will generate an Angular application via the Yeoman tool. Navigate to the farmatrace-ng directory and you will see that the following Angular files have been generated:

4. Make sure you have installed all angular-related packages:

```
npm install -g typings
npm install -g bower
npm install -g @angular/cli
Start angular application by enter command:
ng serve
```

If you run on AWS cloud server, you can run this command:

```
ng serve --host your_private_IP --port 4200
```

You may get an invalid host header message when you run Angular in the cloud server. It is an Angular CLI-related issue as seen at `https://github.com/angular/angular-cli/issues/6070#issuecomment-298208974`. You can fix this by editing `service.js` in `node_modules/webpack-dev-server/lib/Server.js` (line 425); change it to `return true;`.

5. The previous step will bring up the Angular client server. Once the server is up, you can open `http://localhost:4200` or `http://yourserverip:4200`:

```
ubuntu@ip-172-31-14-42:~/farmaTrace/farmatrace-network/farmatrace-ng$ ng serve
Your global Angular CLI version (6.2.3) is greater than your local
version (1.0.1). The local Angular CLI version is used.

To disable this warning use "ng config -g cli.warnings.versionMismatch false".
** NG Live Development Server is running on http://localhost:4200 **
Hash: 4211cda886e66f39542c
Time: 13657ms
chunk    {0} polyfills.bundle.js, polyfills.bundle.js.map (polyfills) 270 kB {5} [initial] [rendered]
chunk    {1} main.bundle.js, main.bundle.js.map (main) 551 kB {4} [initial] [rendered]
chunk    {2} styles.bundle.js, styles.bundle.js.map (styles) 184 kB {5} [initial] [rendered]
chunk    {3} scripts.bundle.js, scripts.bundle.js.map (scripts) 439 kB {5} [initial] [rendered]
chunk    {4} vendor.bundle.js, vendor.bundle.js.map (vendor) 4.12 MB [initial] [rendered]
chunk    {5} inline.bundle.js, inline.bundle.js.map (inline) 0 bytes [entry] [rendered]
webpack: Compiled successfully.
```

6. From here, you can start to update your Angular file to build your web application for `farmatrace`:

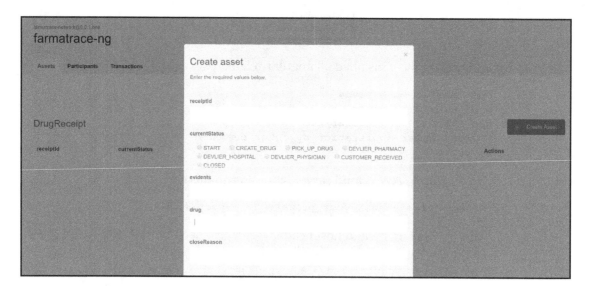

How it works...

The Yeoman Hyperledger Composer tool generates a proxy configuration and connects to the Composer REST server:

```
function getTarget() {
    if (process.env.REST_SERVER_URLS) {
        const restServerURLs = JSON.parse(process.env.REST_SERVER_URLS);
        const restServerURL = restServerURLs['farmatrace-network'];
    ...
    }
    ...
    return 'http://localhost:3000';
}
```

It reads business-network meta-information, then generates the `org.hyperledger.composer.system.ts` typescript file. This file contains the definition of `asset`, `transaction`, and `participant`, as seen in the following code block:

```
export namespace org.hyperledger.composer.system{
    export abstract class Registry extends Asset {
        registryId: string;
        name: string;
        type: string;
        system: boolean;
    }
    ..
```

It also generates `org.packt.farmatrace.ts`, which defines all the classes of `asset`, `participant`, and `transactions` from `org.hyperledger.composer.system.ts`:

```
import {Participant} from './org.hyperledger.composer.system';
import {Transaction} from './org.hyperledger.composer.system';
// export namespace org.packt.farmatrace{
    export class Manufacturer extends Participant {
        manufacturerId: string;
        entityInfo: Entity;
    }
```

The `data.service.ts` file in the Angular application will query or update the transactions API that was explored by Composer REST server:

```
export class DataService<Type> {
    constructor(private http: Http) {
        this.actionUrl = '/api/';
        this.headers = new Headers();
        this.headers.append('Content-Type', 'application/json');
        this.headers.append('Accept', 'application/json');
    }
    public getAll(ns: string): Observable<Type[]> {
        console.log('GetAll ' + ns + ' to ' + this.actionUrl + ns);
        return this.http.get(`${this.actionUrl}${ns}`)
          .map(this.extractData)
          .catch(this.handleError);
    }
```

4
Integrating Hyperledger Fabric with Explorer

Hyperledger Explorer is a powerful utility that allows users to create user-friendly web-based applications. It is a blockchain dashboard and provides the ability to view, invoke, deploy, and query raw blockchain data and network information, including block details, chain codes, and transactions stored in the ledger.

Hyperledger Explorer is a highly maintainable and open source browser that can be configured and built natively on macOS and Ubuntu. At the time of writing, Hyperledger Explorer has not yet gone live. The latest release, v0.3.8, supports Fabric v1.3.

It is common to encounter errors here and there, especially around issues related to versions and/or setting up environments. To save time while debugging, I have included various notes and tips, along with recommended fixes, for some of the errors you might run into while walking through these recipes.

The published official directory structure is a good starting point to examine the basic building blocks of Hyperledger Explorer. Take a look at the snapshot from the Hyperledger Explorer GitHub repository (`https://github.com/hyperledger/blockchain-explorer`) to learn more.

The following screenshot shows the structure of the Hyperledger Explorer directory:

```
├── app                    Application backend root, Explorer configuration
│       ├── rest           REST API
│       ├── persistence    Persistence layer
│             ├── fabric   Persistence API (Hyperledger Fabric)
│       ├── platform       Platforms
│             ├── fabric   Explorer API (Hyperledger Fabric)
│       ├── test           Application backend test
├── client                 Web UI
│       ├── public         Assets
│       ├── src            Front end source code
│             ├── components        React framework
│             ├── services          Request library for API calls
│             ├── state             Redux framework
│             ├── static            Custom and Assets
```

In a nutshell, a Hyperledger Explorer application is composed of six key components:

- **A web server**: Node.js is used to implement the server-side components.
- **A web user interface**: AngularJS is used to implement the frontend framework. Bootstrap is used for its rich UI and responsive features.
- **WebSockets**: WebSocket APIs are used to push information from the server to the clients.
- **A database**: PostgreSQL is the data store. Information about blocks, transactions, and smart contracts will be stored in this database.
- **A security repository**: This will act as a facade for security implementations from different blockchain platforms. The user identities and access management will be implemented using a federated security repository.
- **A blockchain implementation**: This provides updates on transactions, blocks, node logs, and smart contacts to the explorer web server.

We will be covering the following recipes in this chapter:

- Setting up the Hyperledger Explorer environment
- Installing Hyperledger Explorer and setting up the database
- Configuring Hyperledger Explorer with Fabric
- Building Hyperledger Explorer
- Running the Hyperledger Explorer application

Technical requirements

For stability, we will use Hyperledger Fabric v1.3 as the blockchain framework throughout this chapter.

In order to install and run Hyperledger Explorer and other tools successfully, a system with the following minimum settings is required:

- **CPU**: 4 cores, 16 GB RAM
- **Operation system**: Ubuntu Linux 16.04

We will use the Amazon Ubuntu Server version 16.04 throughout this chapter. If you have not had much experience with Ubuntu in the Amazon cloud EC2, refer to the AWS documentation at the following link: `https://aws.amazon.com/getting-started/tutorials/launch-a-virtual-machine/`.

We found using Amazon EC2 environment convenient, especially for test drives or POCs. You may also install Ubuntu locally on your local machine if you prefer, but using a virtual machine is highly recommended to separate the Hyperledger Explorer running environment from other existing environments. This means that, if something unexpected happens, you have a way to recover and rebuild your environment quickly. Some information about setting up virtual machines can be found at the following links: `http://www.psychocats.net/ubuntu/virtualbox` or `https://askubuntu.com/questions/142549/how-to-install-ubuntu-on-virtualbox`.

Setting up the Hyperledger Explorer environment

In this section, we will demonstrate how Hyperledger Explorer works with Hyperledger Fabric. Before we can do that, we will need to install all of the pre-requisites for Hyperledger Explorer and Hyperledger Fabric.

Getting ready

The following is a checklist of the required components along with their required versions:

For Hyperleger Explorer v0.3.8, you will need the following:

- Node.js v8.11.x or greater (v9.x is not yet supported): You can find more details at `https://nodejs.org/en/download/` and `https://nodejs.org/en/download/package-manager/`.
- PostgreSQL (v9.5 or greater) is needed.
- For jq (v1.5), more details can be found at `https://stedolan.github.io/jq/`.

For Hyperledger Fabric v1.3, you will need the following:

- **Node.js v8.11.x or greater (v9.x is not yet supported)**: You can find more details at `https://nodejs.org/en/download/` and `https://nodejs.org/en/download/package-manager/`
- **cURL (v7.47)**: This comes with Ubuntu v16.04: `https://curl.haxx.se/download.html`
- **Docker (v17.06.2-ce or greater)**: Details can be found at `https://www.docker.com/community-edition`
- **Docker Compose (v1.14.0 or greater)**: Check out `https://docs.docker.com/compose/` or `https://github.com/docker/compose/releases/tag/1.14.0`
- **Go (v1.10.x)**: `https://golang.org/dl/`
- **Python (v2.7/v3.5.1)**: Python v3.5.1 comes with Ubuntu v16.04. v2.7 is needed for the Fabric Node.js JDK

How to do it...

The following steps let you create a Hyperledger Explorer environment:

1. Install the Hyperledger Fabric v1.3 pre-requisites. If you have already got Hyperledger Fabric v1.3 successfully installed on your platform, skip this step and move on to step 2. If you have not yet installed Hyperledger Fabric, refer to Chapter 1, *Working with Hyperledger Fabric*, and Chapter 2, *Implementing Hyperledger Fabric*, and follow the instructions to install all of the necessary Fabric dependencies on the platform on which you will be running your Hyperledger Explorer application.

2. Install the Hyperledger Explorer app pre-requisites. Hyperledger Explorer requires Node.js to run. If you have already installed Hyperledger Fabric, you will have Node.js installed already. Hyperledger Explorer does not support Node.js v9.x yet, so if you have v9.x, it is recommended that you uninstall the v9.x version and re-install Node.js v8.x. Run the following command to verify the Node.js version on your system:

```
$ nodejs -v
v8.15.0
```

3. Next, run the following command to install the latest jq version. When prompted, enter Y to proceed:

```
$ sudo apt-get install jq
. . . .
Do you want to continue? [Y/n] Y
```

4. Lastly, install PostgreSQL from the Ubuntu repository. We will need v9.5 or greater. Run the following command and enter Y to proceed when prompted:

```
$ sudo apt-get install postgresql
. . . . . .
Do you want to continue? [Y/n] Y
```

Installing Hyperledger Explorer and setting up the database

With all of the pre-requisites installed, we are now ready to install Hyperledger Explorer.

How to do it...

Execute the following steps to set up your database and Hyperledger Explorer:

1. Run the following command from your home directory. This will clone the latest version of Hyperledger Explorer from GitHub to your system. To make sure we get v0.3.8, do a version checkout in case there is a newer release:

```
$ git clone https://github.com/hyperledger/blockchain-explorer.git
$ git checkout release-3.8
$ cd blockchain-explorer
```

2. Set up the PostgreSQL database. Navigate to Hyperledger Explorer's `app` directory and make a back-up copy of the original explorer configuration file in case you need to rollback to the original configuration:

```
$ cd app or $ cd ~/blockchain-explorer/app
$ cp explorerconfig.json explorerconfig.json.bak
```

3. You can use the vi editor or any other editor to update the PostgreSQL properties in the `explorerconfig.json` file, as shown. You can set the `passwd` to `password` of your preference, then save your changes:

```
"postgreSQL": {
    "host": "127.0.0.1",
    "port": "5432",
    "database": "fabricexplorer",
    "username": "hppoc",
    "passwd": "password"
},
```

4. Next, we need to create a PostgreSQL database. To do this, run the following commands:

```
$ cd ~/blockchain-explorer/app/persistence/fabric/postgreSQL/db
$ sudo bash ./createdb.sh
```

5. If you would like to check the database status, you can connect to the PostgreSQL database with the PostgreSQL command-line interface. Check out the sample commands as follows:

```
$ sudo -u postgres psql
psql (9.5.14)
Type "help" for help.

postgres=# \l
```

You will see the following screenshot with a list of Postgres databases:

```
                                      List of databases
      Name       |  Owner   | Encoding |   Collate   |    Ctype    |   Access privileges
-----------------+----------+----------+-------------+-------------+-----------------------
 fabricexplorer  | hppoc    | UTF8     | en_US.UTF-8 | en_US.UTF-8 |
 postgres        | postgres | UTF8     | en_US.UTF-8 | en_US.UTF-8 |
 template0       | postgres | UTF8     | en_US.UTF-8 | en_US.UTF-8 | =c/postgres          +
                 |          |          |             |             | postgres=CTc/postgres
 template1       | postgres | UTF8     | en_US.UTF-8 | en_US.UTF-8 | =c/postgres          +
                 |          |          |             |             | postgres=CTc/postgres
(4 rows)
```

6. To exit the PostgreSQL, you can use the following command:

```
# to exit from psql:
postgres=# \q
```

Configuring Hyperledger Explorer with Fabric

With Hyperledger Explorer installed, we can now configure the explorer to connect to a blockchain network.

Getting ready

In order to demonstrate how Hyperledger Explorer works, we need a working blockchain network, which in this case is Hyperledger Fabric. We will utilize the `first-network` scripts that should have been installed if you installed all of the pre-requisites for Fabric:

1. To start with, go to the `first-network` directory, which can be found in the Fabric installation:

```
$ cd fabric-samples/first-network
```

2. We will build a Fabric network with four peers, two organizations, one order node, and one channel. Execute the following command to generate the genesis block and all of the necessary certificates, keys, and channel configurations:

```
$ sudo bash ./byfn.sh generate
```

The script should return pretty quickly.

 The previous command must be executed from the `first-network` sub-directory of the `fabric-samples` repository clone. Otherwise, the various provided scripts will be unable to run successfully.

3. Now, let's bring up the network:

```
$ sudo ./byfn.sh up
```

You will see the following screenshot:

```
Starting for channel 'mychannel' with CLI timeout of '10' seconds and CLI delay of '3' seconds
Continue? [Y/n] y
proceeding ...
LOCAL_VERSION=1.3.0
DOCKER_IMAGE_VERSION=1.3.0
Creating network "net_byfn" with the default driver
Creating volume "net_peer0.org2.example.com" with default driver
Creating volume "net_peer1.org2.example.com" with default driver
Creating volume "net_peer1.org1.example.com" with default driver
Creating volume "net_peer0.org1.example.com" with default driver
Creating volume "net_orderer.example.com" with default driver
Creating peer1.org1.example.com ...
Creating peer0.org2.example.com ...
Creating peer1.org2.example.com ...
Creating orderer.example.com ...
Creating peer1.org1.example.com
Creating peer0.org1.example.com ...
Creating peer0.org2.example.com
Creating peer1.org2.example.com
Creating orderer.example.com
Creating peer1.org2.example.com ... done
Creating cli ...
Creating cli ... done


  _____ _____ ___  _____ _____
 / ____|__   __/ _ \ |  __ \|__   __|
 \___ \   | | / /_\ \| |__) |  | |
  ___) |  | | / _____ \|  _  <   | |
 |____/   |_|/_/     \_\_| \_\  |_|


Build your first network (BYFN) end-to-end test

Channel name : mychannel
Creating channel...
```

This will continue to launch all of the containers. Upon successful completion, you will see the following screenshot:

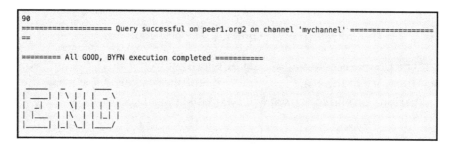

```
90
===================== Query successful on peer1.org2 on channel 'mychannel' ====================
==

========= All GOOD, BYFN execution completed ===========


  _____ _   _ _____
 |  ____| \ | |  __ \
 | |__  |  \| | |  | |
 |  __| | . ` | |  | |
 | |____| |\  | |__| |
 |_____|_| \_|_____/
```

4. You have now successfully set up a Fabric network. To close down the network, run the following command:

```
$ sudo bash ./byfn.sh down
```

You will see the following screenshot upon execution of the previous command:

```
Stopping for channel 'mychannel' with CLI timeout of '10' seconds and CLI delay of '3' seconds
Continue? [Y/n] y
proceeding ...
Stopping cli ... done
Stopping peer0.org1.example.com ... done
Stopping orderer.example.com ... done
Stopping peer1.org2.example.com ... done
Stopping peer0.org2.example.com ... done
Stopping peer1.org1.example.com ... done
Removing cli ... done
Removing peer0.org1.example.com ... done
Removing orderer.example.com ... done
Removing peer1.org2.example.com ... done
Removing peer0.org2.example.com ... done
Removing peer1.org1.example.com ... done
Removing network net_byfn
```

Do not execute the `byfn.sh down` command unless you are done using the blockchain network. This command will kill all of your containers, remove the crypto material and four artifacts, and delete the chaincode images from your Docker registry.

How to do it...

The following steps will help you to configure Hyperledger Explorer:

1. From another Terminal window, go to the `platform/fabric` subdirectory where you installed Explorer:

   $ cd blockchain-explorer/app/platform/fabric

2. Open the `config.json` file using an editor of your choice, such as the following:

   $ vi config.json

3. Update `network-configs` as follows:

   + For keys"adminPrivateKey", "signedCert" , "tlsCACerts" and
   "configtxgenToolPath" :

Change `fabric-path` to your Fabric network path. This is the working directory in which you installed Fabric. My Fabric working directory, for example, is `/cookbook/`, and it is under the `HOME` directory. I will replace `fabric-path` with `$HOME/cookbook`. This will make the `adminPrivateKey` key path look as follows:

```
"adminPrivateKey": {
            "path": "$HOME/cookbook/fabric-samples/first-
network/crypto-
config/peerOrganizations/org1.example.com/users/Admin@org1.example.
com/msp/keystore"
            },
```

For each client, modify `network-id.clients.client-id.channel` to your default channel, which is `mychannel` in our example.

To avoid frustration, when you update `fabric-path`, do not use ~ to represent the user's home directory in the `path`, even though they refer to the same thing. Otherwise, you might run into a confusing error such as this: `{Error: ENOENT: no such file or directory, scandir '~/cookbook/fabric-samples/first-network/.../users/ Admin@org1.example.com/msp/keystore'}`, even when the directory does exist!

How it works...

In order to integrate Hyperledger Explorer with Fabric, we will need to define a blockchain network from which explorer will gather data. This can be done by modifying the `config.json` file to update the `network-configs` property for the Fabric network.

Building Hyperledger Explorer

After completing all of the preceding tasks, we are now ready to build a Hyperledger Explorer application.

How to do it...

Execute the following commands:

1. You will notice that all is running as expected:

    ```
    $ cd ~/blockchain-explorer/
    $ sudo npm install
    > pkcs11js@1.0.16 install /home/ubuntu/blockchain-
    explorer/node_modules/pkcs11js
    > node-gyp rebuild
    make: Entering directory '/home/ubuntu/blockchain-
    explorer/node_modules/pkcs11js/build'
    ....
    make: Leaving directory '/home/ubuntu/blockchain-
    explorer/node_modules/pkcs11js/build'
    added 2 packages from 1 contributor in 392.181s
    ```

2. Otherwise, if you have been running everything with sudo, you might get a
    permission-denied error, as follows:

    ```
    > dtrace-provider@0.8.7 install /home/ubuntu/blockchain-
    explorer/node_modules/dtrace-provider
    > node-gyp rebuild || node suppress-error.js
    gyp ERR! configure error
    gyp ERR! stack Error: EACCES: permission denied, mkdir
    '/home/ubuntu/blockchain-explorer
    /node_modules/dtrace-provider/build'
    ...
    gyp ERR! cwd /home/ubuntu/blockchain-explorer/node_modules/pkcs11js
    gyp ERR! node -v v8.15.0
    gyp ERR! node-gyp -v v3.8.0
    gyp ERR! not ok
    npm ERR! code ELIFECYCLE
    npm ERR! errno 1
    npm ERR! pkcs11js@1.0.16 install: `node-gyp rebuild`
    npm ERR! Exit status 1
    npm ERR!
    npm ERR! Failed at the pkcs11js@1.0.16 install script.
    npm ERR! This is probably not a problem with npm. There is likely
    additional logging output above.
    ```

3. Execute the following commands to change the ownership, and then rerun the
    install:

    ```
    $sudo chown -R $USER:$(id -gn $USER) ./node_modules
    $ npm install
    ```

4. Another possible build error you might face is if you are working on a new machine or a new EC2 instance:

```
> pkcs11js@1.0.16 install /home/ubuntu/blockchain-
explorer/node_modules/pkcs11js
> node-gyp rebuild
gyp ERR! build error
gyp ERR! stack Error: not found: make
gyp ERR! stack at getNotFoundError
(/usr/lib/node_modules/npm/node_modules/which
/which.js:13:12)
gyp ERR! stack at F
(/usr/lib/node_modules/npm/node_modules/which/which.js:68:19)
gyp ERR! stack at E
(/usr/lib/node_modules/npm/node_modules/which/which.js:80:29)
gyp ERR! stack at
/usr/lib/node_modules/npm/node_modules/which/which.js:89:16
gyp ERR! stack at
/usr/lib/node_modules/npm/node_modules/isexe/index.js:42:5
gyp ERR! stack at
/usr/lib/node_modules/npm/node_modules/isexe/mode.js:8:5
gyp ERR! stack at FSReqWrap.oncomplete (fs.js:152:21)
gyp ERR! System Linux 4.4.0-1075-aws
gyp ERR! command "/usr/bin/node"
"/usr/lib/node_modules/npm/node_modules/node-gyp/bin/node-
gyp.js" "rebuild"
gyp ERR! cwd /home/ubuntu/blockchain-explorer/node_modules/pkcs11js
gyp ERR! node -v v8.15.0
gyp ERR! node-gyp -v v3.8.0
gyp ERR! not ok
npm ERR! code ELIFECYCLE
npm ERR! errno 1
npm ERR! pkcs11js@1.0.16 install: `node-gyp rebuild`
npm ERR! Exit status 1
```

5. This means you have not got the GNU make tool installed. Executing the following command should fix the issue:

```
$ sudo apt install build-essential
```

6. We will now build and run the explorer tester:

```
$ cd blockchain-explorer/app/test
$ npm install
npm WARN hyperledger-explorer-test@0.3.3 No repository field.
added 384 packages from 844 contributors in 7.161s
```

7. Run test, as follows:

```
$ npm run test
```

8. You might run into the following authentication error for postgres:

```
(node:12316) UnhandledPromiseRejectionWarning: error: password
authentication failed for user "postgres"
at Connection.parseE (/home/ubuntu/blockchain-
explorer/app/test/node_modules/pg/lib/connection.js:553:11)
at Connection.parseMessage (/home/ubuntu/blockchain-
explorer/app/test/node_modules/pg/lib/connection.js:378:19)
at Socket.<anonymous> (/home/ubuntu/blockchain-
explorer/app/test/node_modules/pg/lib/connection.js:119:22)
at emitOne (events.js:116:13)
at Socket.emit (events.js:211:7)
at addChunk (_stream_readable.js:263:12)
at readableAddChunk (_stream_readable.js:250:11)
at Socket.Readable.push (_stream_readable.js:208:10)
at TCP.onread (net.js:601:20)
(node:12316) UnhandledPromiseRejectionWarning: Unhandled promise
rejection. This error originated either by throwing inside of an
async function without a catch block, or by rejecting a promise
which was not handled with .catch(). (rejection id: 1)
(node:12316) [DEP0018] DeprecationWarning: Unhandled promise
rejections are deprecated. In the future, promise rejections that
are not handled will terminate the Node.js process with a non-zero
exit code.
```

9. If so, execute the following command to change the MD5 authentication to trust for a quick fix:

```
$ sudo sed -i.bak '/^host.*md5/ s/md5/trust/'
/etc/postgresql/*/main/pg_hba.conf
$ sudo service postgresql restart
```

10. Once PostgreSQL restarts, you will have to rerun `test`:

```
$ sudo npm run test
> hyperledger-explorer-test@0.3.3 test /home/ubuntu/blockchain-
explorer/app/test
> mocha *.js --exit
GET /api/blockAndTxList/:channel/:blocknum
should return blockandtx
. . .
# when it is completed, you will see the status:
19 passing (686ms)
1..1
# tests 1
# pass 1
# ok
```

11. From the same Terminal window, install `client`, as follows:

```
$ cd ../../client/
$ npm install
> jss@9.8.7 postinstall /home/ubuntu/blockchain-
explorer/client/node_modules/jss
> node -e "console.log('\u001b[35m\u001b[1mLove JSS? You can now
support us on open collective:\u001b[22m\u001b[39m\n >
\u001b[34mhttps://opencollective.com/jss/donate\u001b[0m']"
. . . .
added 2227 packages from 1353 contributors in 60.754s
```

12. Run some tests, as follows:

```
$ npm test -- -u -coverage
> hyperledger-explorer-client@0.3.8 test /home/ubuntu/blockchain-
explorer/client
> react-scripts test --env=jsdom "-u" "--coverage"
. . .
# you might see some console warnings, ignore it
Test Suites: 26 passed, 26 total
Tests: 171 passed, 171 total
Snapshots: 0 total
Time: 24.283s, estimated 198s
Ran all test suites.
```

13. We can now carry out `build`:

```
$ npm run build
> hyperledger-explorer-client@0.3.8 build /home/ubuntu/blockchain-
explorer/client
> react-scripts build
Creating an optimized production build...
Compiled successfully.
```

 The client build takes time to complete. However, if it takes more than 5 minutes or so and the system appears to freeze without responding, this might be an indication that your current system does not have enough RAM to handle it.

Running the Hyperledger Explorer application

Once Hyperledger Explorer has been built successfully, we are ready to run our Explorer application.

Getting ready

Before running Hyperledger Explorer, we should examine the configuration of Explorer, which is defined in the `explorerconfig.json` file.

Update the following information according to the individual needs of the project:

- Where the synchronization will be running, which is either explorer (local) or from a different location standalone (host)
- The type of blockchain network (Fabric)
- How often the blockchain data will synchronize with explorer

How to do it...

Execute the following steps to run your Hyperledger application:

1. Use the vi editor or your editor of choice to make the modifications as needed:

```
$ cd blockchain-explorer/app
$ vi explorerconfig.json
# Here we will run local with Explorer, update the "sync" property
as needed to # as below:
"sync": {
    "type": "local",
    "platform": "fabric",
    "blocksSyncTime": "3"
    }
}
```

2. Now, start explorer from another Terminal. When you are done using explorer, you should stop explorer and the node server:

```
$ cd blockchain-explorer/
$ sudo ./start.sh
# To stop Explorer, use this command:
$ sudo ./stop.sh
```

3. You can check for error statuses in the log file: [logs/console/console-yyyy-mm-dd.log]. If everything goes well, you will see the following:

```
postgres://hppoc:password@127.0.0.1:5432/fabricexplorer
(node:14817) DeprecationWarning: grpc.load: Use the @grpc/proto-
loader module with
grpc.loadPackageDefinition instead
Please open web browser to access: http://localhost:8080/
pid is 14817
postgres://hppoc:password@127.0.0.1:5432/fabricexplorer
. . .
```

4. The console log might show an explorer error, such as the following:

```
postgres://hppoc:password@127.0.0.1:5432/fabricexplorer
<<<<<<<<<<<<<<<<<<<<<<<<<<< Explorer Error >>>>>>>>>>>>>>>>>>>>>>>
{ Error: The gRPC binary module was not installed. This may be
fixed by running "npm rebuild"
Original error: Cannot find module '/home/ubuntu/blockchain-
explorer/node_modules/grpc/src/node/extension_binary/node-v57-
linux-x64-glibc/grpc_node.node'
at Object.<anonymous> (/home/ubuntu/blockchain-
explorer/node_modules/grpc/src/grpc_extension.js:43:17)
```

```
at Module._compile (module.js:653:30)
at Object.Module._extensions..js (module.js:664:10)
at Module.load (module.js:566:32)
at tryModuleLoad (module.js:506:12)
at Function.Module._load (module.js:498:3)
at Module.require (module.js:597:17)
at require (internal/module.js:11:18)
at Object.<anonymous> (/home/ubuntu/blockchain-
explorer/node_modules/grpc/src
/client_interceptors.js:145:12)
at Module._compile (module.js:653:30) code: 'MODULE_NOT_FOUND' }
Received kill signal, shutting down gracefullyClosed out
connections
```

5. This may be fixed by running `npm rebuild` and then starting explorer again:

```
$ cd ~/blockchain-explorer/
$ npm rebuild
> grpc@1.14.2 install /home/ubuntu/blockchain-
explorer/node_modules/grpc
> node-pre-gyp install --fallback-to-build --library=static_library
...
```

> There is an application log, `[logs/app/app.log]`, that provides more information than the console log if there are any errors when running the explorer application.

6. On the other hand, explorer `start.sh` runs in the background. To observe the progression, you could use the `tail` command for the `app.log` file:

```
$ tail -f logs/app/app.log
```

7. We can now launch explorer from a browser: `http://localhost:8080`.

8. If you are running on AWS EC2, you will need to carry out a further two steps. Replace the localhost with your instance's public IP address and add or modify a security group associate with the EC2 instance to allow inbound traffic from TCP port 8080. If everything is good, you should see the explorer **DASHBOARD** default page. From here, you can navigate to the application to check and monitor various blockchain data:

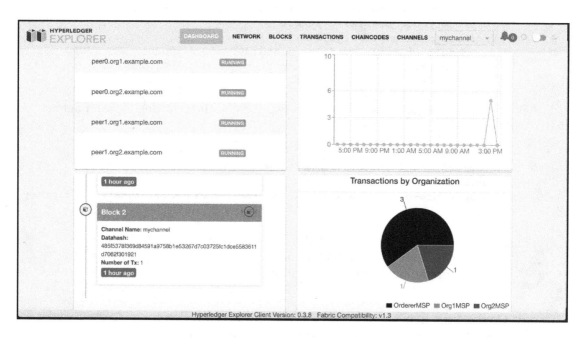

You have now successfully built the Hyperledger Explorer application, integrated it with the Hyperledger Fabric framework, and utilized explorer to visualize the blockchain network data on the browser.

5
Working with Hyperledger Sawtooth

Hyperledger Sawtooth is an enterprise blockchain platform with which to build, deploy, and run **decentralized applications (dApps)** with a highly modular architecture. Hyperledger Sawtooth originated from Intel and is currently an open source project under the Linux Foundation.

The main principles behind Hyperledger Sawtooth are keeping a distributed ledger, distributed data storage, a modular architecture, and a decentralized consensus; these makes smart contracts safe, particularly for enterprise organizations.

This chapter will cover the following recipes:

- Installing Hyperledger Sawtooth
- Configuring Hyperledger Sawtooth
- Designing a namespace and address
- Implementing a transaction family
- Building a transaction processor
- Granting permission on the Sawtooth network
- Developing client applications with the Sawtooth REST API and SDK

Introduction

Hyperledger Sawtooth is an enterprise blockchain platform for building distributed ledger applications and private and permissioned networks that do not require centralized authority or central decision-making services. It simplifies the development of blockchain applications by separating the core system from the application domain with multi-language support.

Sawtooth is open, flexible, and extensible, allowing you to build new services such as membership, ACL, Crypto assets, and data confidentiality. Sawtooth also has a modular architecture, meaning enterprises can choose and customize transaction rules, permissioning, and plug consensus algorithms based on the organization's requirements.

The features offered by Hyperledger Sawtooth are the following:

- **A truly distributed DLT**: The Hyperledger Sawtooth blockchain network is made up of validator nodes. The ledger is shared between all validator nodes and each node has the same information. They participate in a consensus to manage the network.

- **Proof of Elapsed Time (PoET) consensus and support for large-scale networks**: Hyperledger Sawtooth includes a novel consensus algorithm, PoET. PoET is a **Byzantine Fault-tolerance** (**BFT**) consensus algorithm that supports large-scale networks with minimal computing and much more efficient resource consumption compared to proof of work algorithms. PoET was invented by Intel and utilizes the special CPU instruction set called **Software Guard Extensions** (**SGX**), to achieve the scaling benefits of the Nakamoto-style consensus algorithms. Each node waits for a random period of time and the first node to finish is the leader and commits the next block.

- **Fast transaction performance**: Hyperledger Sawtooth keeps the latest version of assets in the global state and transactions in the block chain on each network node. This means that you can look up the state quickly to carry out CRUD actions, which provides fast transaction processing. Sawtooth requires transactions to be processed in batches and supports parallel scheduling of transactions. Parallel transaction execution not only accelerates the execution of transactions but also correctly handles the double spending problem known as **Unspent Transaction Output** (**UTXO**).

- **Support for a broad variety of languages**: Sawtooth supports the implementation of transaction families (safe and smart contracts) in a wide variety of programming languages, including Python, Go, Rust, Java, and Javascript.

- **The ability to configure private, public, and consortium blockchain networks**: Sawtooth can be configured with different permissions to build private, consortium, or public networks by specifying which nodes are allowed to join the validator network and participate in the consensus, and which clients are allowed to submit batches and transactions.

Sawtooth is open and flexible, allowing you to build customized solutions, such as network governance, **know your customer** (**KYC**) processes, **anti-money laundering** (**AML**), and Crypto assets, in addition to its core distribution.

The Sawtooth network is composed of the following components:

- **Validator nodes**: These are peer nodes that shape the network. They are responsible for peer discovery, message communication, blockchain synchronization, managing the global state, consensus, block commits, and so on.
- **Transaction processor**: This is a smart contract for processing business logic.
- **REST API**: This is an API that provides the client application with the ability to interact with Validator nodes:

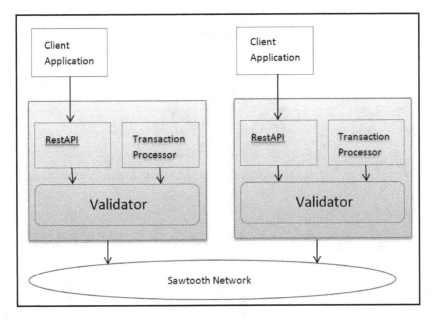

The Sawtooth network

Installing Hyperledger Sawtooth

This recipe will show you how to communicate with Amazon AWS using PuTTy, how to install and launch the Hyperledger Sawtooth network, and how to set up Python for developing Sawtooth applications on AWS. We will also use the Sawtooth command line to test and verify the installed Sawtooth network on AWS.

Getting ready

To set up PuTTy and Python on AWS, perform the following:

1. Install PuTTy (from `https://www.chiark.greenend.org.uk/~sgtatham/putty/`) on your Windows desktop and convert the private key generated by Amazon EC2 into a putty key file using PuTTygen, following the guide that can be found at `https://docs.aws.amazon.com/AWSEC2/latest/UserGuide/putty.html`.

2. In PuTTygen, load the EC2 key file and save the private key:

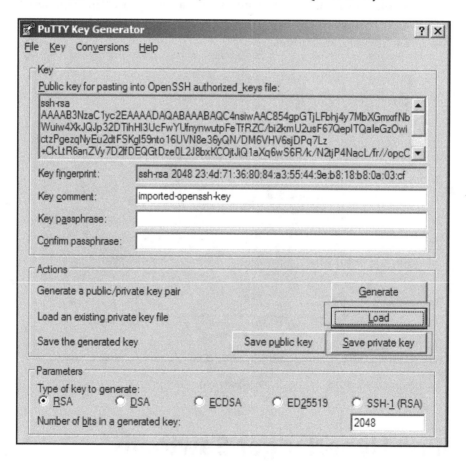

3. Run PuTTy and specify the private key file for PuTTy in **Connection | SSH | Auth**. Log in as ubuntu to the Sawtooth AWS instance:

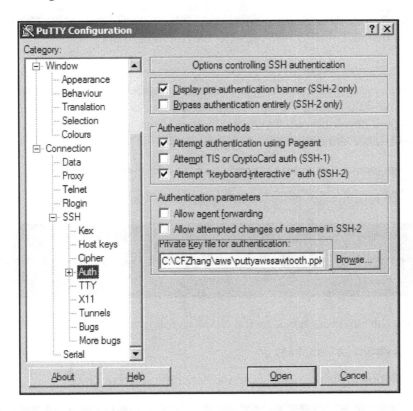

4. Set up Python. Verify that Python version 3.5 or above is pre-installed on the instance:

   ```
   python3 -V
   ```

6. Refresh the Unix package list:

   ```
   sudo apt-get update
   ```

7. Install the Python package manager, pip:

   ```
   sudo apt install python3-pip
   ```

8. Verify that pip has been installed correctly:

   ```
   pip3 -V
   ```

How to do it...

The PuTTy and Python development environment is now ready on AWS. The following commands will install, launch, and verify the Sawtooth network.

1. Subscribe to and install the Hyperledger Sawtooth product 1.0.4 (`https://aws.amazon.com/marketplace/pp/B075TKQCC2`) on the AWS marketplace and launch an AWS EC2 instance, which can be of the `m4.2xlarge` or `t2.mroc` type for personal development. To check whether Hyperledger Sawtooth is running on the instance, enter the following command:

   ```
   systemctl list-units|grep -i sawtooth|less
   ```

   Following screenshot show the list of sawtooth instances:

   ```
   sawtooth-intkey-tp-python.service                loaded active running   Sawtooth Intkey TP Python
   sawtooth-poet-validator-registry-tp.service      loaded active running   Sawtooth PoET TP Validator Registry
   sawtooth-rest-api.service                        loaded active running   Sawtooth REST API
   sawtooth-settings-tp.service                     loaded active running   Sawtooth TP Settings
   sawtooth-validator.service                       loaded active running   Sawtooth Validator Server
   sawtooth-xo-tp-python.service                    loaded active running   Sawtooth XO TP Python
   ```

2. View the Sawtooth block on the chain, as follows:

   ```
   sawtooth block list
   ```

   Following screenshot show the list of the sawtooth block

   ```
   ubuntu@ip-172-31-90-67:~$ sawtooth block list
   NUM  BLOCK ID
    BATS  TXNS  SIGNER
   0    e4d5c459db91048512e45c04f099602d0ba352adcedb3057cd0a141bc2214d861b85438e8d774a7a33c3b51d607dec81a60c411159e8904eb9d746dc918b1ce2
    1    1    02f5d0...
   ```

3. View the Sawtooth global state as follows:

   ```
   sawtooth state list
   ```

   ```
   ubuntu@ip-172-31-90-67:~$ sawtooth state list
   ADDRESS                                                              SIZE  DATA
   000000a87cb5eafdcca6a8cde0fb0dec1400c5ab274474a6aa82c12840f169a04216b7  110   b'\n1\n&sawtooth.settings.vote.authorized_keys\x12B021c9a9d3155d15e5c834b29e.
   HEAD BLOCK: "e4d5c459db91048512e45c04f099602d0ba352adcedb3057cd0a141bc2214d861b85438e8d774a7a33c3b51d607dec81a60c411159e8904eb9d746dc918b1ce2"
   ```

4. Verify that the Sawtooth REST API service is working as follows:

```
curl http://localhost:8008/blocks
```

The following screenshot verifies privous comamnd:

```
ubuntu@ip-172-31-90-67:~$ curl http://localhost:8008/blocks
{
  "data": [
    {
      "batches": [
        {
          "header": {
            "signer_public_key": "021c9a9d3155d15e5c834b29e995d4f3fb7da54e6aa0b1f43ce753bc77cce36138",
            "transaction_ids": [
              "470892276e2e589f8943c4bab48baf6f7193865743901593 99b78a6ed14cf4a27ffe7ffa432e0ac7e131269d2a7f
            ]
          },
        },
```

5. View Sawtooth log files as follows:

```
ls -ll /var/log/sawtooth
```

On execution of the privous command will lead you to the following screen:

```
ubuntu@ip-172-31-90-67:~$ ls -ll  /var/log/sawtooth
total 28
-rw-r--r-- 1 sawtooth sawtooth   59 Sep 22 15:02 intkey-3b435ab4a6784bb3-debug.log
-rw-r--r-- 1 sawtooth sawtooth    0 Sep 22 15:02 intkey-3b435ab4a6784bb3-error.log
-rw-r--r-- 1 sawtooth sawtooth   59 Sep 22 15:02 mkt-0846bd6b792f4413-debug.log
-rw-r--r-- 1 sawtooth sawtooth    0 Sep 22 15:02 mkt-0846bd6b792f4413-error.log
-rw-r--r-- 1 sawtooth sawtooth 1464 Sep 22 15:17 rest_api-debug.log
-rw-r--r-- 1 sawtooth sawtooth    0 Sep 22 15:02 rest_api-error.log
-rw-r--r-- 1 sawtooth sawtooth  327 Sep 22 15:02 settings-b2eeac3aaf78484e-debug.log
-rw-r--r-- 1 sawtooth sawtooth    0 Sep 22 15:02 settings-b2eeac3aaf78484e-error.log
-rw-r--r-- 1 sawtooth sawtooth 5623 Sep 22 15:02 validator-debug.log
-rw-r--r-- 1 sawtooth sawtooth    0 Sep 22 15:02 validator-error.log
```

6. Rename the genesis batch file. If you don't do this, Sawtooth will fail to start if you restart the EC2 instance or the Sawtooth services:

```
mv /var/lib/sawtooth/genesis.batch genesis.batch.bk
```

7. Generate a new public and private key-pair that will be used by the validator node to sign and encrypt messages:

```
sudo sawadm keygen
```

Configuring Hyperledger Sawtooth

This recipe will demonstrate how to configure the Hyperledger Sawtooth validator, the REST API, and much more.

How to do it...

Execute the following steps to configure Hyperledger Sawtooth

1. The Sawtooth validator default configuration file can be found at `/etc/sawtooth/validator.toml`. To set the network bind port and other component bind ports, use the following command:

   ```
   bind = [
       "network:tcp://127.0.0.1:8800",
       "component:tcp://127.0.0.1:4004"
   ]
   ```

2. To set the peer discovery type and peer validator nodes, enter the following:

   ```
   peering = "static"
   peers = ["tcp://127.0.0.1:8801"]
   ```

3. You can find the Sawtooth REST API service default configurations file at `/etc/sawtooth/rest_api.toml`. To set the REST API service host and port, enter the following command:

   ```
   bind = ["127.0.0.1:8008"]
   ```

4. To set the validator connecting point, enter the following:

   ```
   connect = "tcp://localhost:4004"
   ```

5. Sawtooth distributes the example configuration files on EC2. When you view, create, or edit Sawtooth configuration files, you need to use `sudo` and verify that the Sawtooth user has permission to access these files:

   ```
   sudo nano validator.toml
   sudo chmod 777 validator.toml
   ```

6. To check the configuration files used by the validator, you can verify them in the validator log file:

```
less /var/log/sawtooth/validator-debug.log
```

This is shown in the following screenshot:

```
[17:06:29.496 [MainThread] cli INFO] sawtooth-validator (Hyperledger Sawtooth) version 1.0.4
[17:06:29.496 [MainThread] cli INFO] config [path]: config_dir = "/etc/sawtooth"; config [path]: key_dir = "/etc/sawtooth/keys"; config [p
ath]: data_dir = "/var/lib/sawtooth"; config [path]: log_dir = "/var/log/sawtooth"; config [path]: policy_dir = "/etc/sawtooth/policy"
[17:06:29.496 [MainThread] core DEBUG] global state database file is /var/lib/sawtooth/merkle-00.lmdb
[17:06:29.496 [MainThread] core DEBUG] txn receipt store file is /var/lib/sawtooth/txn_receipts-00.lmdb
```

How it works...

The Hyperledger Sawtooth base configuration files include the following:

- conf_dir: The directory to the Sawtooth configuration file
- key_dir: The directory to load key files
- data_dir: The directory for blockchain data files
- log_dir: The directory for log files
- policy_dir: The directory for policy files

The path to these configuration files depends on whether the SAWTOOTH_HOM environment variable is set. When SAWTOOTH_HOME is set, the directories will be as follows:

- conf_dir = SAWTOOTH_HOME/etc/
- key_dir = SAWTOOTH_HOME/keys/
- data_dir = SAWTOOTH_HOME/data/
- log_dir = SAWTOOTH_HOME/logs/
- policy_dir = SAWTOOTH_HOME/policy/

By default, the configuration files for Sawtooth on EC2 are as follows:

- conf_dir = /etc/sawtooth
- key_dir = /etc/sawtooth/keys
- data_dir = /var/lib/sawtooth
- log_dir = /var/log/sawtooth
- policy_dir = /etc/sawtooth/policy

Designing a namespace and address

In this recipe, we will guide you through the main steps of building a Sawtooth transaction family with a case study that implements a marketplace designed to keep track of the owner of a house. The sample application is developed with the Sawtooth Python SDK and uses the Sawtooth XO transaction family as a template. The full code is available with the source code files that come with this book.

The main focus of this case study is on demonstrating how to develop a Sawtooth application as a proof of concept. In a real production environment, state access control, data encryption, confidentiality, and security would be customized based on the different commercial requirements.

The simple business cases for this sample marketplace are creating records to keep track of the owner of a house and transferring the house from one owner to another:

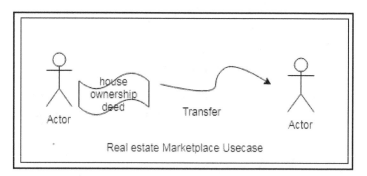

Getting ready

The transaction family is the smart contract or business logic used for your enterprise. To apply the Sawtooth blockchain network in your enterprise system, the following is a good approach to use:

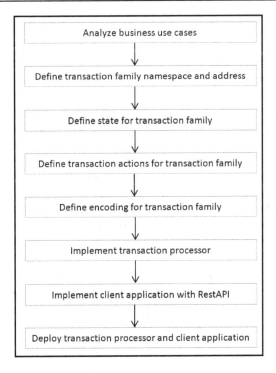

In this recipe, we will cover how to design the transaction family namespace and address. After that, we will explain how Sawtooth stores the global state and accesses data from it using the namespace and address.

How to do it...

The namespace is a three-byte address prefix and must be calculated in the same way within a particular transaction family. The design could be one of the following:

- Map to an arbitrary constant string, such as A00000 or A00001.
- Define a short and meaningful transaction family name that is up to three characters in length and hex-encode it.
- Hash the family name and slice the first six hex characters. Hashing is a useful way to generate an address of a fixed length from family names of various lengths.

The address of the transaction family needs to be 32 bytes and can be constructed with either simple or complicated logic, based on the transaction family. The following list contains a few possible approaches:

- Calculate the address from a set of key attributes using the SHA-512 hash algorithm. As a SHA-512 hash will generate a 512-bits (32-byte) signature for any length of string, it is simple way to calculate the address from a string value of a set of attributes for a transaction family directly.
- Divide the address into segments, and hash each segment, slicing them into different lengths of bytes accordingly. The address could be specified as the `asset type`.`asset` ID. The address can be constructed by hashing the asset type and the asset ID, slicing each into different lengths to compose the 32-byte address. For example, you could slice one asset type with 4 bytes and the asset ID with the remaining 28 bytes.
- Directly hex-encode a name, such as the LDAP distinguished name. The address could simply be a hex-encoded LDAP distinguished name, such as `uid=`, organization unit `(ou)=`, or domain component `(dc)=`, with each set being of a fixed length. For example, the DC could be 4 bytes, the OU could be 4 bytes, and the UID could be the remaining 24 bytes.
- The address must be deterministic and is always calculated in the same way for the same set of key attributes for the transaction family. It may be, however, that two different sets of key attributes result in the same address, based on your address scheme. In this case, the mechanism of serialization and deserialization should correctly handle the address collision and store and retrieve the data correctly for each set of key attributes.

For our application, the namespace and address design will be as follows:

```
Transaction family name = 'mkt'
```

The namespace prefix is the first six hex characters of its hash:

```
hashlib.sha512('mkt'.encode("utf-8")).hexdigest()[0:6]
```

The data address is simply the SHA-512 hash of the name of the address:

```
hashlib.sha512(house.encode('utf-8')).hexdigest()[:64]
```

How it works...

Sawtooth blockchain is not the same as other enterprise blockchain systems, which distribute the ledger among participating nodes in the network and keep a consistent copy of the transactions on each node. It also keeps track of the latest state for all transaction families in a single Radix Merkle tree, which is the global state for the blockchain on each validator node.

The global state is built as a copy-on-write Radix Merkle tree and the root hash is generated by children nodes from the leaf to root and level by level. The root hash will be saved into the block header to make sure each validator can reach a consensus, not only on the transactions in the block but also on the global state for the block. If the root hash is different or modified, the block will be invalidated.

The latest state for an asset in each transaction family is stored in the leaf node of the Radix Merkle tree. The tree could have 35 levels and each parent node in a level could have up to 256 children nodes. The global state Merkle tree for one version looks as follows:

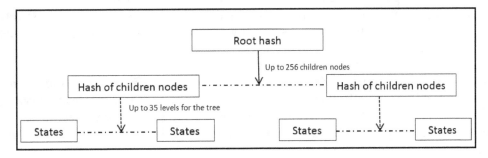

A Radix Merkle tree

The namespace and address scheme

Data is stored in the leaf node of the global state. To access the data from the Merkle tree, the address is used. The address is the unique path that identifies how to access the data from the root to the leaf node in the global state. Sawtooth defines the address with 35 bytes, represented as 70 hex-encoded characters. Each byte in the address defines the next-level node in the tree to the leaf node associated with the address. A byte has 8 bits, so each level would have 2^8 (256) children nodes. The length of the address is 35 bytes, so it could specify up to 35 levels of depth for the global state Merkle tree.

The address scheme for the 35-byte address is that the first 3 bytes (6 hex-encoded characters) are the namespace prefix. The rest of the 32 bytes of the address, represented as 64 hex-encoded characters, can be specified in various ways, based on different business scenarios. In a Sawtooth blockchain, you can define a total of 2^{24} transaction families for your enterprise. The address scheme looks as follows:

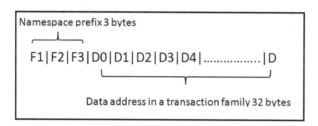

There's more...

The most important guideline to follow for designing a namespace and address for the transaction family states that the address must be deterministic. In the transaction processor and the client application, for the same set of key attributes, the calculated address must be always the same.

As long as the design complies with this rule, how to design the namespace and address for a transaction family is very flexible and completely up to the enterprise. Hashing is a common approach, but it is not obligatory. Your own addressing schema should be designed with your enterprise's business requirements in mind.

Implementing a transaction family

After the namespace and address scheme is defined for the transaction family, the state, transaction, and payload encoding scheme can be defined.

How to do it...

To define the state, you should analyze the data requirements for your organization and follow an appropriate modeling process to define the semantic data model for the system. For example, you could use entity-relationship modeling to represent conceptual data logic in your enterprise. In our example, the state is as follows:

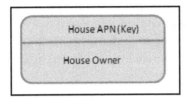

This can be explained as follows:

- **House APN (Key)**: The **Assessor Parcel Number** (APN) for a house is a unique number assigned to each parcel of land by a county tax assessor. The APN is based on formatting codes, depending on the home's location. Local governments use APNs to identify and keep track of land ownership for property tax purposes.
- **House Owner**: The name of the person who currently owns the house.

Defining transactions involves analyzing all your business use cases and the attributes used to perform these business operations. In our example, transactions and their payloads are as follows:

- **House APN (Key)**: The key attribute for the state.
- **Action**: This can be either the `create` keyword or the `transfer` keyword.
- **House Owner**: The name of the house owner.

To define payload encoding schemes, you could choose from one of the following methods:

- **JSON Encoding: JavaScript Object Notation (JSON)** is a lightweight data-interchange format that is popularly used in software systems as an alternative to XML. The standard JSON package for Python can be found here: `https://docs.python.org/3/library/json.html`. The advantages of using JSON are that it is human-readable, it is supported in most programming languages, and it is easy to encode and decode using libraries.

- **Protobuf Encoding**: Protocol buffers are Google's language and platform-neutral mechanism for serializing data. With `protobuf` encoding, you define the message formats in a `.proto` file and compile them using the protocol buffer compiler. To find out more, you can follow the guide that can be found here: `https://developers.google.com/protocol-buffers/`. It is small, fast, and simple, but it is not human-readable. Like JSON, it is also supported in many languages, such as Java, Python, C++, and Go.
- **Simple text encoding**: This involves defining your own message format and carrying out character encoding using your own protocol with a special delimiter, or following common formats, such as `.csv` or `base64`, to represent data in an ASCII format or string. These are human-readable, simple, easy, fast, and language- and platform-neutral.

For our example, the encoding for the state and payload is simple text encoding that encodes the data with UTF8 and the CSV format. We are using the Sawtooth XO family as a template.

For hash collisions, the colliding state will be stored as the UTF-8 encoding of the string with a delimiter, |, such as `entry 1|entry 2`:

```
'|'.join(sorted([','.join([house, owner])
for house, (owner) in house_list.items()])).encode()
```

How it works...

State, transaction, and encoding schemes play an important role when you design the transaction family for your business. In this section, we will explain how each of these work:

- **Defining the state with data modeling for the transaction family**: The state is the data model for your enterprise and it is the data in your system. The state is stored in the global Merkle tree and the actions performed on the state are transactions stored on the blockchain.

- **Defining transactions with a unified command interface for the transaction family**: Transactions are actions performed on the state and the business use cases in your enterprise. Analyzing all your business use cases and defining a unified command interface to abstract all the actions, such as basic **create**, **read**, **update**, **delete** (**CRUD**) actions, in a common way makes your programming model clean and structured. Transaction payloads are messages transferred over the network. The transaction payload is the communication protocol between the client and the validator node and between the validator nodes on the network.
- **Defining the encoding scheme for the transaction family**: The encoding scheme is the serialization and deserialization of the state and the transaction payload. Sawtooth stores arbitrary data in the leaf nodes of the global state, and use an arbitrary message format for the payload on the network. It is up to you to choose a feasible and suitable encoding scheme for your business. Sawtooth provides an infrastructure platform and businesses can customize this based on their own needs.

There are no requirements for encoding the transaction family, but it is a good idea to take the following guidelines into account:

- **Cross-platform, cross-languages**: For Sawtooth, different smart contracts and transaction families can be implemented on different hosts and with different languages. The encoding scheme should support different platforms and different languages.
- **Fast and efficient processing**: Serialization and deserialization are common operations, so they often have an impact on the overall network performance. Fast and efficient encoding improves the network and make it run more healthily.

Building a transaction processor

Sawtooth simplifies the development of applications by separating the core system from the application domain. Application developers only need to focus on implementing their business logic for the enterprise using the transaction processor, with the language of their choice, without needing to know the underlying details of the Sawtooth core system.

Getting ready

In this recipe, we will go through a step-by-step guide to implement a transaction processor, a smart contract, in our example transaction family using the Sawtooth Python SDK.

Python Sawtooth SDK: The Python SDK is installed automatically when you install Hyperledger Sawtooth on AWS. You can import the SDK in Python to verify Python Sawtooth SDK is installed on the computer as follows:

```
ubuntu@ip-172-31-90-67:~/examples/sawtooth_mkt/processor$ python3
Python 3.5.2 (default, Nov 23 2017, 16:37:01)
[GCC 5.4.0 20160609] on linux
Type "help", "copyright", "credits" or "license" for more information.
>>> import sawtooth_sdk
>>> help(sawtooth_sdk)
```

The SDK is installed at `/usr/lib/python3/dist-packages/sawtooth_sdk`.

How to do it...

Let's go through a step-by-step guide to implement a transaction processor. We will highlight the important code segments to explain the logic for each step and the full example code implementation can be downloaded from the GitHub repository.

Registering the transaction handler to the transaction processor

The main module to start the transaction processor and register the transaction handler for the example application is at `sawtooth_mkt/processor/main.py`. The steps to do this are as follows:

1. Instantiate the general transaction processor and set the validator connection URL:

```
processor = TransactionProcessor(url=mkt_config.connect)
```

2. Instantiate the transaction handler and set the namespace prefix for the transaction family:

```
handler = MktTransactionHandler(namespace_prefix=mkt_prefix)
```

3. Register the transaction handler to the transaction processor:

```
processor.add_handler(handler)
```

4. Start the transaction processor to connect to the validator and start the process request for the transaction family:

```
processor.start()
```

Implementing the transaction handler class

The transaction handler class allows us to implement smart contract logic in its `apply` method. The basic steps to implement smart logic are shown in the following diagram:

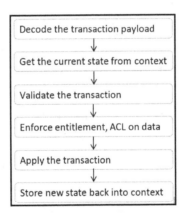

Transaction handler flow

The transaction handler module for our marketplace application can be found in `sawtooth_mkt/processor/handler.py`. The `apply` method skeleton code, as indicated in the preceding diagram, is as follows:

```
def apply(self, transaction, context):
    try:
    # 1. Decode the transaction payload
    house, action, owner, signer = _unpack_transaction(transaction)
    _display("User {} house {} action {} owner {}".format(signer[:6],
```

```
house, action, owner))
    # 2. Get the current state from context
    dbowner, house_list = _get_state_data(context, self._namespace_prefix,
house)
    _display("dbowner {} house list {} ".format(dbowner, house_list))
    # 3. Validate the transaction
    _validate_house_data(action, owner, signer, dbowner)
    # 4. Enforce entitlement, ACL
    # 5. Apply the transaction
    if action == "create":
    _display("User {} created a house {} owner {}.".format(signer[:6],
house, owner))
    elif action == "transfer":
    _display("User {} transfer: {} from {} to {}\n\n".format(signer[:6],
house, dbowner,
owner))
    # 6. Store new state back in context
    _store_state_data(context, house_list, self._namespace_prefix, house,
owner)
    except Exception as e:
        _display("Exception in apply {} \n\n".format(e))
```

We will illustrate each of the preceding steps using the code snippet for the marketplace sample:

1. **Decode the transaction payload**: The transaction header has the signer public key, which identifies the person who submits the transaction. The payload is the encoded transaction data in the client application. For the marketplace sample, we encode the data as a comma-delimited CSV, so the payload will look like (house, action, owner) and the decode function looks as follows:

```
def _unpack_transaction(transaction):
    header = transaction.header
    # The transaction signer is the player
    signer = header.signer_public_key
    try:
        # The payload is csv utf-8 encoded string
        house, action, owner =
transaction.payload.decode().split(",")
    except ValueError:
        raise InvalidTransaction("Invalid payload serialization")
```

2. **Get the current state from the context**: You often need to get the current state for existing assets, which is stored in the global state. You can access this based on the address through the context. The address is the 70-character address, and it includes the 6 characters for the namespace prefix; the remaining 64 characters are for the asset following the scheme that you design for the transaction family. The address for the marketplace example is as follows:

```
def _make_mkt_address(namespace_prefix, house):
    return namespace_prefix + \
        hashlib.sha512(house.encode('utf-8')).hexdigest()[:64]
```

The current state is stored as a multi-house record, each of which is separated by |. Each house and owner is a comma-delimited string:

```
def _get_state_data(context, namespace_prefix, house):
    # Get data from address
    state_entries = \
        context.get_state([_make_mkt_address(namespace_prefix,
house)])
    # context.get_state() returns a list. If no data has been
stored yet
    # at the given address, it will be empty.
    if state_entries:
        try:
            state_data = state_entries[0].data
            _display("state_data {}
\n".format(state_data.decode()))
            house_list = { dbhouse: (dbowner) for dbhouse, dbowner
in
                [ dbhouseowner.split(',') for dbhouseowner
                in state_data.decode().split('|') ] }
            _display("house list in db {} \n".format(house_list))
            dbowner = house_list[house]
            _display("db house {} db owner \n".format(house,
dbowner))
        except ValueError:
            raise InternalError("Failed to deserialize game data.")
    else:
        house_list = {}
        dbowner = None
    return dbowner, house_list
```

3. **Validate the transaction**: Like the normal logic, before you update the current state based on the new action, the transaction data should be validated based on your business rules:

```
def _validate_house_data(action, owner, signer, dbowner):
    if action == 'create':
        if dbowner is not None:
            raise InvalidTransaction('Invalid action: house already
exists.')
    elif action == 'transfer':
        if dbowner is None:
            raise InvalidTransaction(
                'Invalid action: transfer requires an existing
house.')
```

4. **Enforce resource entitlement using access control lists (ACLs)**: Since the signer public key is available as the header, you can enforce resource entitlement to the asset using ACLs before applying the transaction, based on who submitted the transaction. Authorization and resource access can be implemented to keep the data safe.

5. **Apply the transaction**: Once both the transaction and the current state are available, you are ready to apply your business rules, based on the commands and instructions in the transaction. The rules and computation can be applied to the current state to generate a new state.

6. **Store the new state back in the context**: We need to commit the new state back into the global state via the context. This is the same as getting the current state. The new state needs to be encoded to update the global state based on the address:

```
def _store_state_data(context, house_list, namespace_prefix, house,
owner):
    house_list[house] = (owner)
    state_data = '|'.join(sorted([
        ','.join([house, owner]) for house, (owner) in
house_list.items() ])).encode()
    addresses = context.set_state(
        {_make_mkt_address(namespace_prefix, house): state_data})
    if len(addresses) < 1:
        raise InternalError("State Error")
```

Building the command-line script

After the transaction handler is implemented, the transaction processor can be started to connect to the validator and serve the request for your transaction family. We can take advantage of Python Setuptools to create a command line, which makes it easy to run your transaction processor.

Setuptools allows modules to register python functions as console script entry points. When the package has been installed, Setuptools will generate a command-line script that imports your module and calls the registered function. To generate the command line for your transaction processor, enter the following code in `setup.py`:

```
entry_points={
        'console_scripts': [
            'mkt-tp-python = sawtooth_mkt.processor.main:main',
        ]
})
```

After your package is installed, the transaction processor can be started simply by using the command line:

```
ubuntu@ip-172-31-90-67:~$ mkt-tp-python --help
usage: mkt-tp-python [-h] [-C CONNECT] [-v] [-V]
optional arguments:
-h, --help show this help message and exit
-C CONNECT, --connect CONNECT
Endpoint for the validator connection
-v, --verbose Increase output sent to stderr
-V, --version print version information
```

Setting up the transaction processor as a service

`systemd` is an `init` system that provides many features for starting, stopping, and managing processes on the Linux platform. To run a process as a service, a unit file is defined for the process; this is the configuration file that describes how to run the process as a service.

The exec start command is the command line generated in the previous section: `mkt-tp-python` (`sawtooth_mkt/packaging/systemd/sawtooth-mkt-tp-python.service`):

```
[Unit]
Description=Sawtooth MKT TP Python
```

```
After=network.target
[Service]
User=sawtooth
Group=sawtooth
EnvironmentFile=-/etc/default/sawtooth-mkt-tp-python
ExecStart=/usr/bin/mkt-tp-python $SAWTOOTH_MKT_TP_PYTHON_ARGS
Restart=on-failure
[Install]
WantedBy=multi-user.target
```

The `EnvironmentFile` specified in the preceding unit file is used to define environment variables for the service. The environment file for the example marketplace service is at `sawtooth_mkt/packaging/systemd/sawtooth-mkt-tp-python`. Its content is as follows:

```
SAWTOOTH_MKT_TP_PYTHON_ARGS=-v -C tcp://localhost:4004
```

To install both files in the `etc` directory during the installation of the Python package, the following code needs to be added in `setup.py`:

```
if os.path.exists("/etc/default"):
    data_files.append(
        ('/etc/default', ['sawtooth_mkt/packaging/systemd/sawtooth-mkt-tp-
python']))
if os.path.exists("/lib/systemd/system"):
    data_files.append(('/lib/systemd/system',
                       ['sawtooth_mkt/packaging/systemd/sawtooth-mkt-tp-
python.service']))
```

Building a Python egg and installing your python package

Your transaction processor package is now ready to be distributed. It could either be built as a python egg file or you could directly install it from the source on the host:

1. To build a Python egg, enter the following command:

   ```
   sudo python3 setup.py bdist_egg
   ```

2. To install it from source, enter the following command:

   ```
   sudo python3 setup.py install
   ```

3. Your transaction family deployment is done. Your Python package for your transaction family should be installed in the following location if you are installing it from the source on the local host, or in the python default distribute package folder if you are installing it from the built egg files:

```
ubuntu@ip-172-31-90-67:~/examples$ ls -li
/usr/local/lib/python3.5/dist-packages/sawtooth_mkt-1.0.4-py3.5.egg
2157 -rw-r--r-- 1 root staff 31390 Sep 16 17:07
/usr/local/lib/python3.5/dist-packages/sawtooth_mkt-1.0.4-py3.5.egg
```

4. The command line for your transaction processor is as follows:

```
ubuntu@ip-172-31-90-67:~/examples$ which mkt-tp-python
/usr/local/bin/mkt-tp-python
```

5. The system service for your transaction processor is as follows:

```
systemctl list-units|grep -i sawtooth-mkt|less
sawtooth-mkt-tp-python.service loaded active running Sawtooth MKT
TP Python
```

Starting the transaction processor service

You are now ready to start your transaction processor and process clients request for your business:

1. To enable and start the transaction processor service, enter the following:

```
sudo systemctl enable sawtooth-mkt-tp-python.service
sudo systemctl start sawtooth-mkt-tp-python.service
```

2. Check the service status:

```
sudo systemctl status sawtooth-mkt-tp-python.service
```

3. Check the log of your transaction processor in /var/log/sawtooth:

```
[04:36:15.955 [MainThread] core INFO] register attempt: OK
[05:42:59.182 [MainThread] core DEBUG] received message of type:
PING_REQUEST
[06:34:54.718 [MainThread] core DEBUG] received message of type:
TP_PROCESS_REQUEST
```

How it works...

The transaction processor includes two components: a general implemented transaction processor class and one or multiple transaction handler classes. The general-purpose transaction processor connects to the validator, receives the transaction processing request, and dispatches the request to the transaction handler class to be processed.

The general transaction processor is created and started during the start of the transaction processor, the main routine.

The transaction handler class is application-dependent and contains the business logic for a particular family of transactions. The transaction handler class is the real implementation of smart contracts for your applications.

The following diagram shows the relationships between each component:

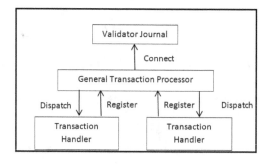

Transaction Processor and Handler

The transaction handler is the smart contract in the Sawtooth blockchain. The main focus of our application development is on implementing the business logic for your enterprise. The transaction handler class interacts with the general transaction processor using two methods:

- **The metadata methods**: The metadata methods are used to register the transaction handler to the transaction processor with the validator. This designates which transaction family and which types of transaction can be handled by the handler. Basically, the `family_name`, `family_versions`, and `namespaces` metadata properties are used by the transaction processor to dispatch transaction requests to the correct transaction handler.

The metadata methods for the marketplace example are as follows:

```
@property
def family_name(self):
    return 'mkt'
@property
 def family_versions(self):
        return ['1.0']
@property
def namespaces(self):
        return [self._namespace_prefix]
```

- **The apply method**: The apply method is the entry point for all the business logic for the transaction family. Its signature is as follows:

```
def apply(self, transaction, context):
```

The `apply` method has two arguments: the transaction and the context. It is very important to understand these two arguments in order to write smart contracts. The argument transaction is the object that is created from the message on the wire based on the `protobuf` definition. It contains a header and a payload, and its `protobuf` definition is as follows:

```
message Transaction {
     // The serialized version of the TransactionHeader
    .bytes header = 1;
    // The signature derived from signing the header
    string header_signature = 2;
    // The payload is the encoded family specific information
    bytes payload = 3;
}
```

The header in the preceding transaction contains the family name, the version, and the public key of the client that signs this transaction, such as `signer_public_key`. Its `protobuf` definition is as follows:

```
message TransactionHeader {
    // Public key for the client who added this transaction to a
batch
    string batcher_public_key = 1;
    // A list of transaction signatures that describe the
transactions that
    // must be processed before this transaction can be valid
    repeated string dependencies = 2;
    // The family name correlates to the transaction processor's
family name
```

```
    // that this transaction can be processed on, for example
'intkey'
    string family_name = 3;
    // The family version correlates to the transaction processor's
family
    // version that this transaction can be processed on, for example
"1.0"
    string family_version = 4;
    // A list of addresses that are given to the context manager and
control
    // what addresses the transaction processor is allowed to read
from.
    repeated string inputs = 5;
    // A random string that provides uniqueness for transactions with
    // otherwise identical fields.
    string nonce = 6;
    // A list of addresses that are given to the context manager and
control
    // what addresses the transaction processor is allowed to write
to.
    repeated string outputs = 7;
    //The sha512 hash of the encoded payload
     string payload_sha512 = 9;
    // Public key for the client that signed the TransactionHeader
    string signer_public_key = 10;
}
```

The payload in the preceding transaction is in the form of bytes and the payload is opaque to the core system, which means that the Sawtooth core will not process the transaction payload; the payload is specific and is handled only by the transaction family. How to encode and decode the payload depends on the approach that you choose for your smart contract. The second argument, context, is an instance of the `Context` class from the Python SDK. The context allows the API to access the current state in the global state on a validator. All validator interactions by the transaction handler should be made through the `Context`.

The APIs in the `Context` are `get_state`, `set_state`, and `delete_state`. Based on the address in the global state, they are defined as follows:

```
class Context:
    def get_state(self, addresses, timeout=None):
    def set_state(self, entries, timeout=None):
    def delete_state(self, addresses, timeout=None):
```

Granting permissions on the Sawtooth network

In this recipe, we will cover how to configure on-chain and off-chain permissions in the Hyperledger Sawtooth network.

How to do it...

To configure off-chain permissions, follow these steps:

1. In the validator configuration file present in /etc/sawtooth/validator.toml, update it with the following lines to set the transactor permission for the marketplace example:

   ```
   [permissions]
   transactor = "policy.toml"
   "transactor.transaction_signer" = "policy.toml"
   ```

2. In the policy file present in /etc/sawtooth/policy/policy.toml, update the following lines:

   ```
   PERMIT_KEY
   021c9a9d3155d15e5c834b29e995d4f3fb7da54e6aa0b1f43ce753bc77cce36138
   DENY_KEY
   02b56f55681409e412fb57b91ba02e16760419d202db40690a6d841e879ec11ee7
   DENY_KEY *
   ```

3. When the client submits a transaction with a key that is not permitted, it will be rejected in the validator log file:

   ```
   [16:26:04.004 [Thread-21] permission_verifier DEBUG] Batch Signer:
   02b56f55681409e412fb57b91ba02e16760419d202db40690a6d841e879ec11ee7
   is not permitted by local configuration.
   ```

4. To configure on-chain roles, the identity transaction family should be installed and the signer of the identity transactions need to have their public key set in the sawtooth.identity.allowed_keys setting:

   ```
   sawset proposal create sawtooth.identity.allowed_keys=
   02f5d0095f9f01e503ad96172bde293b18739860ab988f8b164bc77d3c3b84be00
   ```

5. To create a policy entry, enter the following:

```
sawtooth identity policy create policypermit "PERMIT_KEY
021c9a9d3155d15e5c834b29e995d4f3fb7da54e6aa0b1f43ce753bc77cce36138"
```

6. To specify a policy to the role transactor, enter the following:

```
sawtooth identity role create transactor policypermit
```

How it works...

Hyperledger Sawtooth offers simple and flexible role-policy based permission control to allow the organization to configure different blockchain networks. The policy is a list of entries to permit or deny a party for a particular role and is defined by the entity's public key. The roles are predefined by Sawtooth and are used to define access permissions in the policy file.

There are two categories of role permission provided by Sawtooth:

- **Transactor role permissioning**: A list of policies to control which signers can submit transaction batches. If a signer is not in the permitted policies, the request from the client will be rejected. Sawtooth supports both off-chain and on-chain transactor-role permissioning.
- **Validator role permissioning**: A list of policies to control which peer nodes can join the validator network and participate in the consensus. Sawtooth supports on-chain validator-role permissioning.

The off-chain permissioning is loaded from a local validator configuration file when the validator starts up. While the validator is running, the permission is not updated.

The on-chain transactor and validator permissioning in Sawtooth is supported through the Identity transaction family and it allows us to perform updates on the permissions in real-time on validator nodes across the network. All validator nodes can update and agree on the permission changes at the same time when the validator is running.

The transactor roles are as follows:

- `default`: The default role permits all signers to submit transactions if the entry isn't specified in the policy file
- `transactor`: This role allows clients to sign transactions and batches
- `transactor.transaction_signer.{tp_name}`: This role allows clients to submit transactions for a transaction family

The validator roles are as follows:

- `network`: This controls which nodes can join the validator network
- `network.consensus`: This controls which nodes can participate in the consensus

There's more...

The following table illustrates how to form different networks using transactor and validator role permissions with Sawtooth:

	Transactor permission	Validator permission
Public network	Permit all	Permit all
Consortium network	Permit all	Permit restricted keys
Private network	Permit restricted keys	Permit restricted keys

Developing client applications with the Sawtooth REST API and SDK

Hyperledger Sawtooth provides a pragmatic REST API for clients to interact with a validator using common HTTP standards. There are a many ways to make a REST API request, but the process to build a transaction, batch, encode a payload, and submit them to validator nodes is not easy. Hyperledger Sawtooth provides several SDKs for different languages, such as Python, Go, Java, and JavaScript, to greatly simplify the process of developing client applications to interact with the Sawtooth network.

In this recipe, we will build a client application for our example with the Sawtooth Python SDK and follow the Sawtooth XO transaction family as a template. The full source code for the example is available at GitHub. The basic flow to submit a transaction is shown in the following diagram:

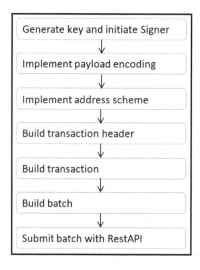

Transaction submission flow

How to do it...

In this section, we will go through each step and present some code snippets to illustrate a sample implementation and logic.

Step 1 – Generating a private/public key-pair and creating a signer instance

1. Generate the private/public key-pair for the client to establish the approach to sign the transaction. To generate a private/public key, run the following command:

```
sawtooth keygen {name}
```

2. This Sawtooth CLI command will generate a private and public key for the client to sign transaction requests. By default, the file is in the user's home directory, `~/.sawtooth/keys/`. To access the generated private key file, you can add the following code in the Marketplace example client (`/sawtooth_mkt/mkt_client.py`):

```
def _get_keyfile(args):
    username = getpass.getuser() if args.username is None else
args.username
    home = os.path.expanduser("~")
    key_dir = os.path.join(home, ".sawtooth", "keys")
    return '{}/{}.priv'.format(key_dir, username)
```

In the client application, after the private key is loaded as shown in the preceding step, the following code snippet is added to create a signer instance from the private key using the Sawtooth signing module in the Python SDK. The signer instance is used to sign the transaction and batch later in the code.

3. To initiate the Signer object used to sign the transaction, enter the following code in the Marketplace sample client (`/sawtooth_mkt/mkt_client.py`):

```
private_key = Secp256k1PrivateKey.from_hex(private_key_str)
self._signer = CryptoFactory(create_context('secp256k1')) \
    .new_signer(private_key)
```

Step 2 – Implementing transaction-payload encoding

For our example, the encoding is just a comma-delimited CSV file and the code snippet can be found at `/sawtooth_mkt/mkt_client.py`:

```
payload = ",".join([house, action, owner]).encode()
```

Step 3 – Implementing the namespace prefix and address scheme

In our case, the namespace prefix is the same as the transaction processor. We encoded the `mkt` namespace and used the first 6 hex characters of its hashing as the prefix; the data address is the SHA-512 hashing of the house APN.

The code file can be found at /sawtooth_mkt/mkt_client.py:

```
def _get_prefix(self):
        return _sha512('mkt'.encode('utf-8'))[0:6]
def _get_address(self, house):
        mkt_prefix = self._get_prefix()
        house_address = _sha512(house.encode('utf-8'))[0:64]
        return mkt_prefix + house_address
```

Step 4 – Building a transaction header and a transaction

To send a transaction in a client application, we first need to build the transaction header in our example client:

```
(/sawtooth_mkt/mkt_client.py):
header = TransactionHeader(
    signer_public_key=self._signer.get_public_key().as_hex(),
    family_name="mkt",
    family_version="1.0",
    inputs=[address],
    outputs=[address],
    dependencies=[],
    payload_sha512=_sha512(payload),
    batcher_public_key=self._signer.get_public_key().as_hex(),
    nonce=time.time().hex().encode()
).SerializeToString()
```

Once the `TransactionHeader` is constructed, a transaction can be created with the header. The header signature is signed with the Signer and the encoded payload created previously. To create a transaction in the Marketplace client, enter the following:

```
(/sawtooth_mkt/mkt_client.py):
signature = self._signer.sign(header)
transaction = Transaction(
    header=header,
    payload=payload,
    header_signature=signature
)
```

Step 5 – Building a batch

The batch header is mainly composed of the public key of the signer and the list of transaction signatures, in the same order that they are listed in the batch. To create a batch header in the marketplace sample client, enter the following:

```
(/sawtooth_mkt/mkt_client.py):
transaction_signatures = [t.header_signature for t in transactions]
header = BatchHeader(
    signer_public_key=self._signer.get_public_key().as_hex(),
    transaction_ids=transaction_signatures
).SerializeToString()
```

Creating a batch is similar to creating a transaction. The batch is constructed with the header, the signature, and the transactions wrapped in the batch. The signer instance in *step 1* could be used to sign the batch if the transaction and batch use the same public key. If they are different, a different signer instance could be created from the batch identity private key, as for the transaction. To create a batch in the marketplace client, enter the following:

```
(/sawtooth_mkt/mkt_client.py):
signature = self._signer.sign(header)
batch = Batch(
    header=header,
    transactions=transactions,
    header_signature=signature)
```

Step 6 – Submitting the batch with REST API

The URL for the REST API service is a configuration file: /etc/sawtooth/rest_api.toml. Check whether the REST API service is running:

```
ubuntu@ip-172-31-90-67:~/examples/sawtooth_mkt$ sudo systemctl status
sawtooth-rest-api.service
sawtooth-rest-api.service - Sawtooth REST API
Loaded: loaded (/lib/systemd/system/sawtooth-rest-api.service; enabled;
vendor preset: enabled)
Active: active (running) since Sun 2018-09-30 15:03:34 UTC; 3h 42min ago
Main PID: 1170 (sawtooth-rest-a)
Tasks: 3
Memory: 25.5M
CPU: 385ms
```

```
CGroup: /system.slice/sawtooth-rest-api.service
  └─1170 /usr/bin/python3 /usr/bin/sawtooth-rest-api --connect
tcp://localhost:4004
Sep 30 15:03:34 ip-172-31-90-67 systemd[1]: Started Sawtooth REST API.
```

To submit a batch in the marketplace client, enter the following:

```
(/sawtooth_mkt/mkt_client.py):
response = self._send_request(
    "batches", batch_list.SerializeToString(),
    'application/octet-stream',
    auth_user=auth_user,
    auth_password=auth_password)
while wait_time < wait:
    status = self._get_status(
        batch_id,
        wait - int(wait_time),
        auth_user=auth_user,
        auth_password=auth_password)
    wait_time = time.time() - start_time
    if status != 'PENDING':
        return response
```

Step 7 – Building the client application

Once one transaction and one basic communication module are implemented for your system, more use cases and business logic can be implemented in the same way for your system. The client application to be implemented depends on the individual business requirements; it may be a desktop or a web application that is using the library:

1. In our case, the client application simply provides a list of command-line tools to interact with the Sawtooth network. The command line tool in our example is implemented at /sawtooth_mkt/mkt_cli.py. To generate a command line script called mkt for the marketplace example during installation, enter the following in setup.py:

    ```
    entry_points={
        'console_scripts': [
            'mkt = sawtooth_mkt.mkt_cli:main_wrapper',
    ```

2. To build a Python egg for the sample client, enter the following:

```
sudo python3 setup.py bdist_egg
```

3. To install the client application from the source, enter the following:

```
sudo python3 setup.py install
```

Step 8 – Testing the sample client

In this step, we will demonstrate how to use the sample client command line to interact with the marketplace sample transaction processor and store data in the Sawtooth blockchain and its global state:

1. For the marketplace sample client, you can find more information about how to run the `mkt` command as follows:

```
ubuntu@ip-172-31-90-67:~/examples$ mkt --help
usage: mkt [-h] [-v] [-V] {create,list,transfer} ...

Provides subcommands to Marketplace sample
optional arguments:
    -h, --help show this help message and exit
    -v, --verbose enable more verbose output
    -V, --version display version information

subcommands:
    {create,list,transfer}
    create      Creates a new house
    list        Displays information for all house
    transfer    transfer house to new owner
```

2. To create a record for a new house with an owner, enter the following:

```
ubuntu@ip-172-31-90-67:~/examples$ mkt create APN-0001-001-001
Kevin
Response: {
"link":
"http://127.0.0.1:8008/batch_statuses?id=ab85aa846f8f289f793e09b535
47b0340315e5217d8d3b00e55af619960257905e5626d56037cb1f0fb1865454dc3
323ae34e3a411ba0fd8948adb1121562f12"
}
```

3. Enter the following, to check the new block to store the transaction in the Sawtooth network for the new record:

```
ubuntu@ip-172-31-90-67:~/examples$ sawtooth block list
NUM  BLOCK_ID BATS  TXNS  SIGNER 1
b5c04df99187acbd898150d2f6bb2a3bd8f2ad6e38b66d9986fe943f6fc8d6fe7f3
0624fafc231655fa434816adfa157d2cc93113d74047aa50efea8ca8673a7  1
1     02f5d0...
ubuntu@ip-172-31-90-67:~/examples$ sawtooth block show
b5c04df99187acbd898150d2f6bb2a3bd8f2ad6e38b66d9986fe943f6fc8d6fe7f3
0624fafc231655fa434816adfa157d2cc93113d74047aa50efea8ca8673a7
batches:
- header:
    signer_public_key:
021c9a9d3155d15e5c834b29e995d4f3fb7da54e6aa0b1f43ce753bc77cce36138
      transaction_ids:
      -
6e18f353ce9222c9e5f5a663907721104897664c94da71864e2f97c63e6455b7552
f506895a8d872c2393c2851c97b45f844efb028cc4b4133ae43f2685dd086
    header_signature:
ab85aa846f8f289f793e09b53547b0340315e5217d8d3b00e55af619960257905e5
626d56037cb1f0fb1865454dc3323ae34e3a411ba0fd8948adb1121562f12
    trace: false
    transactions:
    - header:
        batcher_public_key:
021c9a9d3155d15e5c834b29e995d4f3fb7da54e6aa0b1f43ce753bc77cce36138
        dependencies: []
        family_name: mkt
        family_version: '1.0'
        inputs:    -
50351cbdb56cc9ba06f9e7e2240d37301a53719f3e9509a3b490b191ac8fbe7274a
09f
        nonce: 0x1.6ec496a2e4eeap+30
        outputs:
        -
50351cbdb56cc9ba06f9e7e2240d37301a53719f3e9509a3b490b191ac8fbe7274a
09f
        payload_sha512:
ef86aec70b9068b0326540823556301b6b703a4bd266a75155f0c01b195e8f3f1e8
3bf4ee2448e04496725e7887eb8c20b4dbb4335ac2ff5b1dc51e246f58b2c
        signer_public_key:
021c9a9d3155d15e5c834b29e995d4f3fb7da54e6aa0b1f43ce753bc77cce36138
      header_signature:
6e18f353ce9222c9e5f5a663907721104897664c94da71864e2f97c63e6455b7552
f506895a8d872c2393c2851c97b45f844efb028cc4b4133ae43f2685dd086
      payload: QVBOLTAwMDEtMDAxLTAwMSxjcmVhdGUsS2V2aW4=
header:
```

```
    batch_ids:
    -
ab85aa846f8f289f793e09b53547b0340315e5217d8d3b00e55af619960257905e5
626d56037cb1f0fb1865454dc3323ae34e3a411ba0fd8948adb1121562f12
    block_num: '1'
    consensus: RGV2bW9kZQ==
    previous_block_id:
dc9f9c5d4eb0b4be8cb836f49bb64a7e8be356c2e8510bf0579eb15fcf06834768d
0e998286c9c8188569157a76c943ee3da1398ddb0c30c950eba27b9044b4d
    signer_public_key:
02f5d0095f9f01e503ad96172bde293b18739860ab988f8b164bc77d3c3b84be00
    state_root_hash:
0412b37b75417f753ca9088e4e531a386cbdacbb1f4ba02384ce8e425c555779
header_signature:
b5c04df99187acbd898150d2f6bb2a3bd8f2ad6e38b66d9986fe943f6fc8d6fe7f3
0624fafc231655fa434816adfa157d2cc93113d74047aa50efea8ca8673a7
```

4. To check that the new house record is saved in the global state on the blockchain network, use the following command:

```
ubuntu@ip-172-31-90-67:~/examples$ sawtooth state list
ADDRESS SIZE DATA
000000a87cb5eafdcca6a8cde0fb0dec1400c5ab274474a6aa82c12840f169a0421
6b7 110
b'\n1\n&sawtooth.settings.vote.authorized_keys\x12B021c9a9d3155d15.
..
50351cbdb56cc9ba06f9e7e2240d37301a53719f3e9509a3b490b191ac8fbe7274a
09f 22 b'APN-0001-001-001,Kevin' ...
HEAD BLOCK:
"b5c04df99187acbd898150d2f6bb2a3bd8f2ad6e38b66d9986fe943f6fc8d6fe7f
30624fafc231655fa434816adfa157d2cc93113d74047aa50efea8ca8673a7"
ubuntu@ip-172-31-90-67:~$ sawtooth state show
50351cbdb56cc9ba06f9e7e2240d37301a53719f3e9509a3b490b191ac8fbe7274a
09f
DATA: "b'APN-0001-001-001,Kevin'"
HEAD:
"b5c04df99187acbd898150d2f6bb2a3bd8f2ad6e38b66d9986fe943f6fc8d6fe7f
30624fafc231655fa434816adfa157d2cc93113d74047aa50efea8ca8673a7"
```

5. To list house records with the sample `mkt` command line, enter the following:

```
ubuntu@ip-172-31-90-67:~/examples$ mkt list
HOUSE              OWNER
APN-0001-001-001 Kevin
```

6. To transfer the house to a different owner and check the state at the same address in the global Merkle tree, enter the following:

```
ubuntu@ip-172-31-90-67:~$ mkt transfer APN-0001-001-001 Kathleen
Response: {
"link":
"http://127.0.0.1:8008/batch_statuses?id=47fc39671dee2177222571e97f
637940268d683ea9cedd7fbc9300dfc67d87fb227ff412deb982f83e43575e6894d
2212ae5f1bddf2d8d79bbde9c174edae2eb"
}
ubuntu@ip-172-31-90-67:~$ sawtooth state show
50351cbdb56cc9ba06f9e7e2240d37301a53719f3e9509a3b490b191ac8fbe7274a
09f
DATA: "b'APN-0001-001-001,Kathleen'"
HEAD:
"1800ecc8b36f820aabbbbc076e5cdac02e8541213e518d92ba0d7ad6e74e39fb46
ab2d97312c4e54f2c225c4451e745fd3c4931d5925a3480103d8d6dff2b629"
```

How it works...

To generate the private/public key-pair for a client application, Sawtooth utilizes cryptographic safeguards such as public-key cryptography, secure hashing, and message signing to confirm the client's identity and verify the validity of the data. The private/public key-pair is the foundation of these crypto algorithms. The private key is the client's identity used to communicate with the network. All transaction requests from the client application need to be signed with the client's private key. Also, Sawtooth enforces transactor permissions based on the public key of the client. Authorization and access control lists for resources and data on the network are based on the public key of the client, so it is very important to keep the private key safe. It is impossible to recover your identity if the private key is lost or stolen.

Sawtooth uses the `secp256k1` ECDSA standard for message signing. The `secp256k1` standard is also used in Bitcoin. The Sawtooth signing module in the python SDK provides several classes to make it easy to sign the transaction with the client's private key.

The Signer is defined in the Python file: `signing/sawtooth_signing/__init__.py`. You could create a context first, based on the algorithm, using the `create_context` method. Then, you could use `CryptoFactory` to create a new signer instance and use it to sign the transaction. The `help` doc string on the `create_context` function in the `sawtooth_signing` module is as follows:

```
create_context(algorithm_name)
   Returns an algorithm instance by name.
Help on class CryptoFactory in module sawtooth_signing:
   class CryptoFactory(builtins.object)
     Factory for generating Signers.
     new_signer(self, private_key)
        Create a new signer for the given private key.

Help on class Signer in module sawtooth_signing:
   class Signer(builtins.object)
     A convenient wrapper of Context and PrivateKey
     sign(self, message)
        Signs the given message
```

The payloads are the data and the information that the client sends to the validator in the message. They are just a sequence of bytes to the core system and the communication takes place between the client SDK and the validator nodes. The encoding defines how to serialize and deserialize data into bytes to be transferred on the network. In a client application, the logic for encoding and decoding the transaction payload must be consistent with the encoding implemented in the associated transaction processor by the application (refer to the *Building a transaction processor* recipe for more information).

To implement the namespace and address schema, the client application also needs to be consistent with the transaction processor to follow the same namespace and address design and implementation. The address is specified in the transaction header in the client application (refer to the *Building transaction processor* recipe for the address).

The addresses specified in the transaction in the client application have both input and output addresses. The input addresses are read from the state and the output addresses are written to the state. Both addresses are used by the validator transaction scheduler to efficiently schedule transactions in parallel.

To submit transactions, in order to update the state of the business data, the client application builds a transaction and submits it to the validator. The validator routes the request to the associated transaction processor to apply the request to change the state.

The transaction in the client application follows the same protobuf definition discussed in the *Building a transaction processor* recipe. It is composed of the payload, the header, and the signature. The protobuf definition for the transaction is as follows:

```
message Transaction {
    // The serialized version of the TransactionHeader
    bytes header = 1;
    // The signature derived from signing the header
    string header_signature = 2;
    // The payload is the encoded family specific information
    bytes payload = 3;
}
```

A TransactionHeader in the preceding protobuf contains information for routing a transaction to the correct transaction processor, the input and output state addresses in the transaction, and the public key of the client to sign the transaction. The input and output state addresses in the transaction header are the addresses to read from or write to for the transaction.

A transaction is the protobuf definition. It is simply an object that composes the transaction header and signs the header with the Signer and the encoded payload.

Multiple transactions are always submitted in batches. A batch is the atomic action unit of a state operation. If a batch is processed successfully, all transactions will be committed in the order contained within the batch. If a batch fails, all transactions in the batch will be rolled back and none of the transactions will be applied.

The batch and transaction in the batch could be signed with different public keys. The batcher_public_key field in the transaction header specifies the batch signer public key.

The protobuf definition for the batch and the batch header are as follows:

```
message Batch {
    // The serialized version of the BatchHeader
    bytes header = 1;
    // The signature derived from signing the header
    string header_signature = 2;
    // A list of the transactions that match the list of
    // transaction_ids listed in the batch header
    repeated Transaction transactions = 3;
    // A debugging flag which indicates this batch should be traced through
the
    // system, resulting in a higher level of debugging output.
```

```
      bool trace = 4;
}
message BatchHeader {
    // Public key for the client that signed the BatchHeader
    string signer_public_key = 1;
    // List of transaction.header_signatures that match the order of
    // transactions required for the batch
    repeated string transaction_ids = 2;
}
```

To submit a batch with REST API, the REST API service is a standalone process that runs along with a validator to support a client in communicating with the Sawtooth network using HTTP standards. To submit a batch, simply send a POST request to the /batches endpoint, with a Content-Type header of application/octet-stream, and the body as a serialized batch.

6
Operating an Ethereum Smart Contract with Hyperledger Burrow

Hyperledger Burrow is an enterprise blockchain network that provides a permissioned smart contract interpreter to execute business logic following the **Ethereum Virtual Machine (EVM)** specifications.

Hyperledger Seth is the Sawtooth-Ethereum integration project. It integrates the Hyperledger Burrow implementation of the EVM with Hyperledger Sawtooth to provide support for running Ethereum smart contracts on the Hyperledger Sawtooth platform.

In this chapter, we will cover several recipes regarding how to operate Ethereum smart contracts with Hyperledger Burrow and Seth:

- Installing Hyperledger Burrow on AWS
- Writing smart contracts with Solidity
- Deploying and calling Ethereum smart contracts on Burrow
- Installing Hyperledger Seth with Docker on AWS
- Creating externally owned accounts and writing Solidity contracts on Seth
- Deploying and calling Ethereum contracts with the Seth CLI and RPC
- Permissioning Ethereum EOA and contract accounts on Seth

Introduction

Ethereum is one of the most important public blockchain networks in terms of its impact and market cap. It is sometimes known as a **world computer**, as it is used to run **decentralized applications (DApps)** for everyone and has an open software platform powered by the global infrastructure. It allows different organizations and individuals to build and deploy DApps to execute smart contracts. Ethereum is the next generation of blockchain. It introduced the possibility for blockchain technology to develop from cryptocurrency cash systems to an open, flexible, and distributed global computing platform for a wide variety of applications.

The smart contract running on Ethereum is the application, which can be written in different programming languages to perform all sorts of business logic or fulfill predefined contracts when they are triggered. The EVM is the runtime environment to execute this smart contract. EVM is the heart of Ethereum and is **Turing complete**. Developers can build computer applications that run on the EVM to solve real-world problems or perform business activities with different programming languages. The EVM is a stack machine, on which all computations are performed on an area called the **stack**. It has a maximum size of 1,024 elements and contains words of 256 bits. The EVM executes the opcode compiled from the smart contract on the stack.

Solidity is the high-level and most adopted programming language to write smart contracts. It is contract-oriented and type-safe. It was influenced by C++, Python, and JavaScript, and is designed to target the EVM. Hyperledger Burrow was originally contributed by Monax and co-sponsored by Intel. It is a permissioned EVM that's developed with Golang.

Ethereum smart contracts and the Solidity language are predominate in implementing DApps in the public blockchain network. Burrow offers the permissioned EVM to allow thousands of DApps on the Ethereum network to operate in a permissioned EVM. Burrow is now integrated with Hyperledger Sawtooth and Hyperledger Fabric, and this provides the capability to migrate or run thousands of DApps on the Ethereum network in various blockchain networks in the Hyperledger family.

The Burrow network is composed of Validator peer nodes that run with the Byzantine fault-tolerant Tendermint protocol to reach a consensus. The Tendermint protocol provides high transaction throughput among permissioned validators and also prevents the blockchain from forking.

An introduction to Seth

Burrow is not only becoming more mature, easier to work with, and capable of building robust and fast Burrow networks—it has also started to integrate with other Hyperledger networks, such as Fabric or Sawtooth, to provide EVMs to run Ethereum contracts on these networks.

Seth is the integration between Burrow, Sawtooth, and Ethereum, which provides the capability to run Ethereum smart contracts on the Hyperledger Sawtooth blockchain. Like Burrow, to run an Ethereum smart contract on Sawtooth, you do not need to pay ether or cryptocurrencies as gas, but you do need permission.

Seth is primarily composed of three components on top of the Sawtooth platform, as shown in the following diagram:

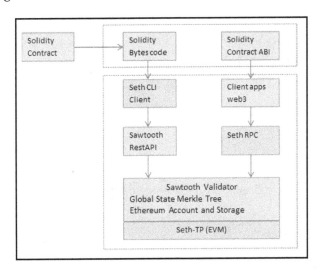

The Seth client is a **command-line interface** tool (**CLI**) that's provided by Seth to interact with the Sawtooth platform, providing Seth-related functionalities such as deploying and calling smart contracts. The Seth CLI communicates with the Sawtooth platform using the normal Sawtooth RestAPI adaptor (more details can be found at `https://sawtooth.` `hyperledger.org/docs/seth/releases/latest/cli_reference.html#seth-cli-` `reference-label`).

Seth-TP is the transaction family that implements the EVM from Burrow within the Sawtooth platform. All business logic and smart contracts are handled and executed in Seth-TP (more details can be found at `https://sawtooth.hyperledger.org/docs/seth/` `releases/latest/cli_reference.html#seth-tp-reference-label`).

The Seth-RPC server is an API gateway to allow existing Ethereum clients to interact with smart contracts on the Sawtooth platform with the Ethereum JSON RPC API (`https://github.com/ethereum/wiki/wiki/JSON-RPC`). More details on API gateways can be found at `https://sawtooth.hyperledger.org/docs/seth/releases/latest/cli_reference.html#seth-rpc-reference-label`.

Installing Hyperledger Burrow on AWS

In this recipe, we will learn how to install Hyperledger Burrow on the AWS Cloud platform.

Getting ready

To install and run the recipes in this chapter, you need an EC2 instance on AWS with the following configuration:

- Operating system: Ubuntu 16.04.5 LTS
- AWS EC2 instance type: `m4.2xlarge` or `t2.mroc`

How to do it...

Execute the following steps to install Hyperledger Burrow:

1. Install Go version 1.10 or higher. The following commands can be used to install Go on an EC2 instance:

   ```
   sudo apt update
   sudo apt install golang-go
   ```

   If you have an old version of Go on AWS, you can install Go with the **Personal Package Archive** (**PPA**), which is provided by the community and not an official source, at `https://launchpad.net/ubuntu/+ppas`:

   ```
   sudo add-apt-repository ppa:gophers/archive
   sudo apt-get update
   sudo apt-get install golang-1.10-go
   ```

2. Add Go into your environment. Create a Go project in the `go` folder in your home directory and make two sub-folders, named `src` and `bin`, using the `mkdir` command under go. Set `GOPATH` to the `go` folder and add Go into the `PATH` environment.

```
export GOROOT=/usr/lib/go-1.10/
export GOPATH=$HOME/go
PATH="$HOME/bin:$HOME/.local/bin:$PATH:$GOROOT/bin:$GOPATH/bin:"
```

   Verify Go install and setup

```
ubuntu@ip-172-31-90-67:~/go/src$ go version
go version go1.10 linux/amd64
```

3. Implement Go `helloworld.go` as follows:

```
package main
import "fmt"
func main() {
fmt.Printf("hello, world\n")
}
```

4. Build and run `helloworld.go`:

```
ubuntu@ip-172-31-90-67:~/go/src/hello$ go run helloworld.go
hello, world
```

5. Get the Burrow source code and build Burrow:

```
ubuntu@ip-172-31-90-67:~/go/src/hello$ go get
github.com/hyperledger/burrow/...
cd github.com/hyperledger/burrow
make install_burrow
```

This will build Burrow and install its execution in the `go/bin` directory. Since the `go/bin` directory is configured in your `PATH`, you can now run the `burrow` command directly.

6. Configure and start Burrow by creating a directory for Burrow under your home directory, such as `~/burrow`. To generate a `burrow.toml` file with one participant and a full account, enter the following command:

```
burrow spec -p1 -f1 | burrow configure -s- > burrow.toml
```

`burrow.toml` is the configuration file for the Burrow validator node. The address and keys for the validator are defined in the file as follows:

```
[[GenesisDoc.Validators]]
Address = "54EF1517D97E7A653D5FA5B05060A82A8856515D"
PublicKey = "{\"CurveType\":\"ed25519\",\"PublicKey
\":\"FF4E4B9D3FB3B4CC0F113661E2E298C7DD7355A1207CA398496550BC162C04
F3\"}"
Amount = 9999999999
Name = "Full_0"
```

7. Once `burrow.toml` is generated, in the same folder, enter the following command to start Burrow:

```
burrow start --validator-index=0 >burrow.log 2>&1 &
```

Enter the following command to view the Burrow log:

```
less burrow.log
```

How it works...

Burrow is implemented with Go. In this recipe, we installed Go on the Ubuntu host and used `go` to download the Burrow source code and its dependencies. Once we built Burrow from source, we generated its configuration file with `burrow spec` and started `Burrow` on the instance.

The most important feature from Burrow is that Burrow is a permissioned EVM. It can execute Ethereum smart contracts when the correct permissions have been granted. Unlike Ethereum, no real ether or cryptocurrency is required to execute smart contracts on Burrow. An arbitrary but finite amount of gas is handed out for every transaction to ensure that the transaction is executed in a finite time. According to the documentation on the Burrow GitHub repository, Burrow's principle is *you don't need money to play when you have permission to play.*

Writing smart contracts with Solidity

Remix (`https://github.com/ethereum/remix`) and Truffle (`https://truffleframework.com`) are popular Ethereum development frameworks. You can use either of these to write smart contracts with Solidity for Burrow. For this recipe, we will use the online version of Remix to write a sample smart contract with Solidity, since this version is simple and easy to use. You can access it here: `https://remix.ethereum.org`.

Getting ready

In this smart contract, we will perform transactions to deposit coins, withdraw coins, and query the account balance. The smart contract looks as follows:

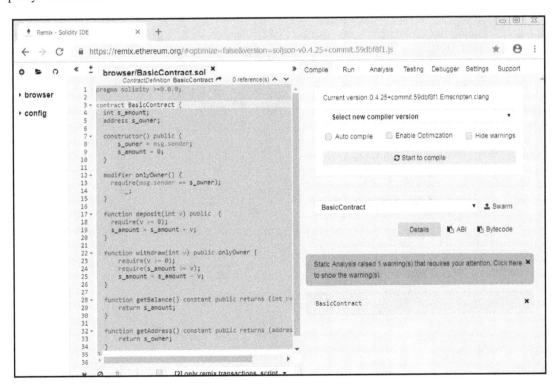

How to do it...

Follow these steps to create your first smart contract using Remix:

1. Create the new smart contract in the Remix browser.
   This BasicContract.sol sample contract will keep the balance of an account, and the contract owner will be able to put deposits into and withdraw from the contract. Its code is as follows:

```solidity
pragma solidity >=0.0.0;
contract BasicContract {
  int s_amount;
  address s_owner;
  constructor() public {
      s_owner = msg.sender;
      s_amount = 0;
  }
  modifier onlyOwner() {
    require(msg.sender == s_owner);
      _;
  }
  function deposit(int v) public  {
    require(v >= 0);
    s_amount = s_amount + v;
  }
  function withdraw(int v) public onlyOwner {
      require(v >= 0);
      require(s_amount >= v);
      s_amount = s_amount - v;
  }
  function getBalance() constant public returns (int retVal) {
      return s_amount;
  }
  function getAddress() constant public returns (address a) {
      return s_owner;
  }
}
```

2. You can use the preceding code to create a new `BasicContract` contract in the Remix browser, as follows. Click on **Compile** to compile the contract to verify that there are no grammar or coding errors, as shown in the following screenshot:

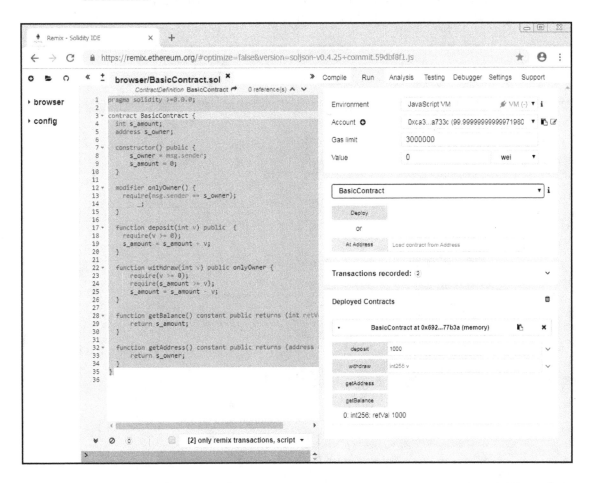

3. Run and test the contract in the Remix browser. After the contract is successfully compiled, you can go to the **Run** tab in the browser.

4. Click **Deploy** to deploy the contract in Remix.

5. Select the **BasicContract** and click on the **deposit**, **withdraw**, and **getBalance** buttons to test the contract in Remix:

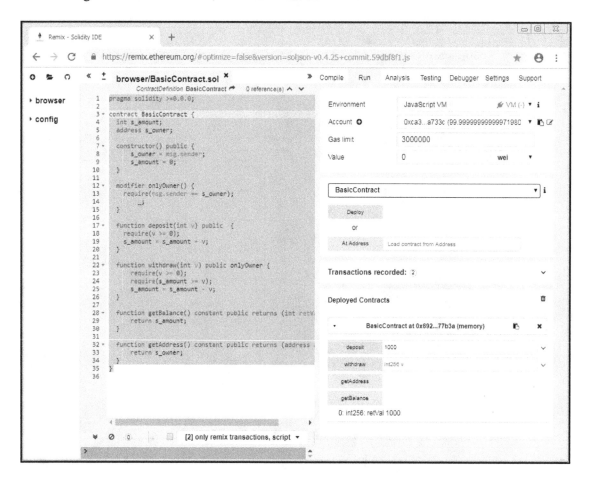

How it works...

We will walk through the structure and features of the Solidity language with our sample smart contract. Solidity is one of the most commonly used programming languages to write smart contracts for Ethereum blockchain, and it can also be adapted to write smart contracts that are executed on the Hyperledger Burrow blockchain network.

Using the pragma version and importing another source file

The Solidity file starts with the pragma version, which annotates the compiler version that the contract is compatible with. It is in the format of 0.x.0. The version could be specified as range, which is a comparator which specifies the versions that satisfy the condition. In the sample contract, it is any compiler after version 0.0.0:

```
pragma solidity >=0.0.0;
```

After the `pragma` version, the Solidity file could also define how to import symbols from other source files. For example, we can import all global symbols from another source file, as follows:

```
import "filename";
```

Similarly, we can import all global symbols from another source file into a new global symbol, whose members are all the global symbols from the file, by using the following statement:

```
import * as symbolname from "filename";
```

Using contracts

Contracts in Solidity are similar to classes in Java, C++, Python, and other object-oriented languages. Solidity is contract-oriented, and contracts can contain declarations of state variables, functions, function modifiers, events, and so on. Click on https://solidity. readthedocs.io/en/v0.4.21/structure-of-a-contract.html#structure-state-variables for more details. A contract is defined as follows:

```
contract BasicContract {
......
}
```

- **State variables** in contracts are values that are permanently stored in contract storage and saved in the blockchain along with the contracts. The type of state variable could be Boolean (`bool`), Number (`int`, `uint`, `fixed`), String, Address, or another type.

The Address type refers to the Ethereum address of a contract or account. The address is 20 bytes, and any contract could explicitly be converted into an address. The address has functions such as balance (which provides the balance of the address in the Ether unit Wei) and transfer (which transfers Ether to the address).

In the sample contract, two state variables are defined. One is the amount, with the int datatype, and the other is the address of the account that is creating the contract:

```
int s_amount;
address s_owner;
```

- **A constructor** is executed when the contract is created. The constructor could be declared with the same name as the contract or the keyword constructor. If there is no constructor, the contract will assume that there is an empty default constructor. The constructor could either be public or internal. In the sample contract, the constructor is defined as follows. It initializes the state variables and assigns the address as the address of the account that created the contract:

```
constructor() public {
    s_owner = msg.sender;
    s_amount = 0;
}
```

- A function can be declared in the contract with the following syntax:

```
function functionname(params) visibility modifier returns (return
values)
```

Functions can have the following visibilities:

- external: External functions are part of the contract interface, which means they can be called from other contracts and via transactions
- public: Public functions are part of the contract interface and can be either called internally or via message calls or transactions
- internal: Internal functions can only be accessed internally from the current contract and derived contracts
- private: Private functions are only visible in the current contract

Functions can also be declared with modifiers such as pure, constant, view, and payable:

- view/constant: Functions will read from the state but will not modify the state
- pure: Functions will neither read from the state nor modify the state
- payable: Functions can receive Ether

Contracts can also define one unnamed function, the fallback function, which is executed if no functions in the contract match the function identifier in the message call.

The following code block contains a function that is defined in the sample contract. The require function is the guard condition or error handler in the contract. If the condition is not satisfied in calling the require function, the EVM will abort the transaction and roll back the state of the contract:

```
function withdraw(int v) public onlyOwner {
        require(v >= 0);
        require(s_amount >= v);
        s_amount = s_amount - v;
}
function getBalance() constant public returns (int retVal) {
        return s_amount;
}
```

- **A function modifier** is a decorator to wrap the marked function, in order to reuse a block of code. The _, in the modifier definition is the placeholder for the marked function.

In our example contract, we define a function modifier to allow only the account that creates the contract to call the withdraw function:

```
modifier onlyOwner() {
    require(msg.sender == s_owner);
        _;
}
```

Solidity also supports **events**, as follows:

- Define an event as follows: event AmountWithdrawedd(int amount);
- Trigger the event as follows: emit AmountWithdrawedd(amount);

Solidity offers a full set of object-oriented features and supports interface, enum, struct, inheritance, and so on. In this section, we went through some basic features that we can use to write a smart contract with Solidity.

Deploying and calling the Ethereum smart contract on Burrow

We will deploy and run the sample contract on Burrow in this recipe.

Getting ready

In order to deploy the sample contract written with Solidity onto Burrow, the Solidity compiler needs to be installed on Linux:

1. Install the Solidity compiler:

```
sudo add-apt-repository ppa:ethereum/ethereum
sudo apt-get update
sudo apt-get install solc
```

2. Verify that the Solidity compiler, solc, is installed with the following command:

```
ubuntu@ip-172-31-90-67:~/go/src/hello$ solc --version
solc, the solidity compiler commandline interface
Version: 0.4.25+commit.59dbf8f1.Linux.g++
```

How to do it...

Execute the following steps to deploy and run smart contract:

1. Define the Burrow deploy configuration file for the Solidity contract. The deploy file for the BasicContract.sol sample contract is the basiccontractdeploy.yaml file. It specifies the job as deploy and the Solidity contract file as follows:

```
jobs:
  - name: BasicContract
    deploy:
      contract: BasicContract.sol
```

2. Deploy the Solidity contract. After both the `BasicContract.sol` contract file and the `basiccontractdeploy.yaml` deploy file are written, the contract can be deployed to the Burrow validator with the `burrow deploy` command:

    ```
    burrow deploy --address=54EF1517D97E7A653D5FA5B05060A82A8856515D -f
    basiccontractdeploy.yaml
    ```

    The output should be as follows:

    ```
    ubuntu@ip-172-31-90-67:~/burrow/example/basic$ burrow deploy --
    address=54EF1517D97E7A653D5FA5B05060A82A8856515D -f
    basiccontractdeploy.yaml
    *****Executing Job***
    Job Name => defaultAddr
    *****Executing Job***
    Job Name => BasicContract
    Deploying Contract name => BasicContract
    addr => 5486CD7F1453396A1C9E4B24CC07AA507C4CD88A
    Saving Binary =>
    /home/ubuntu/burrow/example/basic/bin/BasicContract.bin
    Writing [basiccontractdeploy.output.json] to current directory
    ```

    The deployed contract address is in the preceding output. For our contract, it's `5486CD7F1453396A1C9E4B24CC07AA507C4CD88A`, which will be used when calling this contract.

3. Call the contract. To call the `deposit` function in the sample contract, specify the Burrow deploy configure file, `basiccontractdeposit.yaml`, as follows:

    ```
    jobs:
      - name: deposit
    call:
      destination: 5486CD7F1453396A1C9E4B24CC07AA507C4CD88A
      function: deposit
      data:
        - 1000
    ```

4. Run the Burrow CLI command:

    ```
    burrow deploy --address=54EF1517D97E7A653D5FA5B05060A82A8856515D -f
    basiccontractdeposit.yaml
    ```

5. To call the `withdraw` function in the sample contract, specify the Burrow deploy configure file, `basiccontractwithdraw.yaml`, as follows:

```
jobs:
  - name: withdraw
call:
  destination: 5486CD7F1453396A1C9E4B24CC07AA507C4CD88A
  function: withdraw
data:
  - 200
```

6. Run the Burrow CLI command:

```
burrow deploy --address=54EF1517D97E7A653D5FA5B05060A82A8856515D -f
basiccontractwithdraw.yaml
```

7. To call the `getBalance` function in the sample contract, specify the Burrow deploy configure file, as follows:

```
jobs:
  - name: getBalance
    query-contract:
      destination: 5486CD7F1453396A1C9E4B24CC07AA507C4CD88A
      function: getBalance
  - name: getAddress
    query-contract:
      destination: 5486CD7F1453396A1C9E4B24CC07AA507C4CD88A
      function: getAddress
```

8. Run the Burrow CLI command:

```
burrow deploy --address=54EF1517D97E7A653D5FA5B05060A82A8856515D -f
basiccontractquery.yaml
```

The output for the query should look as follows:

```
ubuntu@ip-172-31-90-67:~/burrow/example/basic$ burrow deploy
--address=54EF1517D97E7A653D5FA5B05060A82A8856515D -f
basiccontractquery.yaml
*****Executing Job***
Job Name => defaultAddr
*****Executing Job***
Job Name => getBalance
Return Value => 800
*****Executing Job***
Job Name => getAddress
Return Value => 54EF1517D97E7A653D5FA5B05060A82A8856515D
Writing [basiccontractquery.output.json] to current directory
```

How it works...

The Burrow blockchain is composed of validator peer nodes. Burrow provides CLI commands to interact with the network. The `burrow deploy` CLI command is used to deploy the smart contract and trigger transactions on the deployed contract account. Its main options are as follows:

```
ubuntu@ip-172-31-90-67:~/burrow/example/basic$ burrow deploy --help
Usage: burrow deploy [OPTIONS]
Deploy and test contracts
Options:
  -u, --chain-url chain-url to be used in IP:PORT format (default
"127.0.0.1:10997")
  -s, --keys IP:PORT of Burrow GRPC service which jobs should or otherwise
transaction
submitted unsigned for mempool signing in Burrow
  -f, --file path to package file which jobs should use. if also using the
--dir flag, give the relative path to jobs file, which should be in the
same directory (default "deploy.yaml")
  -a, --address default address to use; operates the same way as the
[account] job, only before the deploy file is ran
```

To deploy and trigger transactions with the `burrow deploy` command, the validator address and the RPC URL (the default is `127.0.0.1:10997`) will be used. These are defined in the generated Burrow validator configuration file, `burrow.toml`, as follows:

```
[[GenesisDoc.Validators]]
 Address = "54EF1517D97E7A653D5FA5B05060A82A8856515D"
 PublicKey =
"{\"CurveType\":\"ed25519\",\"PublicKey\":\"FF4E4B9D3FB3B4CC0F113661E2E298C
7DD7355A1207CA398496550BC162C04F3\"}"
 Amount = 9999999999
 Name = "Full_0"

[RPC]
 [RPC.Info]
 Enabled = true
 ListenAddress = "tcp://127.0.0.1:26658"
 [RPC.Profiler]
 Enabled = false
 ListenAddress = "tcp://127.0.0.1:6060"
 [RPC.GRPC]
 Enabled = true
 ListenAddress = "127.0.0.1:10997"
```

To deploy and test the contract, the deploy configure file should be provided as an option, indicated by -f. In the file, jobs are defined. To define a job, you need to provide the following:

- **A name**: A user-friendly job name.
- **The job type**: `deploy`, `call`, or `query-contract`. We used the three job types in this recipe to deploy contracts, call transactions to withdraw money, and query the balance of the account.
- **The destination**: The contract account address.
- **The function**: The name of the function in the Solidity contract.
- **The data**: The parameters to call the function.

Installing Hyperledger Seth with Docker on AWS

Seth is packaged separately from the Hyperledger Sawtooth project. Seth provides Docker images to start up the Seth environment. In this recipe, we will install Docker on Ubuntu and start up the Seth Docker image.

How to do it...

1. Install the Docker **Community Edition** (**CE**) by following the Docker documentation. Update the `apt` package index as follows:

   ```
   sudo apt-get update
   ```

2. Install the necessary packages to allow apt to use a repository over HTTPS:

   ```
   sudo apt-get install \
       apt-transport-https \
       ca-certificates \
       curl \
       software-properties-common
   ```

3. Add Docker's official GPG key:

   ```
   curl -fsSL https://download.docker.com/linux/ubuntu/gpg | sudo apt-key add -
   ```

4. Set up the stable repository:

```
sudo add-apt-repository \
    "deb [arch=amd64] https://download.docker.com/linux/ubuntu \
    $(lsb_release -cs) \
    stable"
```

5. Install Docker CE:

```
sudo apt-get update
sudo apt-get install docker-ce
```

6. Verify that Docker CE has installed correctly by running the `hello-world` image:

```
ubuntu@ip-172-31-90-67:~$ sudo docker run hello-world
Hello from Docker!
This message shows that your installation appears to be working
correctly.
```

7. Install Docker Compose. Download the latest version of Docker Compose:

```
sudo curl -L
"https://github.com/docker/compose/releases/download/1.22.0/docker-
compose-$(uname -s)-$(uname -m)" -o /usr/local/bin/docker-compose
```

8. Modify the `docker-compose` executable:

```
sudo chmod +x /usr/local/bin/docker-compose
```

9. Verify the Docker Compose installation:

```
ubuntu@ip-172-31-90-67:~$ docker-compose --version
docker-compose version 1.22.0, build f46880fe
```

10. Build and start Seth. Clone the `sawtooth-seth` GitHub repository:

```
git clone https://github.com/hyperledger/sawtooth-seth.git
cd sawtooth-seth
Build and start up Seth containers:
sudo docker-compose up --build
```

11. Verify the Seth Docker installation. List the Docker container status, as follows:

```
ubuntu@ip-172-31-90-67:~/sawtooth-seth$ sudo docker container ls --
all
CONTAINER ID          IMAGE                                       NAMES
a8e364431895          sawtooth-seth-rpc:latest                    seth-
rpc
c0f26cde1222          sawtooth-seth-cli-go:latest                 seth-
cli-go
6ff3ce573f67          hyperledger/sawtooth-block-info-tp:1.0   block-
info-tp
c28309e8e5c7          sawtooth-seth-tp:latest                     seth-
tp
7babc1b8684b          hyperledger/sawtooth-settings-tp:1.0
settings-tp
9500edea282b          hyperledger/sawtooth-rest-api:1.0        rest-
api
dd65b46253c5          sawtooth-seth-cli:latest                    seth-
cli
6aba65d076ef          hyperledger/sawtooth-validator:1.0
sawtooth-validator
```

12. Inspect the Docker container and view its log. In this case, we are inspecting the `seth-tp` container:

```
ubuntu@ip-172-31-90-67:~/sawtooth-seth$ sudo docker exec -it seth-
cli-go bash
"LogPath":
"/var/lib/docker/containers/c28309e8e5c77dd9839cef91bf2fca00d9b64f9
dc2815ad85fd3ed18c86d32e7/c28309e8e5c77dd9839cef91bf2fca00d9b64f9dc
28
15ad85fd3ed18c86d32e7-json.log",
"Name": "/seth-tp",
```

How it works...

Docker is a platform for developers to develop, deploy, and run applications with containers. It provides a flexible approach to bundle applications and their dependencies into isolated containers with lightweight runtime environments.

Docker Composer is a Docker tool that's use to stack a set of applications or services together and manage multiple containers and their service links for your system. The Docker Compose YAML file is used to define each service and their mapping to the host.

Currently, the best way to install the Seth network is to build Seth Docker containers using the provided Docker composer file from the Seth GitHub repository. The Docker file can be found at `https://github.com/hyperledger/sawtooth-seth/blob/master/docker-compose.yaml`, which is used to build Seth Docker images and start Seth Docker containers for each Seth service.

After building the Seth Docker containers, you can easily set up and run the Seth network without manually installing each Seth service and library, and then configuring each service.

In this recipe, we provided a step-by-step guide to install Docker and Docker Composer, download the Seth repository, and build Seth Docker containers. The Seth network is now ready to launch and work on.

Creating externally owned accounts and writing Solidity contracts on Seth

The easiest way to write Solidity contracts and check their grammar is to write them with Remix (`https://github.com/ethereum/remix`).

We will implement a similar smart contract as we did with Burrow to create an EOA account and perform transactions to deposit, withdraw, and query the account on the Sawtooth network via Seth.

How to do it...

1. Create an **externally owned account (EOA)** with the Seth CLI. Start up shell in the `seth-cli-go` container:

   ```
   sudo docker exec -it seth-cli-go bash
   ```

2. In the container shell, generate a password-encrypted key file with OpenSSL:

   ```
   openssl ecparam -genkey -name secp256k1 | openssl ec -out kevin.pem -aes128
   ```

3. Generate another key file without a password with OpenSSL for the Ethereum JSON RPC client:

```
openssl ecparam -genkey -name secp256k1 | openssl ec -out
jsacct.pem
```

4. Import the key files into Seth and create an alias for the key:

```
seth account import kevin.pem kevin
seth account import jsacct.pem jsacct
```

5. Create accounts on the Sawtooth network:

```
seth account create --nonce=0 --wait kevin
seth account create --nonce=0 --wait jsacct
```

6. List and show the EOA information:

```
root@c0f26cde1222:~# seth account list
Enter Password to unlock kevin:
jsacct: 3b50ebebf7d0de388f6ce229958fcd7c7dfd3a48
kevin: 1dd8fb9b9742d0c6de2c02614e738a72ac872452
root@c0f26cde1222:~# seth show account
1dd8fb9b9742d0c6de2c02614e738a72ac872452
Address: 1dd8fb9b9742d0c6de2c02614e738a72ac872452
Balance: 0
Code :
Nonce : 45
Perms : +root,+send,+call,+contract,+account
(No Storage Set)
```

7. Write a Solidity smart contract. We will write a simple contract called SethContract.sol. Check out the *Writing smart contracts with Solidity* recipe to learn about the basic procedures and features of Solidity before moving onto this one. For SethContract.sol, you can simply copy and paste the following code into Remix to compile the contract:

```
pragma solidity >=0.0.0;
contract SethContract {
    int s_amount;
    address s_owner;
    constructor() public {
        s_owner = msg.sender;
        s_amount = 0;
    }
    function deposit(int v) public {
        require(v >= 0);
```

```
        s_amount = s_amount + v;
    }
    function withdraw(int v) public {
        require(v >= 0);
        require(s_amount >= v);
        s_amount = s_amount - v;
    }
  function reset(int v) public {
        require(v >= 0);
        s_amount = v;
    }
    function getBalance(int v) constant public returns (string
retVal) {
        return int2str(s_amount);
    }
    function getAddress(int v) constant public returns (address a) {
        return s_owner;
    }
    function int2str(int i) internal pure returns (string) {
      if (i == 0) return "0";
      int j = i;
      uint length;
      while (j != 0){
          length++;
          j /= 10;
      }
      bytes memory bstr = new bytes(length);
      uint k = length - 1;
      while (i != 0){
          bstr[k--] = byte(48 + i % 10);
          i /= 10;
      }
      return string(bstr);
    }
}
```

8. Copy the EOA key files from the `seth-go-cli` container into the `seth-rpc` container:

```
sudo docker cp seth-cli-go:/root/.sawtooth/keys/jsacct.pem
jsacct.pem
sudo docker cp jsacct.pem seth-rpc:/root/.sawtooth/keys/jsacct.pem
```

How it works...

Ethereum has two types of accounts: EOAs and contract accounts. Both of these have addresses, but they have a few important differences:

- **EOAs**:
    - Can send transactions to create or execute smart contracts
    - Have a private key for the owner
    - Have no associated code or data storage
- **Contract accounts**:
    - Can send messages to call other contracts but cannot start transactions
    - Have no private key
    - Have code and data storage

All actions on the Ethereum blockchain are started as transactions that are triggered from EOA. EOAs can start transactions to execute smart contract accounts in EVM and update the contract-data storage.

The transaction and contract-data storage will be persisted into the blockchain network.

Seth works in the same way as Ethereum. First, we created the EOAs on the Sawtooth platform. We then used this account to deploy and call the Ethereum contracts.

Seth-RPC is running different containers. It is possible that the Seth-RPC might not be able to find the EOA account key file on its mount volume. To be safe, we copied the EOA account key files into the Seth-RPC container. The existing Ethereum client with the web3 library can communicate with smart contracts on Sawtooth using this EOA account.

Deploying and calling Ethereum contracts with the Seth CLI and RPC

In this recipe, we will compile, deploy, and call Ethereum smart contracts on the Sawtooth platform with the Seth client CLI and the Seth-RPC.

How to do it...

1. Compile the Solidity contract. To deploy a contract, the Seth client expects the contract to be passed in the form of a hex-encoded byte array. The Solidity compiler, `solc`, can be used to generate the byte codes. The command to generate the hex-encoded bytes for a contract is as follows:

```
ubuntu@ip-172-31-90-67:~/seth/example$ solc --bin SethContract.sol
======= SethContract.sol:SethContract =======
Binary:
608060405234801561001057600080fd5b5033600160006101000a81548173fffff
ffffffffffffffffffffffffffffffffffffffff021916908373fffffffffffffffff
fffffffffffffffffffff1602179055506000808......
```

2. Deploy the Solidity contract using the Seth CLI. Start up the shell in the `seth-cli-go` container:

```
sudo docker exec -it seth-cli-go bash
```

3. Deploy the contract with the following command:

```
seth contract create --wait EOA-alias contract-byte-codes
```

4. The output of deploying the sample Solidity contract is as follows:

```
seth contract create --wait kevin
"608060405234801561001057600080fd5b5033600160006101000a81548173ffff
ffffffffff
ffffffffffffffffffffffffffffffffffffffff021916908373fffffffffffffffff
fffffffffffffffff1602179"
Enter Password to unlock kevin:
Contract created
Transaction Receipt: {
  "TransactionID":
"883335adbdbf70b56435697a53b3757e74a65af0d47c9fb09c4ba1749eea263902
42bf51d0c804dd11445d7f6de908518c86d7a03e089a0ae4661d680435978a",
  "GasUsed": 74,
  "Address": "9127865198b6e7280295ea926f14f7fca5560aa9",
  "ReturnValue":
"608060405260043610610006d576000357c0100000000000000000000000000000000
00000000000000000000000000900463ffffffff1680633f2f......
```

5. To show the contract account details, use the following code:

```
root@c0f26cde1222:/project/sawtooth-seth# seth show account
"9127865198b6e7280295ea926f14f7fca5560aa9"
Address: 9127865198b6e7280295ea926f14f7fca5560aa9
Balance: 0
Code : Nonce : 1
Perms : -root,+send,+call,+contract,+account
Storage:
0000000000000000000000000000000000000000000000000000000000000001 ->
00000000000000000000000009127865198b6e7280295ea926f14f7fca5560aa9
0000000000000000000000000000000000000000000000000000000000000000 ->
0000000000000000000000000000000000000000000000000000000000000000
```

6. Call the deployed Solidity contract with the Seth CLI. The Seth CLI expects hex-encoded bytes to call a deployed Solidity contract on the Sawtooth platform. To generate the calling input data for the sample contract, enter the following:

```
node
> var abi = require('ethereumjs-abi')
> abi.simpleEncode("deposit(int)", "0x2").toString("hex")
f04991f0000000000000000000000000000000000000000000000000000000000
00002
abi.simpleEncode("withdraw(int)", "0x01").toString("hex")
7e62eab8000000000000000000000000000000000000000000000000000000000
00001
abi.simpleEncode("getBalance(int):(string)","0x0").toString("hex")
da0a75c8000000000000000000000000000000000000000000000000000000000
00000
```

7. To call the deployed sample contract with the Seth CLI, enter the following:

```
seth contract call --wait EOA-alias contract-address input-
generated-as-ABI
```

8. To call the deposit, withdraw, and `getBalance` functions in the sample contract, enter the following:

```
deposit 2:
seth contract call --wait kevin
"9127865198b6e7280295ea926f14f7fca5560aa9"
"f04991f0000000000000000000000000000000000000000000000000000000000
000002"
withdraw 1:
seth contract call --wait kevin
"9127865198b6e7280295ea926f14f7fca5560aa9"
"7e62eab8000000000000000000000000000000000000000000000000000000000
000001"getbalance:
```

```
seth contract call --wait kevin
"9127865198b6e7280295ea926f14f7fca5560aa9"
da0a75c80000000000000000000000000000000000000000000000000000000000
00000"
```

9. Show the contract account's details:

```
root@c0f26cde1222:/project/sawtooth-seth# seth show account
"9127865198b6e7280295ea926f14f7fca5560aa9"
Address: 9127865198b6e7280295ea926f14f7fca5560aa9
Balance: 0
Code : Nonce : 1
Perms : -root,+send,+call,+contract,+account
Storage:
0000000000000000000000000000000000000000000000000000000000000001 ->
00000000000000000000000009127865198b6e7280295ea926f14f7fca5560aa9
0000000000000000000000000000000000000000000000000000000000000000 ->
0000000000000000000000000000000000000000000000000000000000000001
```

Here, we deposit an amount of 2 and withdraw an amount of 1. The new stored value for the amount state variable becomes 1.

10. Deploy and call the Solidity contract with Seth-RPC. In docker-compose.yaml, unlock the account when starting Seth-RPC with -unlock, as follows:

```
container_name: seth-rpc
  volumes:
    - sawtooth:/root/.sawtooth
  depends_on:
    - validator
  ports:
    - 3030:3030
  command: |
  bash -c "
    seth-rpc --connect tcp://validator:4004 --bind 0.0.0.0:3030 --
  unlock jsacct
    "
```

Stop and restart Docker-Compose.

11. To deploy the contract with Seth-RPC, enter the following:

```
curl -d '{"jsonrpc": "2.0", "method": "eth_sendTransaction", "id":
2, "params": [{"from":
"0x3b50ebebf7d0de388f6ce229958fcd7c7dfd3a48", "data":
"0x60806040523480156100105760080fd5b5033600160006101000a81548173f.
.....a997178a143f9b2be11fc2ec2f1f883f15d3d5f1340029"}]}' -H
"Content-Type: application/json" localhost:3030
```

12. The output will be as follows:

```
{"jsonrpc":"2.0","result":"0xe11a227197b6a6491e67a12979401bc5479743
0616c92cb4989dd6d34fc17bf62f60e589dd6c6512be7dd6eb8e89e1e1c7ed17517
0f9d941921c411abee64556","id":2}
```

13. To list the new contracts that were created as EOA jsacct, enter the following in the `seth-cli-go` container:

```
root@c0f26cde1222:/project/sawtooth-seth# seth contract list jsacct
Address of contracts by nonce for account with alias `jsacct`
4: db8d25c9a87196272b234dd080ba9270d41fa557
```

14. To show the details about the contract account, enter the following:

```
seth show account db8d25c9a87196272b234dd080ba9270d41fa557
```

15. To call the newly deployed contract with Seth-RPC and deposit an amount of 2 into it, enter the following:

```
ubuntu@ip-172-31-90-67:~/sawtooth-seth$ curl -d '{"jsonrpc": "2.0",
"method": "eth_sendTransaction", "id": 2, "params": [{"from":
"0x3b50ebebf7d0de388f6ce229958fcd7c7dfd3a48", "data":
"0xf04991f0000000000000000000000000000000000000000000000000000000000
00000002", "to": "0xdb8d25c9a87196272b234dd080ba9270d41fa557"}]}' -
H "Content-Type: application/json" localhost:3030

{"jsonrpc":"2.0","result":"0x37c1cd1df933ba1f37153a7f9f3a8fbbf7725a
59df4694c15832cab3b4fc46dd02e43e886413161f32c8a58f7ab81bcd69b092f06
e5b5f6f183c65dc7ea29910","id":2}
```

16. To show information about the contract account, enter the following:

```
seth show account db8d25c9a87196272b234dd080ba9270d41fa557
```

How it works...

Seth currently provides two ways to operate and interact with Ethereum contracts on the Sawtooth network: the Seth client CLI and the Seth RPC. To deploy a contract, you compile it with the Solidity compiler, `solc`. Both the Seth CLI and the RPC expect hex-encoded bytes to deploy and call the contract.

The Seth CLI provides the following commands to operate the account and contract:

```
seth [OPTIONS] account <create | import | list>
seth [OPTIONS] contract call [call-OPTIONS] [alias] [address] [data]
```

To generate the hex-encoded bytes to call a deployed Solidity contract on the Sawtooth platform with the Seth CLI, the ABI of the smart contract is used to specify which function in the contract to run and what the function parameters are. The `ethereumjs-abi` library (`https://github.com/ethereumjs/ethereumjs-abi`) can be used to encode the input data that is compatible with the Seth CLI client. The `abi.simpleEncode` method in the library is used to encode the input data, as follows:

```
abi.simpleEncode("function(input argument type list):(return value type)",
"data")
```

The transaction, such as deploying and calling the contract, will be saved in the network. The transaction request also returns a transaction ID for this transaction. You can query the transaction detail with the following command:

```
seth show receipt transaction-id
```

Seth RPC is used to develop Ethereum client applications to communicate with the Sawtooth network. Seth RPC is based on the Ethereum JSON-RPC API, and it is a web server to accept HTTP requests from client applications. It then sends requests to the Sawtooth validator node to perform the request.

In order to submit requests to Seth-RPC, the EOAs in the transaction must be unlocked when Seth-RPC is started. In this recipe, we added the EOA account into the Seth-RPC startup command in the Docker-Compose file.

Seth RPC supports most functions defined in the Ethereum JSON-RPC API, and the most popular API is `eth_sendTransaction`, which is used to create a contract or message-call transaction. The main parameters in this API are as follows:

- `from`: The address the transaction is sent from.
- `to`: The address the transaction is directed to.
- `data`: The compiled code of a contract OR the hash of the invoked method signature and encoded parameters. For more details, see the `Ethereum Contract ABI`.
- `Returns`: The transaction hash.

Permissioning Ethereum EOA and contract accounts on Seth

In this recipe, we will go through how to provision permission to both EOAs and contract accounts on Seth.

How to do it...

1. Start the Seth Docker images with Docker-Compose:

   ```
   sudo docker-compose up
   ```

2. Execute bash on the `seth-cli-go` container:

   ```
   sudo docker exec -it seth-cli-go bash
   ```

3. Check the contract account permissions:

   ```
   seth show account "da9fae99224516db78935d7cb91724e851c5b3fa"
   Address: da9fae99224516db78935d7cb91724e851c5b3fa
   Balance: 0
   Nonce : 1
   Perms : -root,+send,+call,-contract,-account
   Storage:
   0000000000000000000000000000000000000000000000000000000000000001 ->
   00000000000000000000000da9fae99224516db78935d7cb91724e851c5b3fa
   0000000000000000000000000000000000000000000000000000000000000000 ->
   0000000000000000000000000000000000000000000000000000000000000002
   ```

4. The permission for this contract account is as follows:

   ```
   Perms : -root,+send,+call,-contract,-account
   ```

5. Check the EOA account permission using the previous command:

   ```
   root@c0f26cde1222:/project/sawtooth-seth# seth show account
   1dd8fb9b9742d0c6de2c02614e738a72ac872452
   Address: 1dd8fb9b9742d0c6de2c02614e738a72ac872452
   Balance: 0
   Code :
   Nonce : 51
   Perms : +root,+send,+call,+contract,+account
   (No Storage Set)
   ```

6. To set permissions for an EOA or contract account, enter the following:

```
seth permissions set alias --wait --address address --
permissions="-root,+send,+call,+contract,+account"
```

7. The alias is the account alias with root permissions. The address is either the EOA account address or the contract address. We can revoke send and call permissions from the example deployed contract account as follows:

```
root@c0f26cde1222:/project/sawtooth-seth# seth permissions set
kevin --wait --address "da9fae99224516db78935d7cb91724e851c5b3fa" -
-permissions="-root,-send,-call,-contract,-account"
Enter Password to unlock kevin:
Permissions changed of da9fae99224516db78935d7cb91724e851c5b3fa
root@c0f26cde1222:/project/sawtooth-seth# seth show account
"da9fae99224516db78935d7cb91724e851c5b3fa"
Address: da9fae99224516db78935d7cb91724e851c5b3fa
Balance: 0
Perms : -root,-send,-call,-contract,-account
Storage:
0000000000000000000000000000000000000000000000000000000000000001 ->
00000000000000000000000da9fae99224516db78935d7cb91724e851c5b3fa
0000000000000000000000000000000000000000000000000000000000000000 ->
0000000000000000000000000000000000000000000000000000000000000002
```

8. To show the global default address permission, enter the following:

```
root@c0f26cde1222:/project/sawtooth-seth# seth show account
"0000000000000000000000000000000000000000"
Address: 0000000000000000000000000000000000000000
Balance: 0
Code :
Nonce : 1
Perms : +root,+send,+call,+contract,+account
(No Storage Set)
```

9. To set permissions on the global default address, enter the following:

```
root@c0f26cde1222:/project/sawtooth-seth# seth permissions set
kevin --wait --address global --permissions="-
all,+send,+contract,+call,-account"
Enter Password to unlock kevin:
Permissions changed of 0000000000000000000000000000000000000000
```

How it works...

Seth supports a set of predefined permissions for EOA accounts and contract accounts:

- `root`: Change permissions for other accounts
- `call`: Execute deployed contracts
- `contract`: Deploy new contracts from EOA accounts
- `account`: Create new EOA accounts
- `all`: All of the preceding permissions

Permissions can be granted or denied on either an EOA or a contract account using the `seth permission` CLI. The + prefix indicates that permission has been granted, while – indicates that the permission has been denied for a permission on an individual account.

When a new account is created, its permissions are inherited as follows:

- For new EOAs, its permissions are inherited from the global default zero address
- For new contract account, its permissions are inherited from the TOA account that deployed the contract

When Seth is set up initially, by default, all permissions are granted to any new accounts. This includes the `root`, `account`, `contract`, and `call` permissions. In a new deployment, after several super external accounts have been configured, you should evoke the permissions on the global-default zero address to restrict the new account and contract permissions.

Working with Hyperledger Iroha

7

Hyperledger Iroha is a general-purpose permissioned blockchain system hosted by **The Linux Foundation**. It was contributed by Soramitsu, Hitachi, NTT DATA, and Colu. Hyperledger Iroha is written in C++ and incorporates the BFT consensus algorithm, named **Yet Another Consensus** (**YAC**). Hyperledger Iroha consists of simple deployment and fast development. It can be used in applications that manage digital assets, identity, interbank payment, and so on.

Hyperledger Iroha offers the following key features:

- Simple deployment with peer nodes
- Managing accounts and assets in the domain with a role-based permission model
- Fast development with built-in commands and queries
- No extra development for smart contracts for common assets and account management
- An easy and simple Iroha CLI to interact with the network
- A rich set of client libraries for Java, Python, and C++ via Iroha Torii

The Iroha network is illustrated in the following diagram, and each component in the Iroha network is explained here:

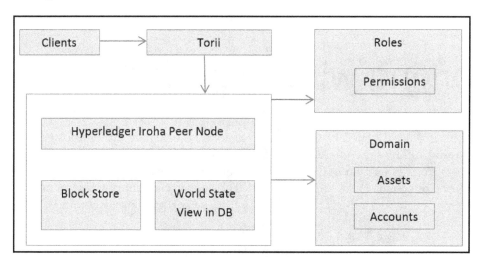

The Iroha network is composed of peer nodes, and these communicate with each other through the **gossip protocol**. Iroha stores its block in a specified block store and stores the current state of the system **World State View** (**WSV**) in a PostgreSQL database.

One of the features of Iroha is to provide permission management and account creation, and each account is assigned with roles for its permission. The role-based permission model is flexible enough to manage the allowed actions and resources for accounts in the system.

Iroha provides a pre-built set of commands and queries to perform common asset and account operations. With the help of built-in commands, you can define assets and accounts into the domain for various applications in your organization.

Iroha also distributes a set of client libraries for different languages, such as Python, Java, and C++, to communicate with the network via **gRPC**-based Torii. Torii is implemented with C++ using gRPC, and it is the entry point for a client to interact with the Iroha network. The gRPC is a remote procedure call framework that was developed by Google. In the gRPC client application, it could call methods on the remote server in the same way as it is calling local objects. The gRPC uses **protobuf** to define its **Interface Definition Language** (**IDL**) and message-interchange formats.

To develop the gRPC application, the service and its methods are first defined in protobuf files. Secondly, the protobuf file is compiled with a gRPC tool to generate the server skeleton code and client stub code for different languages. The real business logic for the server side will be implemented based on the generated server skeleton code. For Iroha, the gRPC server is Torii. The client application could easily call methods on the gRPC server with the generated stud files using a communication channel, such as TCP.

In this chapter, we will cover several recipes about working with **Hyperledger Iroha**:

- Installing Hyperledger Iroha on AWS
- Configuring Hyperledger Iroha
- Interacting with Hyperledger Iroha using the CLI to create cryptocurrency
- Interacting with Hyperledger Iroha using the client library

Installing Hyperledger Iroha on AWS

To install and run the recipes in this chapter, you need an EC2 instance on AWS with the following prerequisite:

- Ubuntu 16.04.5 LTS
- Install Docker CE by referring to the Docker installation guide in `Chapter 8`, *Exploring CLI with Hyperledger Indy*
- Install version control Git by referring to the Git installation guide in `Chapter 8`, *Exploring CLI with Hyperledger Indy*

How to do it...

Execute the following steps to install Hyperledger Iroha on AWS:

1. Create the Hyperledger Iroha Docker network:

   ```
   ubuntu@ip-172-31-90-67:~/iroha$ sudo docker network create iroha-
   network
   7b3be1160967f0021b99cd4e89d05f362590254edde311c391030ccd9c635a5d
   ```

2. To start the Iroha state database, PostgreSQL, enter the following command, which will start the PostgreSQL Docker container:

   ```
   ubuntu@ip-172-31-90-67:~/iroha$ sudo docker run --name postgresDB \
   > -e POSTGRES_USER=postgres \
   > -e POSTGRES_PASSWORD=mysecretpassword \
   ```

```
> -p 5432:5432 \
> --network=iroha-network \
> -d postgres:9.5
Unable to find image 'postgres:9.5' locally
5: Pulling from library/postgres
c1f213be5edb: Pull complete
Digest:
sha256:f4603c7b8aaf418393edb8cd5e2d1abd91d686ab571302dc83f887ea4a56
286b
Status: Downloaded newer image for postgres:9.5
5fe47dbc49027617ad6c6e5c6ba57092bfbb485f3aba6dacc70e2a5183b1d9ba
```

3. Create `blockstore`:

```
ubuntu@ip-172-31-90-67:~/iroha$ sudo docker volume create
blockstore
blockstore
```

4. Configure the network. In this recipe, we are using the configuration file, genesis block, and key pairs from the Iroha example. To configure the Iroha network for real business usage, these need to be generated for your organization:

```
ubuntu@ip-172-31-90-67:~/iroha$git clone
https://github.com/hyperledger/iroha
Cloning into 'iroha'...
remote: Enumerating objects: 1575, done.
remote: Counting objects: 100% (1575/1575), done.
remote: Compressing objects: 100% (1336/1336), done.
remote: Total 1575 (delta 460), reused 596 (delta 182), pack-reused
0
Receiving objects: 100% (1575/1575), 3.58 MiB | 0 bytes/s, done.
Resolving deltas: 100% (460/460), done.
Checking connectivity... done.
```

5. Start the Iroha Docker container:

```
ubuntu@ip-172-31-90-67:~/iroha$ sudo docker run -it --name iroha -p
50051:50051 -v $(pwd)/iroha/example:/opt/iroha_data -v
blockstore:/tmp/block_store --network=iroha-network --
entrypoint=/bin/bash hyperledger/iroha:develop
Unable to find image 'hyperledger/iroha:develop' locally
develop: Pulling from hyperledger/iroha
Digest:
sha256:106030d779109a21412ec2bb58cacb6459653074e813d1c027691f9f3b8a
c85a
Status: Downloaded newer image for hyperledger/iroha:develop
```

6. Launch the Iroha daemon:

```
root@8a0356adcbe3:/opt/iroha_data# irohad --config config.docker --
genesis_block genesis.block --keypair_name node0
[2018-11-03 17:38:04.844225244][th:20][info] MAIN start
[2018-11-03 17:38:04.844847536][th:20][info] MAIN config
initialized
```

How it works...

Iroha can be built from source, but it is easier and faster to install the Iroha network using its Docker image. In this recipe, we installed Iroha with Docker and used its example configuration, key pairs, and so on to set up the Iroha testing environment to work with the blockchain.

In the preceding steps, we created a virtual Docker network to facilitate network communication between the Iroha node and database. Then, we created a block store to persist blocks and started a single Iroha peer network for testing.

Configuring Hyperledger Iroha

In this recipe, we will learn how to configure the Iroha peer node and define the domain, role, permission, and account for the Iroha network.

Getting ready

Before configuring the Iroha network, we will restart the Iroha network that was installed in the *Installing Hyperledger Iroha on AWS* recipe and install a text editor on the Iroha Docker container, which will be used to edit Iroha configuration files in this recipe:

1. Restart the Iroha Docker containers that were installed in a previous recipe with the following commands:

```
ubuntu@ip-172-31-90-67:~/iroha/iroha$ sudo docker start postgresDB
postgresDB
ubuntu@ip-172-31-90-67:~/iroha/iroha$ sudo docker start iroha
iroha
ubuntu@ip-172-31-90-67:~/iroha/iroha$ sudo docker exec -it iroha
/bin/bash
root@8a0356adcbe3:/opt/iroha_data# irohad --config config.docker --
keypair_name node0
```

```
[2018-11-10 02:04:43.703153002][th:19][info] MAIN start
[2018-11-10 02:04:43.705004415][th:19][info] MAIN config
initialized
[2018-11-10 02:04:43.706783634][th:19][info] IROHAD created
```

2. Install the `nano` text editor on the Iroha container:

```
root@b551830ade0e:/opt/iroha_data# apt-get update
Get:1 http://security.ubuntu.com/ubuntu xenial-security InRelease
[107 kB]
root@b551830ade0e:/opt/iroha_data# apt-get install nano
Reading package lists... Done
```

How to do it...

Follow these steps to configure Iroha:

1. Go to the `bash` Iroha container:

   ```
   sudo docker exec -it iroha /bin/bash
   ```

2. Specify the Iroha network parameters in the `config.docker` configuration file:

   ```
   {
     "block_store_path" : "/tmp/block_store/",
     "torii_port" : 50051,
     "internal_port" : 10001,
     "pg_opt" : "host=postgresDB port=5432 user=postgres
   password=mysecretpassword",
     "max_proposal_size" : 10,
     "proposal_delay" : 5000,
     "vote_delay" : 5000,
     "mst_enable" : false
   }
   ```

3. Specify the genesis configuration in the `genesis.block` file. This can be done by first adding a `peer` node when the network is created:

   ```
   "addPeer":{
       "peer":{
           "address":"0.0.0.0:10001",
           "peerKey":"vd1YQE0TFeDrJ5AsXXyOsGAsFiOPAFdz30BrwZEwiSk="
       }
   }
   ```

4. Add the `admin` role:

```
"createRole":{
                    "roleName":"admin",
                    "permissions":[
                      "can_add_peer",
                      "can_add_signatory",
                      "can_create_account",
                      "can_create_domain",
                      "can_get_all_acc_ast",
                      "can_get_all_acc_ast_txs",
                      "can_get_all_acc_detail",
                      "can_get_all_acc_txs",
                      "can_get_all_accounts",
                      "can_get_all_signatories",
                      "can_get_all_txs",
                      "can_get_blocks",
                      "can_get_roles",
                      "can_read_assets",
                      "can_remove_signatory",
                      "can_set_quorum"
                    ]
    }
```

5. Add the domain:

```
"createDomain":{
                    "domainId":"ico",
                    "defaultRole":"user"
    }
```

6. Add the `admin` account and assign an `admin` role to the account:

```
"createAccount":{
                    "accountName":"admin",
                    "domainId":"ico",
    "publicKey":"MToH5jhHdu2VRHcQ0V5ZFIRzzPwFKmgTF6cqafKkmRA="
                    }
    },
    "appendRole":{
                    "accountId":"admin@ico",
                    "roleName":"admin"
    }
```

How it works...

The Iroha daemon command (`irohad`) is used to start the Iroha peer node. The following parameters are set for this:

- `config`: The configuration file for the block store path, client port, peer port, database, and so on.
- `keypair_name`: The public and private key file name used by the peer.
- `genesis_block`: The initial block in the network and domain, role, accounts, and so on to start the hedger. If you're restarting an existing Iroha network, this parameter should be ignored.

In the Iroha daemon configuration file, the parameters are as follows:

`block_store_path`	Path to store blocks.
`torii_port`	Port for client (default `50051`).
`internal_port`	Port for communication between peers (default `10001`).
`pg_opt`	Connection to the PostgresSQL database.
`max_proposal_size`	Maximum size of the block proposal.
`proposal_delay`	The period of time (in ms) to start a proposal.
`vote_delay`	The period of time (in ms) to wait before sending a vote for consensus to the other peer nodes.
`mst_enable`	Switch multi-signatures transactions on/off.

In the `genesis_block` file, peers, domain, role, permission, accounts, and so on can be specified. Hyperledger Iroha provides role-based permission control. The roles and accounts could be set up in the `genesis_block` file when starting the network. It could also be updated using built-in commands when the hedger is started.

The following is a list of main permissions for different categories in the Iroha system:

- Permissions for the account:

`can_create_account`	`can_get_all_acc_detail`	`can_get_domain_acc_ast`
`can_set_detail`	`can_get_domain_accounts`	`can_get_all_acc_ast_txs`
`can_get_all_accounts`	`can_get_all_acc_ast`	`can_get_domain_acc_ast_txs`

- Permissions for the roles:

can_create_role	https://iroha.readthedocs.io/en/latest/maintenance/permissions.html#can-create-role
can_append_role	https://iroha.readthedocs.io/en/latest/maintenance/permissions.html#can-append-role
can_get_roles	https://iroha.readthedocs.io/en/latest/maintenance/permissions.html#can-get-roles

- Permissions for the assets:

can_create_asset	https://iroha.readthedocs.io/en/latest/maintenance/permissions.html#can-create-asset
can_receive	https://iroha.readthedocs.io/en/latest/maintenance/permissions.html#can-receive
can_transfer	https://iroha.readthedocs.io/en/latest/maintenance/permissions.html#can-transfer

- Grantable permissions:

can_set_my_account_detail	https://iroha.readthedocs.io/en/latest/maintenance/permissions.html#can-set-my-account-detail
can_transfer_my_assets	https://iroha.readthedocs.io/en/latest/maintenance/permissions.html#can-transfer-my-assets
can_get_my_acc_detail	https://iroha.readthedocs.io/en/latest/maintenance/permissions.html#can-get-my-acc-detail

The admin accounts can update roles and permissions for other accounts, and the individual account can update grantable permissions for other accounts to access their assets, transactions, and so on to their account.

Interacting with Hyperledger Iroha using the CLI to create cryptocurrency

The Iroha CLI is interactive and flexible, which offers common and basic functions to manage network peers, domains, accounts, assets, and perform transactions and queries to work with the Iroha network.

In this recipe, we will utilize the Iroha CLI to perform the following transactions to demonstrate the ready-to-use asset and account management solution and functionalities offered by Iroha:

- Create a `hotcoin` asset
- Add `hotcoin` to the `admin` account
- Transfer `hotcoin` between accounts
- Query the `hotcoin` account balance

Getting ready

Perform the following steps before moving ahead:

1. Go to the `bash` Iroha container:

   ```
   sudo docker exec -it iroha /bin/bash
   ```

2. Update the `test` domain ID to `ico` using `nano` in the `genesis.block` configuration file. Rename the sample key files to `ico`. For the sake of simplicity, we do not generate private and public key files for this recipe and we reuse the key files from Iroha examples. However, in real usage, all key files for accounts and peers should be generated as follows:

   ```
   root@b551830ade0e:/opt/iroha_data# mv admin@test.priv
   admin@ico.priv
   root@b551830ade0e:/opt/iroha_data# mv admin@test.pub admin@ico.pub
   root@b551830ade0e:/opt/iroha_data# mv test@test.priv user@ico.priv
   root@b551830ade0e:/opt/iroha_data# mv test@test.pub user@ico.pub
   ```

3. Start the Iroha daemon node using the following command:

   ```
   irohad --config config.docker --genesis_block genesis.block --
   keypair_name node0
   ```

How to do it...

Execute the following steps to create cryptocurrency using CLI:

1. Run the Iroha CLI:

   ```
   iroha-cli -account_name admin@ico
   ```

The options that are available on the Iroha CLI menu are as follows:

```
root@b551830ade0e:/opt/iroha_data# iroha-cli -account_name admin@ico
Welcome to Iroha-Cli.
Choose what to do:
1. New transaction (tx)
2. New query (qry)
3. New transaction status request (st)
> :
```

2. Perform a transaction by selecting 1. New transaction (tx). The Iroha CLI's available commands for the transaction are as follows:

```
Forming a new transactions, choose command to add:
1. Detach role from account (detach)
2. Add new role to account (apnd_role)
3. Create new role (crt_role)
4. Set account key/value detail (set_acc_kv)
5. Transfer Assets (tran_ast)
6. Grant permission over your account (grant_perm)
7. Subtract Assets Quantity (sub_ast_qty)
8. Set Account Quorum (set_qrm)
9. Remove Signatory (rem_sign)
10. Create Domain (crt_dmn)
11. Revoke permission from account (revoke_perm)
12. Create Account (crt_acc)
13. Add Signatory to Account (add_sign)
14. Create Asset (crt_ast)
15. Add Peer to Iroha Network (add_peer)
16. Add Asset Quantity (add_ast_qty)
0. Back (b)
```

3. Create the hotcoin asset in the ico domain using the Iroha CLI by selecting 14:

```
> : 14
Asset name: hotcoin
Domain Id: ico
Asset precision: 2
Command is formed. Choose what to do:
1. Add one more command to the transaction (add)
2. Send to Iroha peer (send)
3. Go back and start a new transaction (b)
4. Save as json file (save)
> : 2
```

4. Add the `hotcoin` asset to the `admin` account by selecting option `16`:

```
> : 16
Asset Id: hotcoin#ico
Amount to add, e.g 123.456: 100
Command is formed. Choose what to do:
1. Add one more command to the transaction (add)
2. Send to Iroha peer (send)
3. Go back and start a new transaction (b)
4. Save as json file (save)
> : 2
Peer address (0.0.0.0):
Peer port (50051):
[2018-11-16 18:25:06.198633382][th:267][info] TransactionResponseHandler Trans
Congratulation, your transaction was accepted for processing.
Its hash is b68c625a85bd5f02ecd7a7192562ef8fc9e46f59965daa5f258f779973488ab8
----------------------
```

5. Perform a query to check the coin balance of the `admin` account. This can be done by selecting the first option, `2. New query (qry)`, and the `8. Get Account's Assets (get_acc_ast)` option. The Iroha CLI's available queries are as follows:

```
----------------------
Choose what to do:
1. New transaction (tx)
2. New query (qry)
3. New transaction status request (st)
> : 2
Choose query:
1. Get all permissions related to role (get_role_perm)
2. Get Transactions by transactions' hashes (get_tx)
3. Get information about asset (get_ast_info)
4. Get Account's Transactions (get_acc_tx)
5. Get Account's Asset Transactions (get_acc_ast_tx)
6. Get all current roles in the system (get_roles)
7. Get Account's Signatories (get_acc_sign)
8. Get Account's Assets (get_acc_ast)
9. Get Account Information (get_acc)
0. Back (b)
> : 8
Requested account Id: admin@ico
Requested asset Id: hotcoin#ico
Query is formed. Choose what to do:
1. Send to Iroha peer (send)
2. Save as json file (save)
0. Back (b)
> : 1
Peer address (0.0.0.0):
Peer port (50051):
[2018-11-16 18:30:42.276903040][th:267][info] QueryResponseHandler [Account Assets]
[2018-11-16 18:30:42.277411973][th:267][info] QueryResponseHandler -Account Id:- admin@ico
[2018-11-16 18:30:42.277569686][th:267][info] QueryResponseHandler -Asset Id- hotcoin#ico
[2018-11-16 18:30:42.277580860][th:267][info] QueryResponseHandler -Balance- 100
----------------------
```

6. Perform a transaction to transfer the `hotcoin` asset from the `admin` account to the `user` account by selecting option 5:

```
> : 5
SrcAccount Id: admin@ico
DestAccount Id: user@ico
Asset Id: hotcoin#ico
Amount to transfer, e.g 123.456: 40
Command is formed. Choose what to do:
1. Add one more command to the transaction (add)
2. Send to Iroha peer (send)
3. Go back and start a new transaction (b)
4. Save as json file (save)
> : 2
Peer address (0.0.0.0):
Peer port (50051):
[2018-11-16 18:49:10.742907608][th:300][info] TransactionResponseHandler Trans
Congratulation, your transaction was accepted for processing.
Its hash is a9f7381344a0c06093288d7cfb3b1f311cfe13b455a231505f14a46ad51495e3
--------------------
```

7. Perform a query to check the balance of the `admin` account and `user`. The balance of the `admin` account is now 60:

```
> : 8
Requested account Id (admin@ico):
Requested asset Id (hotcoin#ico):
Query is formed. Choose what to do:
1. Send to Iroha peer (send)
2. Save as json file (save)
0. Back (b)
> : 1
Peer address (0.0.0.0):
Peer port (50051):
[2018-11-16 18:50:46.584175354][th:300][info] QueryResponseHandler [Account Assets]
[2018-11-16 18:50:46.584618395][th:300][info] QueryResponseHandler -Account Id:- admin@ico
[2018-11-16 18:50:46.584677876][th:300][info] QueryResponseHandler -Asset Id- hotcoin#ico
[2018-11-16 18:50:46.584687992][th:300][info] QueryResponseHandler -Balance- 60
--------------------
```

How it works...

In this recipe, we set up the domain, account, and role in the Iroha `genesis.block` file to start a new Iroha network. We also performed different transactions, such as creating an asset, transferring the asset into an account, and querying account balance using the Iroha CLI. The Iroha CLI utilizes a set of Iroha pre-built commands and queries, which are smart contracts on the block chain. Providing pre-built common smart contracts is not only safer, as they are tested and verified by the Iroha community, but it also provides an out-of-the-box solution for small-scale blockchain DApps. You could easily and quickly build the blockchain network and start to create assets, accounts, and perform basic CRUD tractions for your organization.

Iroha commands are smart contracts that perform an action to change the state of an asset and account in Iroha WSV. Commands are applied to the blockchain network using a transaction. The Iroha peer then validates and changes the current state in the WSV, which is the snapshot of the system. Multiple transactions are composed into a block and persisted into the immutable block store, which is used to keep the history of the transactions.

Iroha supports both single and batch transactions. Transactions can consist of one or many commands that will be performed in order and atomically.

The Iroha transaction basic payload and proto definition are as follows:

- Time of creation (time in milliseconds)
- Creator account
- Quorum field (required number of signatures)
- Commands

Command can be defined as follows:

```
message ReducedPayload{
    repeated Command commands = 1;
    string creator_account_id = 2;
    uint64 created_time = 3;
    uint32 quorum = 4;
}
```

Accounts and assets are basic models in the command. The name format to refer to an account is `accountid@domain`, and the name format to refer to an asset is `assetid#domain`. The following commands are implemented in the current Iroha release, and they offer basic CRUD actions for domain, account, asset, role, and permission, as well as their proto definition:

```
message Command {
    oneof command {
    AddAssetQuantity add_asset_quantity = 1;
    AddPeer add_peer = 2;
    AddSignatory add_signatory = 3;
    AppendRole append_role = 4;
    CreateAccount create_account = 5;
    CreateAsset create_asset = 6;
    CreateDomain create_domain = 7;
    CreateRole create_role = 8;
    DetachRole detach_role = 9;
    GrantPermission grant_permission = 10;
    RemoveSignatory remove_sign = 11;
    RevokePermission revoke_permission = 12;
    SetAccountDetail set_account_detail = 13;
    SetAccountQuorum set_quorum = 14;
    SubtractAssetQuantity subtract_asset_quantity = 15;
    TransferAsset transfer_asset = 16;
}
```

Query is the smart contract that is used to request the current state of the system, and it does not update the state. Its basic payload and proto definition are as follows:

- Time of creation (time in milliseconds)
- Creator account
- Query counter (query request count on client side)
- Query

Query can be defined as follows:

```
message QueryPayloadMeta {
    uint64 created_time = 1;
    string creator_account_id = 2;
    // used to prevent replay attacks.
    uint64 query_counter = 3;
}
```

Iroha provides the following built-in queries to inquire about the status of an account, asset, role, and transaction. The query proto definitions are as follows:

```
message Query {
    message Payload {
        QueryPayloadMeta meta = 1;
        oneof query {
            GetAccount get_account = 3;
            GetSignatories get_account_signatories = 4;
            GetAccountTransactions get_account_transactions = 5;
            GetAccountAssetTransactions get_account_asset_transactions = 6;
            GetTransactions get_transactions = 7;
            GetAccountAssets get_account_assets = 8;
            GetAccountDetail get_account_detail = 9;
            GetRoles get_roles = 10;
            GetRolePermissions get_role_permissions = 11;
            GetAssetInfo get_asset_info = 12;
            GetPendingTransactions get_pending_transactions = 13;
        }
    }
}
```

There's more...

The Iroha CLI also provides the functionality to generate key pairs for accounts and so on in the network. You can run this to generate key pairs for admin and user accounts in this recipe rather than using example Iroha key pairs. In a real case, you should choose the secure approach to generate keys for your application.

To generate a public and private key pair to identify a new account, enter the Iroha CLI command, as follows:

```
root@b551830ade0e:/opt/iroha_data# iroha-cli --new_account --account_name
newuser@ico --pass_phrase newuserpassphrase --key_path ./
[2018-11-18 17:03:19.877331834][th:358][info] CLI-MAIN Public and private
key has been generated in current directory
```

Interacting with Hyperledger Iroha using the client library

The Iroha client library is the easiest way to build your own DApps with the Iroha network. The Iroha client application is easy to develop using builders that are present in the Iroha client library, and it communicates with the Iroha network with gRPC transport.

In this recipe, we will use the Iroha Python client library to implement a sample client application to interact with the Iroha network. This will perform the following transactions:

- Transfer the hotcoin asset we created in previous recipe between accounts
- Query the hotcoin account balance

Getting ready

To build and work with the Iroha client library, the following dependencies should be installed:

- automake: This is a tool to automatically generate a Makefile that's compliant with the GNU coding standard for a project, such as the Iroha project on Git:

  ```
  sudo apt install automake
  automake --version
  ```

- bison: This is a general-purpose language parser:

  ```
  sudo apt install bison
  bison --version
  ```

- cmake: This is a tool to manage an application that will be compile and built cross-platform, and it is used to build Iroha from source code:

  ```
  wget https://cmake.org/files/v3.11/cmake-3.11.4.tar.gz
  tar -xvzf cmake-3.11.4.tar.gz
  cd cmake-3.11.4/
  ./configure
  make
  sudo make install
  cmake --version
  # cmake version 3.11.4
  ```

- `git`: To verify the Git version control tool that's present on the computer, use the following command:

```
ubuntu@ip-172-31-90-67:~$ git --version
git version 2.7.4
```

- `python3` and `pip3`: To check whether Python and PIP are installed on the computer, use the following command:

```
ubuntu@ip-172-31-90-67:~$ python3 --version
Python 3.5.2
ubuntu@ip-172-31-90-67:~$ pip3 --version
pip 8.1.1 from /usr/lib/python3/dist-packages (python 3.5)
```

- `boost`: The C++ `boost` library:

```
git clone https://github.com/boostorg/boost /tmp/boost;
cd /tmp/boost ; git submodule update --init --recursive);
(cd /tmp/boost ; /tmp/boost/bootstrap.sh);
(cd /tmp/boost ; /tmp/boost/b2 headers);
(cd /tmp/boost ; /tmp/boost/b2 cxxflags="-std=c++14" install);
ldconfig;
rm -rf /tmp/boost
cat /usr/local/include/boost/version.hpp | grep "BOOST_LIB_VERSION"
ubuntu@ip-172-31-90-67:~$ cat /usr/local/include/boost/version.hpp
| grep "BOOST_LIB_VERSION"
// BOOST_LIB_VERSION must be defined to be the same as
BOOST_VERSION
#define BOOST_LIB_VERSION "1_69"
```

- `swig`: This is a software development tool that provides interoperability between C++ with other programming languages, such as Python, Java, C#, and Go:

```
sudo apt install libpcre3-dev
wget http://prdownloads.sourceforge.net/swig/swig-3.0.12.tar.gz
tar -xvf swig-3.0.12.tar.gz
cd swig-3.0.12
./configure
make
sudo make install
```

- `protobuf` for C++: This is a language-neutral and platform-neutral data serialization from Google:

```
CMAKE_BUILD_TYPE="Release"
git clone https://github.com/google/protobuf /tmp/protobuf;
(cd /tmp/protobuf ; git checkout
```

```
106ffc04be1abf3ff3399f54ccf149815b287dd9);
cmake \
   -DCMAKE_BUILD_TYPE=${CMAKE_BUILD_TYPE} \
   -Dprotobuf_BUILD_TESTS=OFF \
   -Dprotobuf_BUILD_SHARED_LIBS=ON \
   -H/tmp/protobuf/cmake \
   -B/tmp/protobuf/.build;
cmake --build /tmp/protobuf/.build --target install;
ldconfig;
rm -rf /tmp/protobuf
protoc --version
ubuntu@ip-172-31-90-67:~$ protoc --version
libprotoc 3.5.1
```

How to do it...

Let's start by installing the Python client library:

1. You can build the Iroha Python client library from the Iroha source code on the Git repository or install it using `pip3`. In this recipe, we will install it using `pip3` with the following command:

   ```
   ubuntu@ip-172-31-90-67:~/iroha/iroha$ pip3 install iroha
   Collecting iroha
   Installing collected packages: iroha
   Successfully installed iroha-0.0.24
   ```

2. Install the gRPC Python compiling package in the Iroha Python `example` folder:

   ```
   ubuntu@ip-172-31-90-67:~/iroha/iroha/example/python$ pip3 install
   grpcio-toolsCollecting
   grpcio-tools
   Downloading
   https://files.pythonhosted.org/packages/c7/7e/f5f51c104eb41d6cfdc76
   b69c523fb9017747185fe1c0dfe4aea7d8f27fa/grpcio_tools-1.16.1-cp35-
   cp35m-manylinux1_x86_64.whl (22.8MB)
   Installing collected packages: six, grpcio, setuptools, protobuf,
   grpcio-tools
   ```

3. Compile the Iroha `.proto` files for the Python client library in the Iroha Python `example` folder:

   ```
   ubuntu@ip-172-31-90-67:~/iroha/iroha/example/python$ protoc --
   proto_path=../../shared_model/schema --python_out=.
   ../../shared_model/schema/*.proto
   ```

4. A list of *pb2* Python will be generated:

```
ubuntu@ip-172-31-90-67:~/iroha/iroha/example/python$ ls -li *pb2*
539405 -rw-rw-r-- 1 ubuntu ubuntu 5572 Nov 18 17:52 block_pb2.py
539406 -rw-rw-r-- 1 ubuntu ubuntu 41494 Nov 18 17:52
commands_pb2.py
39407 -rw-rw-r-- 1 ubuntu ubuntu 10396 Nov 18 17:52 endpoint_pb2.py
539412 -rw-rw-r-- 1 ubuntu ubuntu 14531 Nov 18 17:52
primitive_pb2.py
539413 -rw-rw-r-- 1 ubuntu ubuntu 2938 Nov 18 17:52 proposal_pb2.py
539415 -rw-rw-r-- 1 ubuntu ubuntu 36901 Nov 18 17:52
qry_responses_pb2.py
539416 -rw-rw-r-- 1 ubuntu ubuntu 31371 Nov 18 17:52 queries_pb2.py
539417 -rw-rw-r-- 1 ubuntu ubuntu 10694 Nov 18 17:52
transaction_pb2.py
```

5. Compile the Iroha gRPC .proto files for the Python client library. Go to the Iroha Python example folder and enter the following command to compile the Iroha gRPC .proto file:

```
ubuntu@ip-172-31-90-67:~/iroha/iroha/example/python$ python3 -m
grpc_tools.protoc --proto_path=../../shared_model/schema --
python_out=. --grpc_python_out=.
../../shared_model/schema/endpoint.proto
```

You may need to delete all serialized_options=None options in endpoint_pb2.py due to an incompatible protoc version. To find and browse the generated gRPC Python file, use the following command:

```
ubuntu@ip-172-31-90-67:~/iroha/iroha/example/python$ ls -li *grpc*
539418 -rw-rw-r-- 1 ubuntu ubuntu 6078 Nov 18 18:03
endpoint_pb2_grpc.py
```

6. Implement the client to submit a transaction using the Iroha Python client library. The client example, ico_hotcoin_client_txn.py, is implemented based on the Iroha Python example. This is a very simple client to transfer 10 hotcoin from admin into the user account in the ico domain. For the sake of simplicity, it does not subscribe to the status of the transaction. The ico_hotcoin_client_txn.py main source code snapshot is as follows:

```
tx_builder = iroha.ModelTransactionBuilder()
crypto = iroha.ModelCrypto()
admin_priv = open("../admin@ico.priv", "r").read()
admin_pub = open("../admin@ico.pub", "r").read()key_pair =
crypto.convertFromExisting(admin_pub, admin_priv)
```

```
def send_tx(tx, key_pair):
  tx_blob =
iroha.ModelProtoTransaction(tx).signAndAddSignature(key_pair).finis
h().blob()
  proto_tx = transaction_pb2.Transaction()
  if sys.version_info[0] == 2:
    tmp = ''.join(map(chr, tx_blob))
  else:
    tmp = bytes(tx_blob)
  proto_tx.ParseFromString(tmp)
  channel = grpc.insecure_channel('127.0.0.1:50051')
  stub = endpoint_pb2_grpc.CommandServiceStub(channel)
  stub.Torii(proto_tx)

def transfer_hotcoin_from_admin_to_user():
  """
  Transfer 10 hotcoin from admin@ico to user@ico
  """
  tx = tx_builder.creatorAccountId(creator) \
    .createdTime(current_time()) \
    .transferAsset("admin@ico", "user@ico", "hotcoin#ico",
"Transfer 10 from admin to user", "10.00").build()
  send_tx(tx, key_pair)
  print("Hash of the transaction: ", tx.hash().hex())


transfer_hotcoin_from_admin_to_user()
```

To run `ico_hotcoin_client_txn.py`, transfer `hotcoin` from `admin` to `user` with the following command:

```
ubuntu@ip-172-31-90-67:~/iroha/iroha/example/python$python3
ico_hotcoin_client_txn.py
Hash of the transaction:
360b30b88374b49898568a0fbd1f4b9d409fb5429f972949f176a11a27ef084e
```

7. Implement the client to query the account asset balance using the Iroha Python client library. The client example, `ico_hotcoin_client_query.py`, is also implemented based on the Iroha Python example. This is a very simple client to query the balance of `hotcoin` in the `admin` account in the `ico` domain. The `ico_hotcoin_client_query.py` main source code snapshot is as follows:

```
query_builder = iroha.ModelQueryBuilder()
query_counter = 1

def send_query(query, key_pair):
  query_blob =
iroha.ModelProtoQuery(query).signAndAddSignature(key_pair).finish()
```

```
  .blob()
    proto_query = queries_pb2.Query()
    if sys.version_info[0] == 2:
      tmp = ''.join(map(chr, query_blob))
    else:
      tmp = bytes(query_blob)
    proto_query.ParseFromString(tmp)
    channel = grpc.insecure_channel('127.0.0.1:50051')
    query_stub = endpoint_pb2_grpc.QueryServiceStub(channel)
    query_response = query_stub.Find(proto_query)
    return query_response


def get_admin_hotcoin_balance():
    """
    Get the hotcoin balance after the transfer for amin@ico asset
hotcoin#ico
    """
    global query_counter
    query_counter += 1
    query = query_builder.creatorAccountId(creator) \
      .createdTime(current_time()) \
      .queryCounter(query_counter) \
      .getAccountAssets("admin@ico") \
      .build()
    query_response = send_query(query, key_pair)
    print(query_response)
get_admin_hotcoin_balance()
```

8. To run `ico_hotcoin_client_query.py` in order to query the balance of account `admin`, enter the following command:

```
ubuntu@ip-172-31-90-67:~/iroha/iroha/example/python$python3
ico_hotcoin_client_query.py
account_assets_response {
  account_assets {
    asset_id: "hotcoin#ico"
    account_id: "admin@ico"
    balance: "100.00"
  }
}

query_hash:
"9ff8b6f891efc377e8dd3fa0dabc6319621b9101b217da5d6bc33aefb9fd8e9f"
```

How it works...

In this recipe, we installed the Iroha Python client library and its dependencies to develop the Iroha client application with the Python programming language. The sample application is implemented based on the Iroha Python client template. In this sample application, we performed a transaction to transfer coins between accounts and to develop a query to check the balance of accounts to demonstrate how a client application interacts with the Iroha network using the Iroha SDK.

In this recipe, we generated the gRPC stub files for the Iroha client with Python and the IDL service definition for Iroha Torii, which is in the `.proto` file, `endpoint.proto`. Its `Transaction` and `query` definition are as follows:

- For `Transaction`:

```
service CommandService {
    rpc Torii (Transaction) returns (google.protobuf.Empty);
    rpc ListTorii (TxList) returns (google.protobuf.Empty);
    rpc Status (TxStatusRequest) returns (ToriiResponse);
    rpc StatusStream(TxStatusRequest) returns (stream ToriiResponse);
}
```

- For `Query`:

```
service QueryService {
    rpc Find (Query) returns (QueryResponse);
    rpc FetchCommits (BlocksQuery) returns (stream
BlockQueryResponse);
}
```

In our transaction sample file, `ico_hotcoin_client_txn.py`, we are calling the `Torii` method in `CommandServiceStub` to send a transaction to our Iroha Troii endpoint, as follows:

```
channel = grpc.insecure_channel('127.0.0.1:50051')
stub = endpoint_pb2_grpc.CommandServiceStub(channel)
stub.Torii(proto_tx)
```

In our query sample file, `ico_hotcoin_client_query.py`, we are calling the `Find` method in `QueryService` to send a query to our Iroha Troii endpoint, as follows:

```
channel = grpc.insecure_channel('127.0.0.1:50051')
query_stub = endpoint_pb2_grpc.QueryServiceStub(channel)
query_response = query_stub.Find(proto_query)
```

To help people easily build a transaction and query to send to Torii, Iroha provides both `ModelTransactionBuilder` and `ModelQueryBuilder` in its Python client library, `iroha.py`. `iroha.py` is a utility module that uses `swig` to expose the Iroha C++ logic and functionalities to the Python client. Both builder classes, `ModelTransactionBuilder` and `ModelQueryBuilder`, are easy to use and provide methods to a command or query in a fluent way. In our `ico_hotcoin_client_txn.py` example, the builder is used as follows:

```
tx = tx_builder.creatorAccountId(creator) \
   .createdTime(current_time()) \
   .transferAsset("admin@ico", "user@ico", "hotcoin#ico", "Transfer 10 from
admin to user", "10.00").build()
```

In this recipe, we implemented an example Iroha client application using the Iroha client SDK. The basic structure for the Iroha client application is as follows:

- Loading key pairs for the creator
- Using the builder to build a transaction or query
- Signing the transaction or query using loaded key pairs
- Sending a transaction or query request using the gRPC stub

8
Exploring the CLI with Hyperledger Indy

Hyperledger Indy is a distributed ledger in The Linux Foundation family which is built for decentralized digital-identity management. Hyperledger Indy is in its incubation stage, and we will explore the Indy CLI to look at the concept and functions offered by Hyperledger Indy with the current distribution.

In this chapter, we will cover several recipes about exploring the CLI with Hyperledger Indy:

- Installing Hyperledger Indy and the Indy CLI on AWS
- Exploring the Indy CLI with Hyperledger Indy

Introduction

Hyperledger Indy is a public permissioned blockchain network for identity, which is built with privacy by design. It provides decentralized and self-sovereign identity management with a distributed ledger technology. An identity owner takes full control of its personal data in order to expose select information or avoid compromising the underlying personal data. Hyperledger Indy offers an alternative solution to managing identities and tackling increasing identity security demands, such as privacy, personal information leakage, data breach, and identity theft.

Here are Hyperledger Indy's key concepts:

- **Self-sovereign identity**: The individuals and businesses entities could manage and prove their own identity, credentials, and claims on the blockchain network without the need of a central identity authority.
- **Zero knowledge proof**: Only your required information is shared and exposed between different parties. Your credential (claim/proof) is proofed between agents without revealing your sensitive data completely.

Hyperledger Indy is composed of the following projects:

- `indy-node`: The **indy-plenum-based** implementation of the distributed ledger with the **Redundant Byzantine Fault-tolerance** (**RBFT**) consensus protocol. RBFT is intended for better consensus performance, where means the ordering is calculated on master instance and redundantly calculated and monitored on backup instances.
- `indy-sdk`: The client library to interact with the Indy network. This is basically the c-callable library, which has different wrappers for different programming languages. It is also used by the Indy CLI tool.
- `indy-crypto`: The crypto library for Indy based on the **Apache Milagro Cryptographic Library** (**AMCL**). This supports C, Rust, the Python API, and more.

The Hyperledger Indy network is a distributed ledger that was designed specifically for decentralized identities with the following characteristics:

- A collection pool of nodes running the RBFT consensus protocol
- The distributed ledger has several different-purpose ledgers replicated on each node:
    - **Pool ledger**: Transactions related to the node transaction
    - **Config ledger**: Transactions for pool configuration
    - **Domain ledger**: Transactions to identity application specific
- Two types of genesis transactions to define the initial transaction on the ledger:
    - Pool genesis transactions define bootstrap nodes in the network
    - Domain genesis transactions define initial trusted identities

Installing Hyperledger Indy and the Indy CLI on AWS

In this recipe, we will be learning more about Hyperledger Indy and how to install Indy on AWS.

Getting ready

To install and run the recipes in this chapter, you need an AWS EC2 instance with the following configuration:

- Ubuntu 16.04.5 LTS (GNU/Linux 4.4.0-1069-aws x86_64)
- Install Docker CE by referring to the Docker installation guide in Chapter 6, *Operating an Ethereum Smart Contract with Hyperledger Burrow*
- Install Git by referring to the Git installation guide in Chapter 6, *Operating an Ethereum Smart Contract with Hyperledger Burrow*

How to do it...

Follow the steps to install Indy and Indy CLI:

1. Get the indy-sdk source code. Make a folder named ~/indy and download the indy-sdk source code:

   ```
   git clone -b rc --depth=1
   https://github.com/hyperledger/indy-sdk.git
   ```

2. Build the Indy Docker image from its Docker file. Go to the indy-sdk folder and build the Indy Docker image:

   ```
   sudo docker build -f ci/indy-pool.dockerfile -t indy_pool .

   ubuntu@ip-172-31-90-67:~/indy/indy-sdk$ sudo docker build -f
   ci/indy-pool.dockerfile -t indy_pool .
   Sending build context to Docker daemon 119.4MB
   Step 1/22 : FROM ubuntu:16.04
   ---> a597cf115cd3
   ......
   Successfully built ad625c5e93d9
   Successfully tagged indy_pool:latest
   ```

3. Start up the Indy network using the built Docker image on a localhost:

```
sudo docker run —itd —p 9701-9708:9701-9708 indy_pool
```

Verify that the `indy_pool` container is running and get the `indy_pool` Docker container name with the following command. You'll need the Docker container name to stop and restart the Indy Docker container using the Docker command later. The Indy Docker container name for the recipe is `stoic_mendeleev`:

```
ubuntu@ip-172-31-90-67:~/indy/indy-sdk$ sudo docker ps —a
CONTAINER ID IMAGE COMMAND CREATED STATUS PORTS NAMES
c6feb453b2b9 indy_pool "/usr/bin/supervisord" 6 days ago Up 2
seconds 0.0.0.0:9701-9708->9701-9708/tcp stoic_mendeleev
```

Log into the shell of the running Indy container by entering the following command:

```
ubuntu@ip-172-31-90-67:~/indy/indy-sdk$ sudo docker exec —it
stoic_mendeleev /bin/bash
indy@c6feb453b2b9:/$
```

4. To install `indy-sdk` on the Ubuntu AWS host, perform the following commands in the `~/indy` folder on the AWS host:

```
sudo apt-key adv --keyserver keyserver.ubuntu.com --recv-keys
68DB5E88
sudo add-apt-repository "deb https://repo.sovrin.org/sdk/deb xenial
stable"
sudo apt-get update
sudo apt-get install —y libindy
ubuntu@ip-172-31-90-67:~/indy$ sudo apt-get install —y libindy
Reading package lists... Done
Building dependency tree
Reading state information... Done
......
Get:1 http://us-east-1.ec2.archive.ubuntu.com/ubuntu
xenial/universe amd64 libsqlite0 amd64
2.8.17-12fakesync1 [139 kB]
Get:2 https://repo.sovrin.org/sdk/deb xenial/stable amd64 libindy
amd64 1.6.8 [2,662 kB]
......
Setting up libsqlite0 (2.8.17-12fakesync1) ...
Setting up libindy (1.6.8) ...
Processing triggers for libc-bin (2.23-0ubuntu10) ...
```

5. Install `indy-cli`:

```
sudo apt-get install -y indy-cli
ubuntu@ip-172-31-90-67:~/indy$ sudo apt-get install -y indy-cli
Reading package lists... Done
......
Preparing to unpack .../indy-cli_1.6.8_amd64.deb ...
Unpacking indy-cli (1.6.8) ...
Setting up indy-cli (1.6.8) ...
```

How it works...

In this recipe, we downloaded the Indy source code repository, then built the Indy Docker container and started testing the Indy network on the AWS localhost. We also installed `indy-sdk` and `indy-cli` to interact with the Indy testing pool for the next recipe.

In the Indy Docker container, the command to start Indy node is `/usr/bin/python3 /usr/local/bin/start_indy_node Node1 0.0.0.0 9701 0.0.0.0 9702`.

The parameters for the `start_indy_node` Python module are `node_name node_ip node_port client_ip client_port`.

The Indy network nodes use two pairs of IPs or ports for running the node and communicating between nodes and clients. The first IP or port pair is for the node-to-node communication, and the second IP or port pair is for client-to-node communication.

There's more...

To browse the configuration and genesis transactions definition files for the Indy network that was installed in this recipe, you can log into the Indy Docker container using the following command:

```
sudo docker exec -it stoic_mendeleev /bin/bash
```

In the shell of the Indy container, you can browse the Indy system configuration file and the configuration directories for different parts of the Indy node under `/etc/indy`:

```
# Current network
# Disable stdout logging
enableStdOutLogging = False
# Directory to store ledger.
LEDGER_DIR = '/var/lib/indy'
# Directory to store logs.
```

```
LOG_DIR = '/var/log/indy'
# Directory to store keys.
KEYS_DIR = '/var/lib/indy'
# Directory to store genesis transactions files.
GENESIS_DIR = '/var/lib/indy'
# Directory to store backups.
BACKUP_DIR = '/var/lib/indy/backup'
# Directory to store plugins.
PLUGINS_DIR = '/var/lib/indy/plugins'
# Directory to store node info.
NODE_INFO_DIR = '/var/lib/indy'
NETWORK_NAME = 'sandbox'
```

For example, the node genesis transaction files are specified as GENESIS_DIR = /var/lib/indy. For the sandbox testing network, its genesis files are under the /var/lib/indy/sandbox folder as domain_transactions_genesis and pool_transactions_genesis. The sample transaction to create an initial identity in the network is as follows:

```
{"reqSignature":{},"txn":{"data":{"dest":"Th7MpTaRZVRYnPiabds81Y","role":"2
","verkey":"~7TYfekw4GUagBnBVCqPjiC"},"metadata":{"from":"V4SGRU86Z58d6TV7P
BUe6f"},"type":"1"},"txnMetadata":{"seqNo":2},"ver":"1"}
```

Exploring the Indy CLI with Hyperledger Indy

In this recipe, we will explore the design and intention for the wallet, **Decentralized Identifier (DID)**, pool, and ledger transaction in Indy network:

- **Wallet**: Hyperledger Indy manages identity with a new approach, **Decentralized Key Management System (DKMS)**, which manages identities on distributed ledger technologies such as the blockchain network. DKMS is different from the conventional **public key infrastructure (PKI)**-based approach to manage identities per certificate, as issued by the centralized CA. In Hyperledger Indy, identities are self-sovereign and are managed by each participant. An identity owner fully controls its identities and credentials and is also independent from any centralized identity providers or certificate authorities.

Identity owners generate and store their private keys, identities, secrets, credentials, and other cryptographic material in the wallet. Each participant in the network communicates, signs, and proofs its identities and credentials to the network with private data in the wallet. Consequently, the safety of the wallet is vital to the owner and entities.

The `wallet` for the client is stored in the user's home directory, named '`~/.indy_client`', by default. It is also stored in a SQLite data file, as follows:

```
ubuntu@ip-172-31-90-67:~/.indy_client/wallet/mywallet$ ls -lia
total 132
539445 drwxrwxr-x 2 ubuntu ubuntu 4096 Dec 10 04:24 .
534504 drwxrwxr-x 3 ubuntu ubuntu 4096 Dec 10 04:22 ..
539448 -rw-r--r-- 1 ubuntu ubuntu 57344 Dec 10 04:24 sqlite.db
539453 -rw-r--r-- 1 ubuntu ubuntu 32768 Dec 14 16:52 sqlite.db-shm
539451 -rw-r--r-- 1 ubuntu ubuntu 32992 Dec 10 04:34 sqlite.db-wal
```

- **DID**: DID is a globally-unique identifier for an entity or individual owner that is not managed by a centralized authority but can be registered with the distributed ledger (`https://w3c-ccg.github.io/did-spec/#dfn-dlt`), the technology's decentralized network, and resolvable on the ledger without requiring any centralized authority. To maintain privacy, an entity or identity owner can own multiple DIDs. The DID in Indy has the following characters:
    - Persistency
    - Globally resolvable
    - Cryptographically verifiable
    - Decentralized

In Hyperledger Indy, there are two types of DID. The first type is **Verinym**. A Verinym DID is the unique identifier of a legal identity or identity owner. The second type is a **pseudonym**, which is used to maintain the privacy of a digital relationship or connection between participants. If the pseudonym is used to maintain only one digital relationship, it is also called a **pairwise identifier**, which maintains secure connections between two participants.

Hyperledger Indy is a permissioned network. DIDs have different types of roles in the Indy network, such as **Steward** and **Trust Anchor**. The Steward role is for the person or organization who operates the Indy network. The person or organization with the Steward role could not only create and configure Indy nodes and node pool, but also can create, update, or delete other DIDs and post NYM transactions. The Trust Anchor is mainly used to publish DIDs and post NYM and schema transactions into the ledger. In order to register the other DID into the ledger, the DID to send the NYM transaction should have the Trust Anchor role, or the transaction will be rejected by the Indy pool.

The new DID could be registered to `ledger` via the `nym` transaction through the Indy CLI. In the recipe, we first imported the `did` named `Th7MpTaRZVRYnPiabds81Y`, which is defined as the Steward role in the bootstrap network genesis file for the testing network. Then, we activated the DID and used it to send the `nym` transaction to register a new `did`, as follows:

```
pool(sandbox):wallet(mywallet):did(Th7...81Y):indy> ledger nym
did=JRAoDbiV2tRfWSL3jcRKCk verkey=~6iKD9dkZEypiugWbDEHsXw
role=TRUST_ANCHOR
```

- **Credential schema and credential definition**: Credential schema is the base semantic structure to describe the list of attributes that a verifiable credential would contain. Credential definition is used to define the issuer to sign and issue the verifiable credential that was satisfied with a specific credential schema.

  The following diagram illustrates the concept of verifiable credentials and DID in the Hyperledger Indy system:

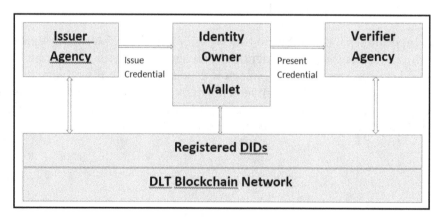

The organization could be the issuer agency or the verifier agency in the Indy network. The organization as the issuer agency would issue a credential to an individual identity owner, such as birth certificate, driving license, or college degree. The organization as the verifier agency could verify credentials that are presented by identity owners and it could also verify that the credential is issued by the trusted issuer agency through the Indy network. Each entity registers their DID on the ledger blockchain network. The published DIDs on the ledger allow entities and identity owners to identify the ownership of the DID and verify whether the credential that was issued by the DID is trustworthy and tamperproof.

The basic workflow is as follows: when a verifier agency requires information from an identity owner (such as whether the user has a driver's license), the verifier agency sends a proof request to the identity owner. The identity owner will then create a credential request to an issuer agency, such as the DMV. The issuer agency will issue the credentials to the identity owner if the owner has a driver's license and signs the credentials. The identity owner would then send back the credentials to the verifier agency. The verifier agency can verify the issuer agency DID, as well as the signature presented in the credentials, and register them in the ledger. If the issuer agency DID is matched with the DID registered in the ledger, the credential is trusted. Any manipulation of the credentials will change the cryptographic signature of the issuer agency.

Note that what is being verified in a verifiable credential is the identity and signature of the issuer agency. Different digital signature formats require different cryptography. In Indy, credentials use zero-knowledge proof signatures (http://groups.csail.mit.edu/cis/pubs/lysyanskaya/cl02b. pdf—**Camenisch-Lysyanskaya (CL)**) that enable the identity owner to present proof about the credentials without revealing the underlying data.

- **Transaction**: The ledger command group in the Indy CLI is sending NYM, schema, node, and other similar transactions to the ledger. These transactions are stored in the Indy blockchain network. Each transaction in Indy consists of transaction metadata and transaction-specific data. Its basic structure is as follows:

```
{
    "ver": < transaction version>,      "txn": {
        "type": < transaction type>,
        "data": < transaction specific data fields>,
    },
    "txnMetadata": {
        "txnTime": < transaction POSIX timestamp>,
```

```
        "seqNo": < unique sequence number of the transaction in
    ledger >,
        },
        "reqSignature":< submitter's signature >
    }
```

Here are the supported transaction types:

- NODE = 0
- NYM = 1
- ATTRIB = 100
- SCHEMA = 101
- CLAIM_DEF = 102
- POOL_UPGRADE = 109
- NODE_UPGRADE = 110
- POOL_CONFIG = 111

And here are the supported roles in a NYM transaction:

- None (common USER)
- 0 (TRUSTEE)
- 2 (STEWARD)
- 101 (TRUST_ANCHOR)

One of the genesis transactions to create the initial transaction on the testing network is defined as follows:

```
{"reqSignature":{},"txn":{"data":{"dest":"Th7MpTaRZVRYnPiabds81Y","role":"2
","verkey":"~7TYfekw4GUagBnBVCqPjiC"},"metadata":{"from":"V4SGRU86Z58d6TV7P
BUe6f"},"type":"1"},"txnMetadata":{"seqNo":2},"ver":"1"}
```

From the preceding transaction structure, you can see that the transaction is a NYM transaction (type is 1), which is used to create a new DID, Th7MpTaRZVRYnPiabds81Y, is being used as the Steward (the role is 2) in the ledger.

The Indy CLI is the official command-line tool provided by the Heperledger Indy project to interact with the Indy pool blockchain network. It currently provides the following commands, which we will explore in this recipe:

- Manage the wallet
- Manage the DID

- Manage the Indy pool
- Post the NYM, schema, and node transactions to the Indy pool ledger

Getting ready

If the Indy Docker container is stopped, use the following command to start the Indy Docker container:

```
ubuntu@ip-172-31-90-67:~/indy/indy-sdk$ sudo docker start
stoic_mendeleev
```

How to do it...

Executing the following steps will help you understand more about the Indy CLI.

Running the Indy CLI

In the `indy-sdk` directory, run `indy-cli`, as follows:

```
ubuntu@ip-172-31-90-67:~/indy/indy-sdk$ indy-cli
indy>
```

Creating, opening, and listing the wallet

Execute the following steps:

1. Create the wallet:

   ```
   indy> wallet create mywallet key
   Enter value for key:
   Wallet "mywallet" has been created
   ```

2. Open the wallet:

   ```
   indy> wallet open mywallet key
   Enter value for key:
   Wallet "mywallet" has been opened
   wallet(mywallet):indy>
   ```

3. List the wallet:

```
wallet(mywallet):indy> wallet list
+----------+---------+
| Name | Type |
+----------+---------+
| mywallet | default |
+----------+---------+
Current wallet "mywallet"
```

Creating, importing, and using the DID

Execute the following steps:

1. Import the predefined Steward DID from the `sandbox` testing network domain genesis file, `domain_transactions_genesis`. The `admindid.txt` import file is as follows:

```
{
"version": 1,
"dids": [{
"did": "Th7MpTaRZVRYnPiabds81Y",
"seed": "000000000000000000000000Steward1"
}]
}
```

2. Import the predefined Steward DID for the `sandbox` testing network:

```
wallet(mywallet):indy> did import /home/ubuntu/indy/indy-
sdk/admindid.txt
Did "Th7MpTaRZVRYnPiabds81Y" has been created with
"~7TYfekw4GUagBnBVCqPjiC" verkey
DIDs import finished
```

3. Create a new DID:

```
wallet(mywallet):indy> did new
Did "JRAoDbiV2tRfWSL3jcRKCk" has been created with
"~6iKD9dkZEypiugWbDEHsXw" verkey
```

4. List the DID in the wallet:

```
wallet(mywallet):indy> did list
+-------------------------+-------------------------+----------+
| Did | Verkey | Metadata |
+-------------------------+-------------------------+----------+
| JRAoDbiV2tRfWSL3jcRKCk | ~6iKD9dkZEypiugWbDEHsXw | - |
```

```
+-------------------------+-------------------------+-----------+
| Th7MpTaRZVRYnPiabds81Y  | ~7TYfekw4GUagBnBVCqPjiC |  -  |
+-------------------------+-------------------------+-----------+
```

5. Specify the identity that was used to send a transaction request to the Indy network. To do this, you can enter the following command:

```
wallet(mywallet):indy> did use Th7MpTaRZVRYnPiabds81Y
Did "Th7MpTaRZVRYnPiabds81Y" has been set as active
wallet(mywallet):did(Th7...81Y):indy>
```

Creating, connecting, and listing the Indy node pool

Execute the following steps:

1. Create the Indy pool configuration on the CLI using the genesis file for the sandbox testing network:

```
wallet(mywallet):did(Th7...81Y):indy>pool create sandbox
gen_txn_file=
/home/ubuntu/indy/indy_sdk/cli/docker_pool_transactions_genesis
Pool config "sandbox" has been created
```

2. To connect the Indy CLI to the created Indy pool's sandbox, use the following command:

```
wallet(mywallet):did(Th7...81Y):indy> pool connect sandbox
Pool "sandbox" has been connected
```

3. List the pool in the CLI using the pool list command:

```
pool(sandbox):wallet(mywallet):did(Th7...81Y):indy> pool list
+----------+
| Pool |
+----------+
| sandbox |
+----------+
Current pool "sandbox"
```

Sending NYM transactions to the ledger

Execute the following steps:

1. Post the new DID to the testing Indy pool's `sandbox` and assign a new DID `role` named `TRUST_ANCHOR`:

```
pool(sandbox):wallet(mywallet):did(Th7...81Y):indy> ledger nym
did=JRAoDbiV2tRfWSL3jcRKCk verkey=~6iKD9dkZEypiugWbDEHsXw
role=TRUST_ANCHOR
Nym request has been sent to Ledger.
Metadata:
+-------------------------+------------------+----------------------+-
---------------------+
| From | Sequence Number | Request ID | Transaction time |
+-------------------------+------------------+----------------------+-
---------------------+
| Th7MpTaRZVRYnPiabds81Y | 17 | 1544417908972843261 | 2018-12-10
04:58:29 |
+-------------------------+------------------+----------------------+-
---------------------+
Data:
+-------------------------+------------------------------+----------------+
| Did | Verkey | Role |
+-------------------------+------------------------------+----------------+
| JRAoDbiV2tRfWSL3jcRKCk | ~6iKD9dkZEypiugWbDEHsXw | TRUST_ANCHOR |
+-------------------------+------------------------------+----------------+
```

2. Get the NYM transaction for the DID from `ledger`:

```
pool(sandbox):wallet(mywallet):did(Th7...81Y):indy> ledger get-nym
did=JRAoDbiV2tRfWSL3jcRKCk
Following NYM has been received.
Metadata:
+-------------------------+------------------+----------------------+-
---------------------+
| Identifier | Sequence Number | Request ID | Transaction time |
+-------------------------+------------------+----------------------+-
---------------------+
| Th7MpTaRZVRYnPiabds81Y | 17 | 1544418107983346566 | 2018-12-10
04:58:29 |
+-------------------------+------------------+----------------------+-
---------------------+
Data:
+-------------------------+------------------+-------------------+------------------
-----------+----------------+
| Identifier | Dest | Verkey | Role |
+-------------------------+------------------+-------------------+------------------
```

```
---------+--------------+
| Th7MpTaRZVRYnPiabds81Y | JRAoDbiV2tRfWSL3jcRKCk |
~6iKD9dkZEypiugWbDEHsXw | TRUST_ANCHOR |
+-----------------------+-----------------------+---------------
---------+--------------+
```

Posting the credential schema and credential definition transaction to the ledger

Execute the following steps:

1. Create a sample credential schema for `ledger`:

```
pool(sandbox):wallet(mywallet):did(Th7...81Y):indy> ledger schema
name=mydriverlicense version=1.0 attr_names=name,age,licensenumber
Schema request has been sent to Ledger.
Metadata:
+-----------------------+---------------+----------------------+--
---------------------+
| From | Sequence Number | Request ID | Transaction time |
+-----------------------+---------------+----------------------+--
---------------------+
| Th7MpTaRZVRYnPiabds81Y | 18 | 1544418399030903286 | 2018-12-10
05:06:39 |
+-----------------------+---------------+----------------------+--
---------------------+
Data:
+-----------------+---------+----------------------------+
| Name | Version | Attributes |
+-----------------+---------+----------------------------+
| mydriverlicense | 1.0 | "licensenumber","age","name" |
+-----------------+---------+----------------------------+
```

2. Query the sample credential schema from `ledger`:

```
pool(sandbox):wallet(mywallet):did(Th7...81Y):indy> ledger get-
schema did=Th7MpTaRZVRYnPiabds81Y name=mydriverlicense version=1.0
Following Schema has been received.
Metadata:
+-----------------------+---------------+----------------------+--
---------------------+
| Identifier | Sequence Number | Request ID | Transaction time |
+-----------------------+---------------+----------------------+--
---------------------+
| Th7MpTaRZVRYnPiabds81Y | 18 | 1544418499351543236 | 2018-12-10
05:06:39 |
```

```
+-------------------+---------+-------------------------+--
-------------------+
Data:
+-------------------+---------+-------------------------+
| Name | Version | Attributes |
+-------------------+---------+-------------------------+
| mydriverlicense | 1.0 | "licensenumber","age","name" |
+-------------------+---------+-------------------------+
```

3. Send the testing credential definition to `ledger`. This is only necessary in order to demonstrate how the `cred-def` command works. `schema_id` and `primary` should be set based on your use case:

```
pool(sandbox):wallet(mywallet):did(Th7...81Y):indy>
ledger cred-def schema_id=18 signature_type=CL tag=1
primary={"n":"1","s":"2","rms":"3","r":{},"rctxt":"4","z":"5"}
NodeConfig request has been sent to Ledger.
Metadata:
+-------------------------+---------------+-----------------+--
-------------------+
| From | Sequence Number | Request ID | Transaction time |
+-------------------------+---------------+-----------------+--
-------------------+
| Th7MpTaRZVRYnPiabds81Y | 21 | 1544419102597743998 | 2018-12-10
05:18:22 |
+-------------------------+---------------+-----------------+--
-------------------+
Data:
+-----------------------------------------------------------+
| Primary Key |
+-----------------------------------------------------------+
| {n:"1",r:{"master_secret":"3"},rctxt:"4",s:"2",z:"5"} |
+-----------------------------------------------------------+
```

4. Query the credential definition from `ledger`:

```
pool(sandbox):wallet(mywallet):did(Th7...81Y):indy>
ledger get-cred-def schema_id=18 signature_type=CL tag=1
origin=Th7MpTaRZVRYnPiabds81Y
Following Credential Definition has been received.
Metadata:
+-------------------------+---------------+-----------------+--
-------------------+
| Identifier | Sequence Number | Request ID | Transaction time |
+-------------------------+---------------+-----------------+--
-------------------+
| Th7MpTaRZVRYnPiabds81Y | 21 | 1544419207049800109 | 2018-12-10
05:18:22 |
```

```
+-----------------------+-----------------+---------------------+--
---------------------+
Data:
+----------------------------------------------------------+
| Primary Key |
+----------------------------------------------------------+
| {n:"1",r:{"master_secret":"3"},rctxt:"4",s:"2",z:"5"} |
+----------------------------------------------------------+
```

How it works...

In the Indy CLI, you interactively specify a command to execute. The commands in Indy CLI have the following format:

```
<command-group> <command> < param-name>=<param-value>...
```

The command groups in the current version are mainly the wallet, DID, pool, and ledger.

9
Hyperledger Blockchain Scalability and Security

In previous chapters, we covered Hyperledger blockchains and tools, exploring how to set up and run smart contracts in each blockchain. But we haven't talked much about blockchain scalability, performance, and security. In this chapter, we will explore these topics. We will cover the following recipes:

- Hyperledger blockchain scalability and performance
- Hyperledger blockchain security
- Hyperledger performance measurement

Hyperledger blockchain scalability and performance

In the public blockchain, anyone can join the network to execute a transaction. Bitcoin runs a **Proof of Work** (**PoW**) based consensus algorithm with 1 block creation time of 10 minutes and a fixed block size of 1 MB. The transaction processing peak throughput is between 3.3-7 transactions per second. The six-block confirmation latency takes around one hour.

At the high-level flow process, the transaction messages are submitted to the ordering service. The orderer then receives transactions from various channels and queues up these messages per channel. The orderer creates a new block of transactions per channel and delivers the block to all peers through the gossip protocol. The gossip protocol connects the peers in the channel and broadcasts ledger and channel data in a scalable fashion. The transaction message can be communicated in the same organization or between peers in different organizations in the same channel. When adding more peers to the network, it should only affect the performance on the channel peers attended. Other channels will not be affected. The protocol decouples network operations to ensure data integrity, data consistency, and scalability. In the public bitcoin blockchain, all transactions are handled through a series of sequential operations in blocks and are added to the ledger. This sequential process will not gain much performance benefit when using powerful hardware.

In Hyperledger Fabric, consensus is taken at the ordering service. By adding more peers, you can achieve better concurrency. The ordering service is designed in a modular way as it is totally pluggable. You can also select scalable consensus mechanisms (Solo, Kafka, and BFT) for application use cases. Kafka is primarily a distributed, fault-tolerant, high-throughput message platform, which is batch-handling-capable. The Hyperledger Fabric Kafka ordering mechanism utilizes Apache Kafka to handle real-time endorsed transaction data. The ordering service, which can be set up as a cluster of orderers, processes messages with a Kafka cluster, which ensures that each orderer process receives transactions and generates blocks in the same order. This event-driven sync design makes for better performances. Kafka consensus is recommended for production use.

How to do it...

Some performance constraints in Hyperledger Fabric are as follows:

- Block-size scaling
- Endorser scaling
- Endorser policy
- Channels and resource allocation

Block-size scaling

When we increase the block size, related transaction throughput in the block will be increased, but there are many other things that can impact performance. When the block size is increased, it requires more computing power; the storage requirement will go up, and more network bandwidth will be required.

You can tune message-transaction throughput through a control-related configuration (`configtx.yaml`), provided by Fabric as follows:

```
Orderer: &OrdererDefaults

    # Orderer Type: The orderer implementation to start
    # Available types are "solo" and "kafka"
    OrdererType: solo

    Addresses:
    # Batch Timeout: The amount of time to wait before creating a batch
    BatchTimeout: 2s

    # Batch Size: Controls the number of messages batched into a block
    BatchSize:

        # Max Message Count: The maximum number of messages to permit in a batch
        MaxMessageCount: 10

        # Absolute Max Bytes: The absolute maximum number of bytes allowed for
        # the serialized messages in a batch.
        AbsoluteMaxBytes: 99 MB

        # Preferred Max Bytes: The preferred maximum number of bytes allowed for
        # the serialized messages in a batch. A message larger than the preferred
        # max bytes will result in a batch larger than preferred max bytes.
        PreferredMaxBytes: 512 KB
```

Here are some configurations:

- `MaxMessageCount`: This defines the maximum number of messages/transactions to permit in a block per batch.
- `AbsoluteMaxBytes`: This is the absolute maximum number of bytes allowed for serialized transactions/messages in a batch.
- `PreferredMaxBytes`: This is the preferred maximum number of bytes allowed in a batch. A transaction/message larger than the preferred maximum bytes will result in a batch larger than the preferred max bytes.

To get a higher throughput, you can increase `MaxMessageCount` to maximize throughput. In other cases, you can tweak parameters in `configtx.yaml` to optimize your transaction throughput.

Here is the research result, which looks at the impact of the block size and **Transaction Arrival Rate** on performance:

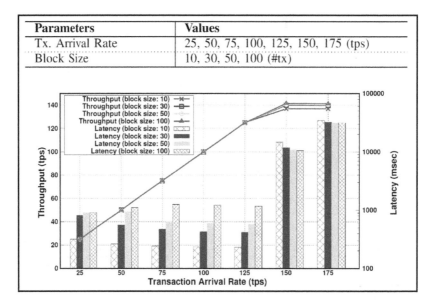

Parameters	Values
Tx. Arrival Rate	25, 50, 75, 100, 125, 150, 175 (tps)
Block Size	10, 30, 50, 100 (#tx)

When the **Transaction Arrival Rate** increases, the **Throughput** linear increases. At around **140** tps, the **Throughput** reaches the saturation point and the **Latency** increases significantly. All block sizes will have similar **Latency**. This is because, when a peer receives an ordered transaction, it invokes the **Validation System Chaincode** (**VSCC**) to determine the validity of the transaction. During the VSCC phase, the number of validation requests can grow rapidly, which can impact commit latency. When the transaction rate increases before the saturation point, a smaller block size will be faster. When the **Arrival Rate** increases, there is no impact on the endorsement and broadcast latency, but there is an impact on the **Transaction Latency**. The result of this is shown as follows:

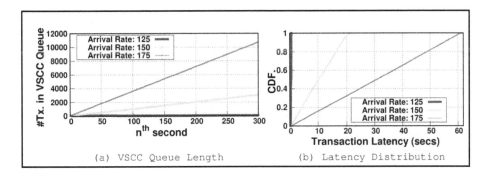

(a) VSCC Queue Length   (b) Latency Distribution

Endorser scaling

The peer message communication occurs on the same channel. When adding an endorser's node to a different channel, it should not impact the channel's performance. However, in the same channel, adding endorser nodes will significantly impact the performance throughput.

Here, we mainly focus on endorser scaling on the same channel this will add endorsers on different channels that would not have any impact on the performance. Consequently, we limit the test to one channel.

Here is the result of some research on adding **tps vs Endorsers** nodes:

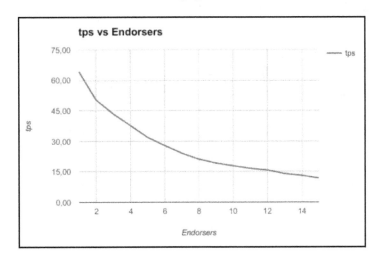

We can see that throughput drops dramatically when endorser nodes increase. When endorse execute chain code, these endorse nodes runs independently from one another. Each endorse has to exchange a message for every endorse node in the same channel. This will significantly add process efforts for each message network communication, and it will impact performance throughput. Consequently, it is typically configured to limit the number of endorsers in the same channel.

The endorser policy

Hyperledger Fabric allows the user to define an endorsement policy to instruct a peer to execute a chaincode. This invokes the VSCC to validate the transaction; the transaction result can be added to the ledger. The endorsement policy can be expressed over principals using Boolean logic syntax.

The syntax of the language is as follows:

```
EXPR (E [, E...])
```

Here are a few examples of an endorsement policy:

```
AND('Org1.member', 'Org2.member') requests 1 signature from each of the two
principals
```

```
AND('Org1.member', OR('Org2.member', 'Org3.member')) requests a member of
the Org1 MSP and either 1 signature from a member of the Org2 MSP or 1
signature from a member of the Org3 MSP.
```

Here are some research results on the impact of the endorsement policy:

CONFIGURATION TO IDENTIFY THE IMPACT OF ENDORSEMENT POLICIES.	
Parameters	**Values**
Endorsement Policy (AND/OR)	1) OR [a, b, c, d]
	2) OR [AND(a ,b), AND(a, c), AND(a, d), AND(b, c), AND(b, d), AND(C, D)]
	3) OR [AND(a ,b, c), AND(a, b, d), AND(b, c, d), AND(a, c, d)]
	4) AND [a, b, c, d]
Endorsement Policy (NOutOf)	1) 1-OutOf [a ,b ,c, d]
	2) 2-OutOf [a ,b ,c, d]
	3) 3-OutOf [a ,b ,c, d]
	4) 4-OutOf [a ,b ,c, d]
Tx. Arrival Rate	125, 150, 175 (tps)

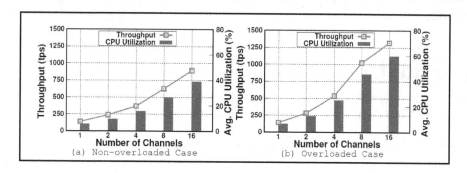

To reduce the VSCC latency and resource consumption, we can decrease the number of Fabric identities, signatures, and sub-policies.

Channels and resource allocation

Research shows that, when adding more channels, the throughput increases and latency decreases. The resource utilization also increases:

Only network members in the same channel will involve validation and then commit ledger process. Each channel transaction is isolated from the other channel. The transaction endorsement, validation, and commit can be executed in parallel when increasing the number of channels. This increases resource utilization with higher throughput.

Hyperledger blockchain security

Being different from the public blockchain, Hyperledger Fabric is a permission-based blockchain network. Here, the identity of each node is known and all participants know each other. Since all nodes can trust each other, mining power is not required in order to build trust. This allows us to select various consensus mechanisms, such as the BFT protocol. In the permission blockchain, more centralized identity management prevents Sybil attacks. Participants in the network can transfer, query, and invoke transactions that are controlled by the chain code. Enterprise applications often require complex enterprise security standards. A permissioned network is highly suitable for this scenario.

Hyperledger Fabric provides a modular CA component to issue a certificate for each member in the network. Fabric CA allows user enrollment, issuing, renewing and revoking certificates, and so on. Network users can prove their identity and ownership by providing a certificate. Authorized certificates can be used to sign the transaction and verify operations that are performed on the network. This enables ACL-based control over network activity and ensures that the network can trace every transaction for a registered user. Members of the network can be controlled to access private and confidential channel, applications, and data with ACL-based control. The authorized participants in the channel can share and exchange digitized assets in a secure manner. The secure channel has a corresponding ledger that contains the transaction ledger data and updatable world state data. Each peer in the channel stores their own copy of ledger.

In this section, we will set up the Fabric CA client and server. We will then generate a user identity and register and enroll the identity.

How to do it...

You need the prerequisite software before you install the Fabric CA server. Install the Go 1.10+ installation and ensure that the GOPATH environment variable is set correctly.

You can refer to Chapter 1, *Working with Hyperledger Fabric*, for more information on how to install Go.

The Fabric CA server

Execute the following steps:

1. Set up the Golang development environment:

   ```
   mkdir go
   export GOPATH=/home/ubuntu/go
   export PATH=/usr/local/go/bin:$GOPATH/bin/:$PATH
   ```

2. Install the `libtool` and `libtdhl-dev` packages:

   ```
   sudo apt install libtoollibltdl-dev
   ```

3. Install `fabric-ca-server` and `fabric-ca-client`:

   ```
   go get -u github.com/hyperledger/fabric-ca/cmd/...
   ```

   This will install the `fabric-ca-server` and `fabric-ca-client` binary. Once installed, check to make sure you have `fabric-ca-client` and `fabric-ca-server` installed under `$GOPATH/bin`:

   ```
   ubuntu@ip-172-31-7-32:~/go$ ls -lrt
   total 12
   drwxrwxr-x 3 ubuntu ubuntu 4096 Jan 25 05:30 src
   drwxrwxr-x 3 ubuntu ubuntu 4096 Jan 25 05:30 pkg
   drwxrwxr-x 2 ubuntu ubuntu 4096 Jan 25 05:30 bin
   ubuntu@ip-172-31-7-32:~/go$ cd bin
   ubuntu@ip-172-31-7-32:~/go/bin$ ls -lrt
   total 41340
   -rwxrwxr-x 1 ubuntu ubuntu 19629432 Jan 25 05:30 fabric-ca-client
   -rwxrwxr-x 1 ubuntu ubuntu 22698344 Jan 25 05:30 fabric-ca-server
   ```

4. Start `fabric-ca-server` by entering the following command:

   ```
   fabric-ca-server start -b admin:adminpw
   ```

The output is as follows:

This starts `fabric-ca-server`, which is listening on port `7054`.

The Fabric CA client

You just started `fabric-ca-server`. Open the second Terminal and make sure you have set up the Go path in the same way as the `admin` Terminal. Let's enroll `admin` by running the `fabric-ca-client` enroll:

```
fabric-ca-client enroll -u http://admin:adminpw@localhost:7054
```

The `fabric-ca-client` command points to the Fabric CA server's default address, `localhost:7054`. If all goes well, you should see the following client and server Terminal screen:

The Fabric CA server received the enroll request from a Fabric CA client-signed certificate with a serial number. In the Fabric CA client window, we can see root CA, **Enrollment Certificate** (**ECert**), corresponding private key and CA certificate chain PEM files are stored under the `fabric-ca/clients/admin/msp` directory.

The Fabric CA database

By default, Fabric CA uses SQLite as a database to store user information. In the previous step, we enrolled an admin user in the SQLite database. Let's check whether this user is stored in our SQLite database. Let's install SQLite first:

1. Execute the following install command to install `sqlite3`:

   ```
   sudo apt-get update
   sudo apt-get install sqlite3
   ```

2. Once installation is complete, start the SQLite server and connect to `fabric-ca-server.db`:

   ```
   sqlite3 fabric-ca-server.db
   ```

   This will enter the SQLite CLI. For this, we can issue a few SQLite commands.

3. Let's check the existing database by entering the following command:

   ```
   sqlite3> .database
   ```

4. Now we will check the existing table:

   ```
   sqlite3> .table
   ```

   Here are the results:

```
ubuntu@ip-172-31-7-32:~$ sqlite3 fabric-ca-server.db
SQLite version 3.11.0 2016-02-15 17:29:24
Enter ".help" for usage hints.
sqlite> .database
seq  name                 file
---  -------------------  -------------------------------------------------------------
0    main                 /home/ubuntu/fabric-ca-server.db
sqlite> .table
affiliations              properties
certificates              revocation_authority_info
credentials               users
nonces
sqlite>
```

5. Let's check enrolled user records from the `users` table:

```
sqlite3> select * from users;
```

```
sqlite> select * from users;
admin|$2a$10$uw23OvnwyeZMOBGfbP5eDerBAdoj7VNSXg48vQQ58jdvkrJltdU52|client|||[{"name":"hf.GenCRL","value":"1"},{"name":"hf.Registrar.Attributes","value":"*
"},{"name":"hf.AffiliationMgr","value":"1"},{"name":"hf.Registrar.Roles","value":"*"},{"name":"hf.Registrar.DelegateRoles","value":"*"},{"name":"hf.Revok
er","value":"1"},{"name":"hf.IntermediateCA","value":"1"}]|1|-1|2|0
sqlite>
```

We can see that the `admin` user was stored under a `users` table. Now we can register new user with the enrollment ID as `admin2`, `affiliation` as `org1.department1`, the `hf.Revoker` attribute set as `true`, and the `admin` attribute set as `true:ecert`. The `:ecert` suffix means that a user's enrollment certificate will contain the `admin` attribute, and can be used for later access-control decisions. Here is the command:

```
fabric-ca-client register --id.name admin2 --id.affiliation
org1.department1 --id.attrs 'hf.Revoker=true,admin=true:ecert'
```

6. In SQLite, run `select * from users` again. You can now see that a new user, `admin2`, was added to the database successfully:

```
sqlite> select * from users;
admin|$2a$10$uw23OvnwyeZMOBGfbP5eDerBAdoj7VNSXg48vQQ58jdvkrJltdU52|client|||[{"name":"hf.GenCRL","value":"1"},{"name":"hf.Registrar.Attributes","value":"*
"},{"name":"hf.AffiliationMgr","value":"1"},{"name":"hf.Registrar.Roles","value":"*"},{"name":"hf.Registrar.DelegateRoles","value":"*"},{"name":"hf.Revok
er","value":"1"},{"name":"hf.IntermediateCA","value":"1"}]|1|-1|2|0
sqlite> select * from users;
admin|$2a$10$uw23OvnwyeZMOBGfbP5eDerBAdoj7VNSXg48vQQ58jdvkrJltdU52|client|||[{"name":"hf.GenCRL","value":"1"},{"name":"hf.Registrar.Attributes","value":"*
"},{"name":"hf.AffiliationMgr","value":"1"},{"name":"hf.Registrar.Roles","value":"*"},{"name":"hf.Registrar.DelegateRoles","value":"*"},{"name":"hf.Revok
er","value":"1"},{"name":"hf.IntermediateCA","value":"1"}]|2|-1|2|0
admin2|$2a$10$XV5qKgg2ZwbnEfpd0CUbAOKxR053d3N9R26r.cDHaWigk/.hD.BC|client|org1.department1|[{"name":"hf.Revoker","value":"true"},{"name":"admin","value"
:"true","ecert":true},{"name":"hf.EnrollmentID","value":"admin2","ecert":true},{"name":"hf.Type","value":"client","ecert":true},{"name":"hf.Affiliation",
"value":"org1.department1","ecert":true}]|0|-1|2|0
sqlite>
```

How it works...

The following diagram illustrates the Fabric CA architecture:

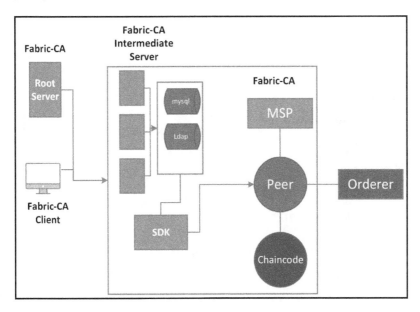

The Fabric CA **Root Server** is the root node of the entire CA tree. This connects a cluster of intermediate Fabric CA servers to manage the Fabric identity and certificates. The intermediate Fabric CA server connects to a database of stored user data to keep track of a user's identity and certificate. The Fabric CA client connects to these severs through the Fabric SDK.

When the fabric CA server starts, the server will generate several default configuration files and the `.pem` key files:

`fabric-ca-server-config.yaml, ca-cert.pem, IssuerPublicKey, fabric-ca-server.db`

`fabric-ca-server-config.yaml` defines various `fabric-ca-server` commands, including the `port` number, `db` configuration, `registry` identities information, and `ca` configuration.

Here is an example of `fabric-ca-server-config.yaml`:

```yaml
port: 7054
tls:
  enabled: false
  certfile:
  keyfile:
  clientauth:
    type: noclientcert
    certfiles:
ca:
  name:
  keyfile:
  certfile:
  chainfile:
registry:
  maxenrollments: -1
  identities:
    - name: <<<adminUserName>>>
      pass: <<<adminPassword>>>
      type: client
      affiliation: ""
      attrs:
        hf.Registrar.Roles: "*"
        hf.Registrar.DelegateRoles: "*"
        hf.Revoker: true
        hf.IntermediateCA: true
        hf.GenCRL: true
        hf.Registrar.Attributes: "*"
        hf.AffiliationMgr: true
db:
  type: sqlite3
  datasource: fabric-ca-server.db
  tls:
      enabled: false
      certfiles:
      client:
        certfile:
        keyfile:
affiliations:
  org1:
    - department1
    - department2
  org2:
    - department1
signing:
    default:
      usage:
        - digital signature
      expiry: 8760h
```

The configuration file can be modified per application need.

The `fabric-ca-client` tool reads the `fabric-ca-client-config.yaml` configuration to communicate with `fabric-ca-server`. By executing a client-side command, it can enroll, register, and invoke a user from `fabric-ca-client`. Here is a high-level `fabric-ca-client` config file:

```yaml
# URL of the Fabric-ca-server (default: http://localhost:7054)
url: <<<URL>>>
mspdir: msp
tls:
    # TLS section for secure socket connection
    certfiles:
    client:
      certfile:
      keyfile:
csr:
    cn: <<<ENROLLMENT_ID>>>
    keyrequest:
      algo: ecdsa
      size: 256
    serialnumber:
    names:
       - C: US
         ST: North Carolina
         L:
         O: Hyperledger
         OU: Fabric
    hosts:
      - <<<MYHOST>>>
    name:
    type:
    affiliation:
    maxenrollments: 0
    attributes:
enrollment:
    profile:
    label:
caname:
bccsp:
    default: SW
    sw:
        hash: SHA2
        security: 256
        filekeystore:
            # The directory used for the software file-based keystore
            keystore: msp/keystore
```

The config file defines the connection URL to the `fabric-ca-server`. `msp` location, `tlsconfiguration`, enrollment details, and so on. By tuning these configurations, `fabric-ca-client` can control how we generate client security files and environment variables.

Hyperledger performance measurement

In a blockchain system, we are expecting to get its optimum performance. The goal of any performance evaluation is to cover system-wide measures' transaction throughput or latency, as well as the overall OS, network- and blockchain-level IO, and its availability.

A benchmark should be relevant and understandable. It is the process of making standard measurements to run a test plan based on a set of criteria, conditions, or a program by which the performance is evaluated. The results of the analysis should be easily understandable, and both users and vendors must be satisfied that the results of the analysis are unbiased.

One of the Hyperledger projects develops a blockchain benchmark tool for blockchain-performance benchmarking. This tool is **Hyperledger Caliper**. It integrates with multiple existing enterprise blockchains and allows the user to measure blockchain performance with a predefined use case as well as generating performance test reports. These reports contain a standard performance indicator defined by the Hyperledger performance and Scale Working Group. Caliper provides **Northbound Interfaces** (**NBIs**) interfaces to help to implement test cases. Currently, Caliper supports multiple blockchain solutions including the following:

- Fabric (v1.0+)
- Burrow 1.0
- Sawtooth 1.0+
- Iroha 1.0 beta-3
- Hyperledger Composer

Caliper measures several key metrics for blockchain in the test result. These are as follows:

Success rate, fail rate, transaction send rate, transaction/read latency (maximum, minimum, average) and transaction/read throughput:

Following is a test result:

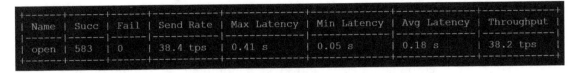

Name	Succ	Fail	Send Rate	Max Latency	Min Latency	Avg Latency	Throughput
open	583	0	38.4 tps	0.41 s	0.05 s	0.18 s	38.2 tps

Here is another test result:

```
info: [bench-flow.js]: ###test result:###
info: [bench-flow.js]:
+--------+------+------+-----------+-------------+-------------+-------------+------------+
| Name   | Succ | Fail | Send Rate | Max Latency | Min Latency | Avg Latency | Throughput |
+--------+------+------+-----------+-------------+-------------+-------------+------------+
| query  | 0    | 15   | 7.3 tps   | 0.00 s      | 100000.00 s | NaN s       | 0.0 tps    |
+--------+------+------+-----------+-------------+-------------+-------------+------------+
```

Transaction/latency is the time between the response being received and the request being submitted. Transaction/read throughput is calculated using the following formula:

Transaction Throughput = Total committed transactions / total time in seconds @ #committed nodes

This is the rate in which valid transactions are committed across all of the nodes in a blockchain network. This rate is typically expressed as **Transaction Per Second** (**TPS**). Resource statistics are also included in the report summary. This shows resource TYPE (Process, Docker), Memory (max, avg), CPU (max, avg), network IO (Traffic In, Traffic Out) and disc IO (Disc Read, Disc Write):

Getting ready

Before we start, make sure you have installed required prerequisites for the following tools:

- Node.js 8.x
- node-gyp
- Docker
- Docker Compose

How to do it...

Log in to Ubuntu and get the Caliper project under the default home directory. Execute the following git command:

```
git clone https://github.com/hyperledger/caliper.git
```

This will download all of the Caliper project source code. Here is the Caliper project structure:

```
ubuntu@ip-172-31-5-77:~/caliper$ ls -lrt
total 248
-rw-rw-r--   1 ubuntu ubuntu    1538 Jan 21 03:32 README.md
-rw-rw-r--   1 ubuntu ubuntu    1580 Jan 21 03:32 PULL_REQUEST_TEMPLATE.md
-rw-rw-r--   1 ubuntu ubuntu   11358 Jan 21 03:32 LICENSE
-rw-rw-r--   1 ubuntu ubuntu    1318 Jan 21 03:32 ISSUE_TEMPLATE.md
-rw-rw-r--   1 ubuntu ubuntu    2571 Jan 21 03:32 CONTRIBUTING.md
drwxrwxr-x   2 ubuntu ubuntu    4096 Jan 21 03:32 config
drwxrwxr-x   7 ubuntu ubuntu    4096 Jan 21 03:32 benchmark
drwxrwxr-x   2 ubuntu ubuntu    4096 Jan 21 03:32 scripts
drwxrwxr-x   8 ubuntu ubuntu    4096 Jan 21 03:32 network
drwxrwxr-x   4 ubuntu ubuntu    4096 Jan 21 03:32 test
drwxrwxr-x   6 ubuntu ubuntu    4096 Jan 21 03:32 src
drwxrwxr-x   2 ubuntu ubuntu    4096 Jan 21 06:23 log
drwxrwxr-x   4 ubuntu ubuntu    4096 Jan 21 06:23 coverage
drwxrwxr-x 340 ubuntu ubuntu   16384 Jan 21 07:04 node_modules
-rw-rw-r--   1 ubuntu ubuntu    2834 Jan 21 07:04 package.json
-rw-rw-r--   1 ubuntu ubuntu  169315 Jan 21 07:04 package-lock.json
```

Installing dependencies

In this section, we will use Caliper to test Fabric blockchain performance. Currently, Caliper's stable version is v1.1.0. We need to make sure all of our dependency's libraries match this version. We first need to install `grpc`, `fabric-ca-client`, and `fabric-client` under the `Caliper` folder and make sure all three of these node libraries are `1.10.0`:

```
npm install grpc@1.10.0
npm install fabric-ca-client@1.10.0
npm install fabric-client@1.10.0
```

Running the benchmark

Once all dependencies are installed, navigate to the benchmark folder. There are several predefined benchmarks under this folder:

```
ubuntu@ip-172-31-5-77:~/caliper/benchmark$ ls -lrt
total 20
drwxrwxr-x 3 ubuntu ubuntu 4096 Jan 21 03:32 smallbank
drwxrwxr-x 2 ubuntu ubuntu 4096 Jan 21 03:32 marbles
drwxrwxr-x 2 ubuntu ubuntu 4096 Jan 21 03:32 drm
drwxrwxr-x 4 ubuntu ubuntu 4096 Jan 21 03:40 composer
drwxrwxr-x 2 ubuntu ubuntu 4096 Jan 21 07:06 simple
```

You can run these benchmarks by entering npm test - benchmark_name. Let's run a simple benchmark:

```
ubuntu@ip-172-31-5-77:~/caliper/benchmark$ npm test -- simple
```

This will run a simple benchmark-performance test. If everything runs fine, you should see that the following report stats are printed in the console:

```
info: [bench-flow.js]: ###test result:###
info: [bench-flow.js]:
+------+------+------+-----------+-------------+-------------+-------------+------------+
| Name | Succ | Fail | Send Rate | Max Latency | Min Latency | Avg Latency | Throughput |
+------+------+------+-----------+-------------+-------------+-------------+------------+
| open | 583  | 0    | 38.4 tps  | 0.41 s      | 0.05 s      | 0.18 s      | 38.2 tps   |
+------+------+------+-----------+-------------+-------------+-------------+------------+

info: [bench-flow.js]: ### resource stats ###
info: [bench-flow.js]:
+---------+------------------------------+-------------+-------------+----------+----------+------------+-------------+-----------+------------+
| TYPE    | NAME                         | Memory(max) | Memory(avg) | CPU(max) | CPU(avg) | Traffic In | Traffic Out | Disc Read | Disc Write |
+---------+------------------------------+-------------+-------------+----------+----------+------------+-------------+-----------+------------+
| Process | node local-client.js(avg)    | 102.9MB     | 101.1MB     | 33.01%   | 10.24%   | --         | --          | --        | --         |
| Docker  | dev-peer0.org2.example.co...1e-v0 | 43.9MB  | 41.6MB      | 8.67%    | 5.49%    | 1.1MB      | 579.9KB     | 0B        | 0B         |
| Docker  | dev-peer0.org1.example.co...1e-v0 | 44.1MB  | 41.8MB      | 8.83%    | 5.46%    | 1.1MB      | 581.2KB     | 0B        | 0B         |
| Docker  | dev-peer0.org1.example.co...es-v1 | 45.7MB  | 45.7MB      | 0.00%    | 0.00%    | 0B         | 0B          | 0B        | 0B         |
| Docker  | dev-peer0.org2.example.co...es-v1 | 45.7MB  | 45.7MB      | 0.00%    | 0.00%    | 0B         | 0B          | 0B        | 0B         |
| Docker  | peer0.org2.example.com       | 273.9MB     | 271.4MB     | 26.53%   | 15.46%   | 3.7MB      | 6.4MB       | 56.0KB    | 3.8MB      |
| Docker  | peer0.org1.example.com       | 277.0MB     | 274.3MB     | 26.40%   | 15.75%   | 3.7MB      | 8.8MB       | 0B        | 3.0MB      |
| Docker  | orderer.example.com          | 18.1MB      | 15.0MB      | 12.43%   | 7.25%    | 2.6MB      | 4.9MB       | 56.0KB    | 2.7MB      |
| Docker  | ca.org2.example.com          | 4.9MB       | 4.9MB       | 0.00%    | 0.00%    | 0B         | 0B          | 0B        | 0B         |
| Docker  | ca.org1.example.com          | 7.6MB       | 6.7MB       | 0.00%    | 0.00%    | 0B         | 0B          | 0B        | 0B         |
+---------+------------------------------+-------------+-------------+----------+----------+------------+-------------+-----------+------------+
```

The test report present under the `simple` folder:

```
ubuntu@ip-172-31-5-77:~/caliper/benchmark/simple$ ls -lrt
total 60
-rw-rw-r-- 1 ubuntu ubuntu  675 Jan 21 03:32 query.js
-rw-rw-r-- 1 ubuntu ubuntu 2033 Jan 21 03:32 open.js
-rw-rw-r-- 1 ubuntu ubuntu 2704 Jan 21 03:32 main.js
-rw-rw-r-- 1 ubuntu ubuntu  689 Jan 21 03:32 config-zookeeper.yaml
-rw-rw-r-- 1 ubuntu ubuntu  914 Jan 21 03:32 config.yaml
-rw-rw-r-- 1 ubuntu ubuntu  545 Jan 21 03:32 config-sawtooth.yaml
-rw-rw-r-- 1 ubuntu ubuntu 1763 Jan 21 03:32 config-record-replay-rate.yaml
-rw-rw-r-- 1 ubuntu ubuntu  607 Jan 21 03:32 config-linear-rate.yaml
-rw-rw-r-- 1 ubuntu ubuntu  553 Jan 21 03:32 config-iroha.yaml
-rw-rw-r-- 1 ubuntu ubuntu  611 Jan 21 03:32 config-file.yaml
-rw-rw-r-- 1 ubuntu ubuntu  985 Jan 21 03:32 config-feedback-rate.yaml
-rw-rw-r-- 1 ubuntu ubuntu  911 Jan 21 03:32 config-composite-rate.yaml
-rw-r--r-- 1 root   root   8740 Jan 21 07:06 report-20190121T070659.html
```

If you open a generated HTML report file, you should see the following report page:

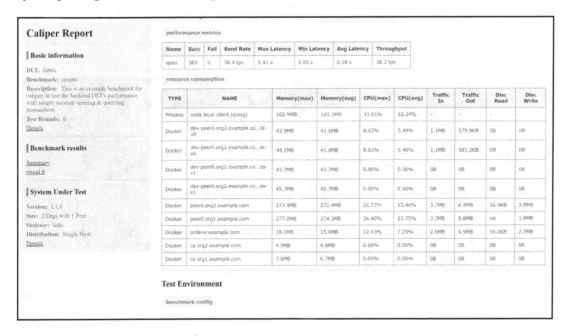

This gives a lot of detailed information about the performance-measurement matrix. This information will help you to diagnose and troubleshoot various performance problems.

How it works...

The following diagram gives you an overview of Caliper's entire architecture and the hierarchy of each of the components:

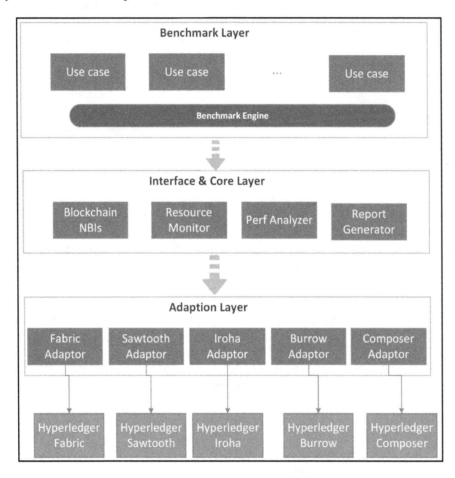

There are four layers in Caliper: **Benchmark Layer**, **Interface** and **Core Layer**, **Adaption Layer**, and the actual blockchain. These layers, which decouple each other, can easily plug in and out to call the needed components.

The adaption layer

The adaption layer is directly connected to an existing blockchain network. There are various types of adapter, including Fabric, Burrow, Sawtooth, Iroha, and Composer. Each adaptor implements the Caliper blockchain NBI by using a related blockchain SDK or RESTful API. Caliper NBIs are interfaces that define common blockchain operation methods, which can interact with blockchain network. Similarly to the Fabric CLI container, you can install, instantiate, invoke, and query smart contacts from the ledger. The NBIs can be used for an application's client to write tests for multiple supported blockchain systems.

The interface and core layer

The interface and core layer connects the adaption layer and benchmark application layer. It provides an NBI interface to interact with the application layer. This layer implements core functions defined in the NBI. Here are four kinds of NBI provided in the NBI interface:

- **Blockchain operating interfaces**: These define deploying smart contracts, invoking contracts, and querying ledger state data.
- **Resource monitor**: This reads key-resource metrics information from blockchain, including transaction latency, read throughput, and resource stats. It provides two kinds of monitors: one to watch local processes, and one to watch local or remote docker containers.
- **Performance analyzer**: This is a utility that analyzes the predefined performance statistics (including TPS, delay, and success ratio) during the performance test with the help of the predefined configuration file. It also provides a benchmark result. The tool records the system's key metrics while invoking NBI functions, such as committing transaction, querying the blockchain data, and updating the state.
- **Report generator**: This is responsible for generating an HTML-format testing report and printing a report summary in the console.

The application layer

The application layer is known as the **benchmark layer**; this contains a predefined benchmark test case. Caliper has some predefined test cases. Each test has a set of configuration files. It defines the test flow, blockchain network configuration, and performance-related test arguments. Here are simple test case configuration files:

```
test:
  name: simple
  clients:
    type: local
    number: 5
  rounds:
  - label: query
    txNumber:
    - 1000
    rateControl:
    - type: fixed-rate
      opts:
        tps: 100
    callback: benchmark/simple/query.js
monitor:
  type:
  - docker
  - process
  docker:
    name:
    - all
  process:
  - command: node
    arguments: local-client.js
    multiOutput: avg
  interval: 1
```

The `rounds` configuration defines how many rounds are needed to execute `test`. For each round, `label` defines a `test` function, `name`, while `txNumber` defines an array of sub-round test numbers. `rateControl` specified the `type` of rate and submission rate for the transaction. In the `monitor` section, `type` defines the supported resources type (for example, `docker` and `process`). The `docker` container list in the file will be watched. The `process` section defines how to execute a command during the test.

Caliper also provides a default network configuration file under the `network` folder. For example, our simple Fabric test case network file can be found under `caliper/network/fabric-v1.2`.

These configuration files specify how to interact with **System Under Test** (SUT):

```
{
  "caliper" : {
    "blockchain": "fabric",
    "command" : {
      "start": "docker-compose -f network/fabric-v1.2/customdomain/docker-compose-tls.yaml up -d"
      "end" : "docker-compose -f network/fabric-v1.2/customdomain/docker-compose-tls.yaml down;do
    }
  },
  "fabric": {
    "cryptodir": "network/fabric-v1.2/customdomain/crypto-config",
    "network": {
      "orderer": {
        "url": "grpcs://localhost:7050",
        "mspid": "OrdererMSP",
        "domain": "mydomain.com",
        "user": {
          "key": ".../key.pem",
          "cert": ".../Admin@mydomain.com-cert.pem"
        },
        "server-hostname": "orderer.mydomain.com",
        "tls_cacerts": ".../tls/ca.crt"
      },
      "org1": {
        "name": "peerOrg1",
        "mspid": "org1MSP",
        "domain": "org1.mydomain.com",
        "user": {..},
        "ca": {...},
        "peer1": {..},
      }
    },
    "channel": [
      {
        "name": "mychannel",
        "config": "network/fabric-v1.2/customdomain/mychannel.tx",
        "organizations": ["org1", "org6"],
        "deployed": false
      }
    ],
    "chaincodes": [
      {"id": "simple",
       "path": "src/contract/fabric/simple/node",
       "language":"node", "version": "v0", "channel": "mychannel"}
    ]
  }
}
```

The Fabric network configuration file defines the node's (`orderer` and `org1`) information; these configurations control how to submit and validate a transaction. It also contains channel configuration and the participant's information. Chain code specifies the channel `id`, deploy `path`, chaincode `language`, and the `information` channel.

Once we have started running the Caliper test, the benchmark engine will start to benchmark the master. It will then execute a default test flow, which consists of four stages:

- **Preparation stage**: In this stage, the master prepares the test context, deploys and installs smart contract to the network, and then starts the monitor tool to watch resource consumption of the backend blockchain system.
- **Test execution stage**: In this stage, the master assigns tasks to the test client. Each test client is used to execute the test case according to the specific benchmark configuration, such as the rate controller and transaction count. Each test case script defines interactions with the SUT. In this stage, the master starts a loop to perform tests according to the benchmark configuration file. Tasks will be generated and assigned to clients according to the defined workload. Performance statistics returned by clients will be stored for later analysis.
- **Performance analysis stage**: During the test run, performance statistics were returned by the test client. The performance analyzer utilized this data to analyze and measure the key-performance matrix.
- **Test report stage**: The report generator gathers test results and generates an HTML-format test report.

Here is the benchmark engine test process:

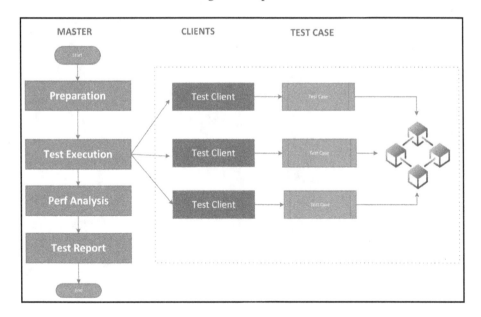

See also

- Parth Thakkar. (2018). *Performance Benchmarking and OptimizingHyperledger Fabric Blockchain Platform*. Retrieved on January 23, 2019 from `https://arxiv.org/pdf/1805.11390.pdf`
- Mattias Scherer. (2018). *Performance and Scalability of Blockchain Networks and Smart Contracts*. Retrieved on January 23, 2019 from `http://www.diva-portal.org/smash/record.jsf?pid=diva2%3A1111497dswid=-8085`

Hyperledger Blockchain Ecosystem

This chapter mainly targets those who are relatively new to distributed ledger technology and permissioned blockchains. The primary goal is to explore Hyperledger blockchain concepts, to equip you with the necessary knowledge and important technical design methodology of the Hyperledger ecosystem, and then learn when to apply these technologies through real-world use cases. The materials included in this chapter will help you better understand later chapters, and will make it easier for you to complete the recipes included in this cookbook.

A good analogy would be the making of a delicious dish. A chef would first need to know what ingredients and seasonings they should use, then prepare them before they can actually start creating the recipe.

For those who already have a good understanding of how the Hyperledger ecosystem works, this chapter would be a good *one-stop shop* review. Or feel free to jump to the chapter that interests you the most and come back for information when needed.

The following recipes will be covered in this chapter:

- An introduction to the Hyperledger family
- Building the Hyperledger framework layers
- Solving business problems with Hyperledger

Without further ado, let's take a look at the Hyperledger ecosystem and gear you up for the rest of the book.

An introduction to the Hyperledger family

The Linux Foundation has made significant accomplishments since its inception in 2000. In December 2015, The Linux Foundation announced the Hyperledger project as an open source environment for analyzing, building, and collaborating on the development of distributed ledger systems. The creation of the Hyperledger project has helped to attract many major participants including IBM, Oracle, Cisco, Red Hat, and Accenture.

Notably, Hyperledger focuses primarily on building distributed ledger solutions for permissioned blockchains and consortium networks. It is gaining popularity among large technology companies. Financial players have undoubtedly given blockchain technology substantial exposure as well.

At its core, Hyperledger is an umbrella project of modular open source frameworks and tools for building and experimenting with blockchains. Hyperledger refers to its design as *the greenhouse for enterprise blockchains*. It aims to be an incubator for developing practical applications and business solutions with blockchain technology.

New projects are being added to the Hyperledger ecosystem constantly. At the time of writing, it consists of 10 active projects. Each project has its unique advantages and offers various functionalities. Among the 10 current projects with stable releases, 5 are frameworks and 5 are utility tools.

We will do a high-level overview of the projects here. More details on individual frameworks and tools can be found in throughout the book.

The framework projects

The framework projects aim to provide platforms to build a variety of distributed ledgers and their components. They are as follows:

- **Hyperledger Fabric**: Fabric is the most popular Hyperledger framework. Smart contracts (also known as **chaincode**) are written in Golang and JavaScript, and run in Docker containers. Fabric is known for its extensibility and allows enterprises to build distributed ledger networks on top of an established and successful architecture.

- **Hyperledger Sawtooth**: Sawtooth is the second project to reach 1.0 release maturity. Sawtooth-core is written in Python, while Sawtooth Raft and Sawtooth Sabre are written in Rust. It also has JavaScript and Golang components. Sawtooth supports both permissioned and permissionless deployments. It supports the EVM through a collaboration with the Hyperledger Burrow.
- **Hyperledger Burrow**: Burrow is the first permissioned ledger that supports EVM. It is written in Go and heavily focuses on being a deterministic smart contract engine.
- **Hyperledger Indy**: Indy is built explicitly for decentralized identity management. The server portion, Indy node, is built in Python, while the Indy SDK is written in Rust. It offers tools and reusable components to manage digital identities on blockchains or other distributed ledgers.
- **Hyperledger Iroha**: Iroha is designed to target the creation and management of complex digital assets and identities. It is written in C++ and is end user friendly. Iroha has a powerful role-based model for access control and supports complex analytics.

The tool projects

The tool projects provide a set of utilities to make working with blockchain networks easier. These tools range from performance measurement, on-demand deployment, and building a business network with existing business models. The following are the highlights of the Hyperledger tools:

- **Hyperledger Composer**: Composer is a suite of tools used for the fast creation of blockchain business networks and is written in JavaScript. It is the most active tool in terms of development activities. Composer is designed to accelerate the integration of blockchain applications and smart contracts with existing business models.
- **Hyperledger Explorer**: Explorer provides a dashboard for peering into block details which are primarily written in JavaScript. Explorer can also be integrated with authentication platforms and supports the Hyperledger Sawtooth framework with its typescript-based, Angular-built iteration.

- **Hyperledger Caliper**: Caliper is a benchmark tool for measuring blockchain performance and is written in JavaScript. It utilizes indicators such as **Transactions Per Second** (**TPS**), transaction latency, and resource utilization. Caliper is a unique general tool and has become a useful reference for enterprises to measure the performance of their distributed ledgers.
- **Hyperledger Cello**: Cello brings the on-demand deployment model to blockchains and is written in the Go language. Cello is an automated application for deploying and managing blockchains in the form of plug-and-play, particularly for enterprises looking to integrate distributed ledger technologies. It also provides a real-time dashboard for blockchain statuses, system utilization, chain code performance, and the configuration of blockchains. It currently supports Hyperledger Fabric.
- **Hyperledger Quilt**: Quilt is the interoperability tool between ledger systems and is written in Java by implementing the **Interledger Protocol** (**ILP**) for atomic swaps. Quilt is an enterprise-grade implementation of the ILP, and provides libraries and reference implementations for the core Interledger components used for payment networks.

Now that we have the big picture of the Hyperledger ecosystem, we are ready to discuss some key design concepts of Hyperledger business blockchains .

Building the Hyperledger framework layers

Before we deep dive into how the Hyperledger framework works, it would be a good idea to have a basic understanding of the Hyperledger philosophy.

The Hyperledger design philosophy at a glance

To address the diversity of requirements from different industries, all Hyperledger projects must follow the same design philosophy, which is as follows:

- **Modular**: The Hyperledger architecture working group defines functional modules to address common issues, including policy, consensus, cryptography, identity, and smart contracts. This modular approach allows different developer communities to work independently, while developing extensible frameworks using reusable common building blocks.

- **Highly secure**: It is essential to provide robust security for distributed ledgers in order to keep valuable data safe and enable enterprise blockchains to involve. Hyperledger projects follow the best practices, specified by The Linux Foundation's core infrastructure initiative, and support security by design. All Hyperledger algorithms and protocols are reviewed and audited by security experts and open source communities on a regular basis. More information can be found at https://www.coreinfrastructure.org/.

- **Interoperable**: In order to support interoperability and increased demand for distributed ledger technologies, most Hyperledger smart contracts and applications should be portable across different blockchain networks.

- **Cryptocurrency-agnostic**: Hyperledger projects are independent and agnostic of all tokens, altcoins and cryptocurrencies. However, Hyperledger will not issue its own cryptocurrencies. The purpose of Hyperledger is to build enterprise blockchain software, not to manage cryptocurrencies of any sort.

- **APIs**: Each Hyperledger project provides a rich set of APIs to support interoperability with other systems. These easy-to-use APIs help blockchain technologies expand across a variety of industries.

 Refer to the official Hyperledger website and publications for more detail about these ideas.

Now let's take a look at how the Hyperledger framework works.

Framework architecture overview

The Hyperledger architecture working group has defined nine business blockchain components, as shown in the following table:

Table 1: Hyperledger Business blockchain components	
Business Blockchain Component	**Key Functions / Responsibilities**
Consensus Layer	+ Generates an order agreement + Confirms correctness of block transactions; depends on Smart Contract Layer to validate transactions
Smart Contract Layer	+ Processes transaction requests + Validates transactions by executing business logic
Communication Layer	+ Transports peer-to-peer messages between nodes within a shared ledger instance
Data Store Abstraction	+ Allows other modules to use different data stores
Crypto Abstraction	+ Allows swap-out of different crypto algorithms with no impact to other modules
Identity Services	+ Establishes root of trust during initial setup of a blockchain instance + Enable identities and/or system entities enrollment, registration and changes management during network operation + Provides authentication and authorization
Policy Service	+ Manages various policies as specified by the system, including endorsement, consensus and group management policy + Interfaces and relies on other modules to enforce the polices
APIs	+ Enables applications/clients to interface with blockchains
Interoperation	+ Supports interoperation between different instances

Among the nine components, the consensus layer and smart contract layer are fundamental to a business blockchain. So, let's learn more about them.

The consensus layer

To satisfy various business requirements, several different consensus mechanisms are being worked on within the Hyperledger community. There are two major types of consensus:

- **Permissioned lottery-based algorithms**: Including **Proof of Elapsed Time (PoET)** and **Proof of Work (PoW)**
- **Permissioned voting-based algorithms**: Including **Redundant Byzantine Fault Tolerance (RBFT)** and Paxos

For a list of consensus algorithms and types, their pros and cons, along with the corresponding Hyperledger framework, check out the following table:

Table 2: Hyperledger Framework Consensus Algorithms / Types			
Hyperledger Framework	**Consensus Algorithm/ Type**	**Consensus Pros**	**Consensus Cons**
Fabric	Kafka / Permissioned voting-base; Order is done by leader; Only in-sync replicas can be leader	Offers crash fault tolerance, good speed of finality	Not Byzantine fault tolerant, system might not reach agreement in the case of malicious nodes
Sawtooth	PoET / Permissioned lottery-based, pluggable elect -ion strategy	Provides scalability and Byzantine fault tolerance	Moderate speed of finality, might need to resolve forks
Indy	RBFT / Permissioned voting-based strategy. Only orders requested by master instance are executed.	Offers Byzantine fault tolerance, good speed of finality	All nodes in the network are known and must be all connected; more nodes will need more time to reach consensus
Iroha	Sumeragi / Permissioned server reputation system	Offers Byzantine fault tolerance, good speed of finality	All nodes in the network are known and must be all connected; more nodes will need more time to reach consensus

Smart contracts

A smart contract is code that contains the business logic. It can be a simple data update, or it can be a more complex transaction with various conditions and involving multiple parties. These programs are stored on a blockchain network and can be executed on all nodes simultaneously. Business logic pre-installed on the validators in the blockchain before the network is launched is called an **installed smart contract**.

Another type of smart contract is called an **on-chain smart contract**. The code becomes part of the ledger when business logic is deployed to the blockchain as a committed transaction, which is then used by subsequent transactions. The smart contract layer works very closely with the consensus layer, including consensus on other peers, the identity service, and the client application.

The job of the smart contract layer is to process transaction requests and execute business logic to determine whether transactions are valid. Currently, there are four Hyperledger frameworks that support smart contracts:

- Hyperledger Fabric
- Hyperledger Sawtooth
- Hyperledger Burrow
- Hyperledger Iroha

 A Hyperledger framework may choose to implement the workflow differently. Refer to other chapters of this book and the official Hyperledger website for more information (https://www.hyperledger.org/).

Let's take a look at the high-level generic workflow that shows how smart contracts process transaction request in a blockchain network. This is common in all Hyperledger frameworks, as illustrated in the following diagram:

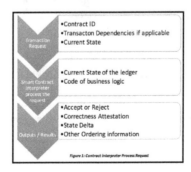

When a request is sent to the smart contract, the contract ID, the transaction request information, the current ledger state, and any dependencies, are processed by the contract interpreter, where the smart contract code is executed. The contract interpreter either rejects the request if it is invalid, or generates results accordingly.

OK, it is now time to look into how we can utilize the Hyperledger ecosystem to solve real-world business problems.

Solving business problems with Hyperledger

The majority of the real-world production implementations are Hyperledger Fabric with Hyperledger Sawtooth and Indy in the production stage. In this section, we will use three examples to demonstrate how we can solve real-world business problems with Hyperledger. We will look at examples for Hyperledger Fabric, Hyperledger Sawtooth, and Hyperledger Indy in the following use cases.

IBM and Walmart – blockchain for food safety with Hyperledger Fabric

Our use case is divided into different parts: the problem itself, the approach to the problem, and the end result using Hyperledger Fabric.

The problem

Food safety is a global concern—every, year 1 in 10 people fall ill and about 400,000 people die due to contaminated food. The global food supply chain has multiple participants, such as farmers, suppliers, processors, distributors, retailers, regulators, and consumers. When an outbreak of a food-borne disease happens, it can take days, even weeks, to trace the origin and the state of food.

The approach

Walmart and IBM are envisioning a fully-transparent, 21st century, digitized, decentralized food supply ecosystem. The company created a system based on Hyperledger Fabric to test their hypothesis, known as food-traceability system which was put to the test using a two proof-of-concept project. Mangos that were sold in Walmart's US stores and pork that was sold in Chinese Walmart stores were traced.

The results

In the end, the Hyperledger Fabric blockchain-based food-traceability system worked in both instances. For pork in China, this system allowed a certificate of authenticity to be uploaded to the blockchain, which brought more trust to the system which was a big issue before. For mangos in the US, the time needed to trace their provenance went from 7 days to 2.2 seconds.

The following records are tracked in the system:

- Farm-origin data
- Batch number
- Factory and processing data
- Expiration dates
- Storage temperatures
- Shipping details
- Results

During the pilot project, Walmart could trace the origin of more than 25 products from 5 different suppliers using Hyperledger Fabric. The company recently announced rolling out the system to more products and categories, and it will start requiring all of its suppliers of fresh leafy greens (such as lettuce and spinach) to trace their products using this system too.

Along with Walmart, many other companies, including Dole, Unilever, Golden State Foods, Tyson Foods, Kroger, and Nestle, announced expanded blockchain collaboration.

This union of using IBM's enterprise-grade blockchain platform reduced the time taken to isolate another food-borne outbreak source:

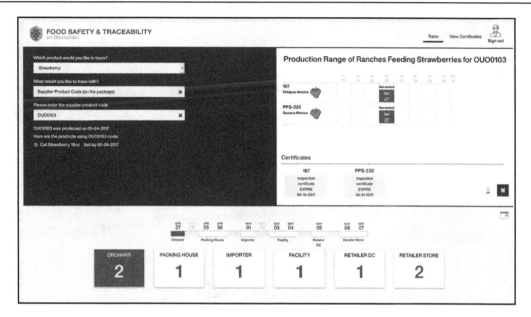

Source: IBM FoodTrust

ScanTrust and Cambio Coffee – supply-chain blockchain with Hyperledger Sawtooth

ScanTrust SA provides a blockchain-based IoT platform that connects products and packaging using secure unique identifiers. This enables the authentication of supply-chain visibility and mobile-products. ScanTrust allows packaging and label partners to receive orders from brand owners, and integrate secure codes into existing automated product packaging and labeling methods.

The problem

When you buy a product, it is hard to find out where it comes from. ScanTrust wanted to enhance its offering in supply-chain traceability and help their client, Cambio Coffee, bring more transparency to their ethical trade business.

The approach

Hyperledger Sawtooth supports both permissioned and permissionless deployments. It includes a novel consensus algorithm, PoET, which targets large distributed validator populations with minimal resource consumption.

The Hyperledger Sawtooth workflow is as follows:

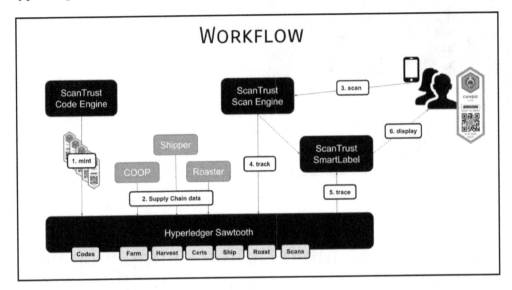

Source: ScanTrust

The results

There are two useful takeaways. First, once you add a barcode to a product for anti-counterfeiting or track-and-trace, you might as well use it for customer engagement as well (and vice versa). Second, for anti-counterfeit and customer engagement, you need customers to interact with the barcode to reap the full benefits. You may need some incentives to do so, with tokens being a logical route:

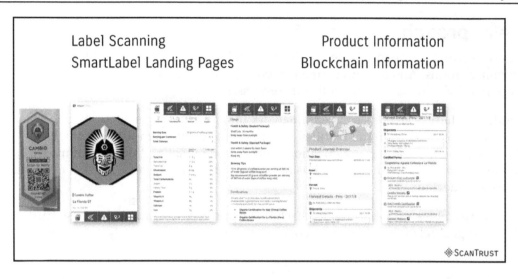

Label Scanning   Product Information
SmartLabel Landing Pages   Blockchain Information

Source: ScanTrust

Hyperledger Sawtooth was used to build a blockchain-enabled traceability function by ScanTrust. For example, if you buy a pack of coffee from Cambio, a direct-trade organic coffee company, and scan the label with your smartphone, you will see the journey the coffee has made to get to your breakfast table: from harvest in Peru to shipment, to roasting in Shanghai, and then being delivered to your home. Each stop on the journey is recorded on the blockchain so that the data cannot be tampered with.

BC and VON – cutting government red tape with Hyperledger Indy

Let's look at the **Verifiable Organizations Network** (**VON**), started by the governments of British Columbia, Ontario, and Canada.

The problem

Nearly one-third of the C$36,000,000,000 cost of regulation in Canada is unnecessary red tape, according to the latest survey of Canadian companies. Companies with fewer than 5 people pay C$6,744 per worker just to meet regulations. Even a sole proprietor in Canada must use at least three different tax numbers (SIN, GST/HST, and CRA BN).

The approach

Businesses with government-issued digital credentials could save hours filling in government forms. And any government agency could shorten or eliminate forms, improve the accuracy of its data, and streamline its processes.

Hyperledger Indy is an open source framework that provides tools, libraries, and reusable components for decentralized identities. It supports self-sovereign IDs controlled by individuals that work across organizations and silos, eliminating the need for multiple passwords and logins, and enabling business people to control who sees what information. All this was ideal for VON.

The team assembles an open software stack that helps business people establish trusted and enduring digital relationships to help governments cut red tape.

The results

Those things include Hyperledger Indy-based components that make it easy for government services to verify and issue digital credentials. The VON team wanted to cover a wide range of use cases beyond government forms, such as professional associations that register members such as doctors, nurses, and engineers; standards groups that certify food as organic or kosher; or businesses that need to prove their facilities have been inspected.

In the following example, the VON can operate through the following steps:

1. Mary registers her eco-tour business and receives a digital incorporation credential.
2. Mary needs a loan for a new tour bus. When the bank's online loan service asks for proof of incorporation, she presents her digital incorporation credential.
3. Using Hyperledger Indy-based software, the bank verifies Mary's credential and completes the loan transaction.

This is also shown in the following diagram:

Source: Verifiable Organizations Network

Also, you can use OrgBook BC to look up the correct name for a potential supplier or partner, in this case, Lululemon, the maker of athletic wear found at `https://orgbook.gov.bc.ca/en/organization/BC0578072`

The first demonstration project, OrgBook BC, announced in January 2019, includes digital IDs for 529,000 companies and 1,400,000 credentials. Similar services are coming soon from other jurisdictions.

The team plans to grow OrgBook BC by adding more services from the BC government. But that's not all. They'd like to help British Columbia's 160 municipalities that issue permits and licenses, most of them small towns with limited IT skills.

Other Books You May Enjoy

If you enjoyed this book, you may be interested in these other books by Packt:

Blockchain By Example
Bellaj Badr, Richard Horrocks, Xun (Brian) Wu

ISBN: 9781788475686

- Grasp decentralized technology fundamentals to master blockchain principles
- Build blockchain projects on Bitcoin, Ethereum, and Hyperledger
- Create your currency and a payment application using Bitcoin
- Implement decentralized apps and supply chain systems using Hyperledger
- Write smart contracts, run your ICO, and build a Tontine decentralized app using Ethereum
- Implement distributed file management with blockchain
- Integrate blockchain into existing systems in your organization

Hands-On Blockchain with Hyperledger
Nitin Gaur

ISBN: 9781788994521

- Discover why blockchain is a game changer in the technology landscape
- Set up blockchain networks using basic Hyperledger Fabric deployment
- Understand the considerations for creating decentralized applications
- Learn to integrate business networks with existing systems
- Write Smart Contracts quickly with Hyperledger Composer
- Design transaction model and chaincode with Golang
- Deploy Composer REST Gateway to access the Composer transactions
- Maintain, monitor, and govern your blockchain solutions

Leave a review - let other readers know what you think

Please share your thoughts on this book with others by leaving a review on the site that you bought it from. If you purchased the book from Amazon, please leave us an honest review on this book's Amazon page. This is vital so that other potential readers can see and use your unbiased opinion to make purchasing decisions, we can understand what our customers think about our products, and our authors can see your feedback on the title that they have worked with Packt to create. It will only take a few minutes of your time, but is valuable to other potential customers, our authors, and Packt. Thank you!

Index